HISTORY AND LITERATURE

The Chorus of History
1485-1558

1485-1558

The Chorus of History
Literary-historical relations in Renaissance Britain

A. M. KINGHORN
*Reader in English Literature
in the University of
the West Indies*

BARNES AND NOBLE, INC.
PUBLISHERS, BOOKSELLERS
SINCE 1873

First published 1971

© 1971 Blandford Press Ltd

Published in the United States by Barnes & Noble, Inc.

ISBN 389 04117 3 (*Hardbound*)

ISBN 389 04131 9 (*Paperback*)

FOR MARION
"this flour of wyfly pacience"

Printed in Great Britain

Contents

ACKNOWLEDGMENTS

Acknowledgment is due to the following for their kind permission to reproduce photographs:

Crown Copyright: reproduced by permission of the Ministry of Public Building and Works, Edinburgh, Nos. 1, 2, 3

Crown Copyright, The Royal Commission on Historical Monuments (England), Nos. 4, 5

National Galleries of Scotland, Nos. 19, 21

National Portrait Gallery, London, Nos. 10, 24, 26, 29, 30

Radio Times Hulton Picture Library, Nos. 6, 7, 9, 11, 15

Trustees of the British Museum, Nos. 12, 16, 18, 25, 28

Trustees of the National Library of Scotland, Nos. 22, 23

University of London Library, Nos. 13, 14

Victoria and Albert Museum, No. 8

Nos. 17, 20 and 27 are reproduced by gracious permission of Her Majesty The Queen

List of Illustrations

For 'tis your thoughts that now must deck our kings,
Carry them here and there; jumping o'er times,
Turning the accomplishment of many years
Into an hour-glass: for the which supply,
Admit me Chorus to this History.

Henry V, Prologue, 28–32

AUTHOR'S NOTE

A quotation is given either in its original form with meanings of difficult words and phrases explained, or with a literal translation into modern English appended. Where no useful purpose would appear to be served by preserving Tudor spelling, a modernised version has been provided or used as source. Texts used as sources are identified as the quotations occur. The bibliography lists standard editions together with a number of other works which the author has found especially valuable.

The author would like to express his thanks to the Librarian and Staff of the University of the West Indies.

1 : Introduction

THIS is neither history nor literary history, nor, properly speaking, is it literary criticism, though it partakes of all three. It is based on standard historical investigations of the period, on studies of specific authors and on textbooks explaining the nature of contemporary political, economic and social conditions. Many volumes have been produced by experts which provide exhaustive accounts of the European Renaissance in art and in letters, of the state of the Roman Catholic Church prior to the Reformation and of Henry VIII's autocracy in England. Detailed biographies of major and minor personalities associated with the Henrician revolution are readily available and critical studies of literary figures from Malory to the Earl of Surrey offer themselves in increasing numbers. In an age of ultra-specialism, such as our own, one goes first to specialists for information and then tries to relate one kind of expertise to another. Unfortunately, this process can cause, initially at least, much confusion and misunderstanding, firstly, because these relations are often hard to discern, secondly, because they are usually more subtle than at first sight appears and thirdly, because it is not always necessary, or even desirable, that such links be forged at all. The alliance between history and literature has always been very far from ideal. It is easy to lose sight of a literary work by burying it in a compost of facts, statistics and items of so-called "background" information—this is the pitfall for the unwary literary critic, occupied, from time to time, by even the most distinguished of them.

The historian is likewise faced by traps, perhaps more obvious ones. He is supposed to deal in facts, but he must not only select them according to agreed principles but must then communicate them unequivocally, clothe them in language which by its very nature is highly emotive and draw unbiased conclusions from his own complex arguments. That school of historians whose members think of their discipline as a "science" and claim that their arguments emerge as a result of inductive reasoning are particularly open to attack by rivals of a more philosophic turn of mind and especially by adherents to the old-fashioned methods of Macaulay, for whom the writing of history went hand in hand with the achievement of a glowing literary style of exceptional emotive power. The poetic prose of the great Victorians recreated history as a living force for their generation, but nowadays their rhetoric is regarded with mistrust as a distorting element, imposing a potentially fallacious viewpoint. The light of history is not to be admitted by the ear alone, for the influence of scientific method is strong even among those of us who profess to reject the notion that history is a science.

The Greeks thought that history was a lower kind of activity than poetry and that the poet rather than the historian was a guide for society. Such phrases as 'the grown world learns from the poet' or 'we, the poets, are the teachers of men' indicate the high esteem in which the imaginative writer in Athens held himself. Some philosophers, like Plato, were not so sure, and maintained that the poet did not tell the truth because he was unable to perceive reality directly, so was a menace to society, not a benefit. Yet we still talk about 'poetry and history', 'history and philosophy' and 'poetry and philosophy', seeking to establish relations among them. In fact, we go even farther and accord recognition to specialists in 'the literature of society' who are prepared to argue, with the help of economics, theories of political institutions and a battery of statistics, that no art can be properly understood in a purely 'aesthetic' vacuum. The classical Renaissance disciplines of language-training and wide reading are, it would seem, no longer considered adequate grounding for the study of literature. This is a dismaying thought, especially since it is clear that the art is long and the life is short, and possibly nasty and brutish as well.

As a student of literature, rather than of history or of philosophy, the author recognises the main danger facing him, namely, that of overcrowding. In a book like this, both the wood and the trees should be visible. Yet the period which it covers contains no literary figures of the dimensions of Chaucer, Langland, Spenser, Shakespeare or Milton. In fact not even many major-minor writers emerge to stand as prominent signposts or, to borrow a favoured sixteenth-century analogy, safe anchorages. The anonymous poet of *Sir Gawain and the Green Knight*, or 'Grene Kniʒt' as some scholars persist in calling this primitive apparition, has few, if any, rivals from Gower to Sidney. The most important poets from a literary-critical point of view are Henryson, Dunbar, Skelton, Wyatt and Surrey, of whom two are Scotsmen and one of the Englishmen so atypical as to be neglected until the present century. On a lower poetic level names like Barclay, Sackville and Lyndsay suggest themselves, together with a host of named and anonymous composers of verse representative of what C. S. Lewis unflatteringly called the 'Drab Age'.

In addition, prose authors are numerous, imaginative, purely descriptive, didactic, practitioners of Latinised English, translators from classical and vernacular languages into English and writers of official and personal documents—Malory, Caxton, Elyot, Cheke, Wilson, Ascham, Grimald and Whythorne, each deserving of a place in the annals of English letters. To these one must add prose originals in Latin, like More's, or in Italian, like Castiglione's; translated into English prose, they became English works. Monumental translations of classical authors like Virgil, such as that of Gawain Douglas, made in 1512–3 after a labour of only eighteen months, are rare examples of how a vernacular version of a Latin original may serve as a substitute for its model, substantiating Goethe's definition of the highest type of translation. The same may be said for the vernacular Bible of Tyndale and Coverdale, a work of immense erudition and painstaking research, undertaken by men whose political positions were often precarious.

As well as all these active and sometimes voluminous producers of poetry and prose, the large number of playwrights, of whom one named example is John Bale, a disseminator of current political and religious ideas by way of the stage as it then was, have to be given their due credit in a study of literary-historical relations, even if many of their plays were of dramatically poor quality. John Rastell, More's brother-in-law, was a scholar-printer, would-be explorer, translator and playwright who in a standard history of English drama might receive no more than passing mention as the author of *The Four Elements*, a poor and incomplete play; in this volume it is quoted extensively because it serves as a good example of how history and literature, voyages of discovery and the ideals of humanism, may be seen embodied in one personage, though Rastell himself is really a very shadowy figure from a biographer's standpoint.

The sixteenth century was the first to develop a recognisable historical method—one based on documentary evidence, for both Henry VII and his son provided later historians with solid evidence in the form of account books, state papers, personal directives and letters, Chamber and Household records and diplomatic documents, which proliferated as the network of government administration grew more complex. This habit of keeping records, descending through society to merchant houses and private individuals, made certain that sources of information about all kinds of social phenomena were made available for future students of the social life of England during this time. For the first time family portraits began to emerge of relatively ordinary middle-class people, representatives of the new prosperous merchant group, like the Johnsons, and comparable with the Pastons of the previous century, who were upper-middle-class country squires. People could now own printed books, obtainable at relatively reasonable prices, and their sons and daughters were offered better opportunities of education than had been the case in earlier times. The different interests of the social historian are well exemplified in a collection of extracts such as C. H. Williams edited in the volume called *English Historical Documents 1485–1558*, a valuable adjunct to a literary study of the period.

Leaving aside individual figures, one may consider the era as one of new movements and trends, to which labels, some useful, others misleading, have regularly been attached; for instance, 'Renaissance', 'Reformation', 'Humanism', 'New Learning', 'Rise of Modern English', 'Copernican Revolution', 'Age of Discovery', 'Era of Adventure', 'Coming of Protestantism', and other optimistic-sounding expressions implying a heartfelt dislike of the 'Middle Ages', 'Monasticism', 'Papal Supremacy' and all that medieval scholastic learning was thought to stand for. Other all-embracing descriptive words and phrases are intended to apply to groups having a common interest or design, such as 'translators', 'courtly makers', 'educationists', 'social satirists', 'chroniclers', 'polemical writers' and 'reformers' of several persuasions.

Any of these subjects is in itself extensive enough to enable a scholar to write a large book examining its implications for the Tudors. Each one warrants treatment in depth, yet, in a study of how history touches literature and of its rarer concomitant, the effects of literature on history, how is it possible to escape super-ficiality and the mere juggling with labels that is the deadly vice of the 'survey'? What to omit, how much abbreviated factual informa-tion to include, the extent of historical matter to be introduced and the limitations of treatment in the case of each writer considered have all been determined by considerations of clarity as a main end of the volume. Not all the works of all the men named above, nor all the categories and movements referred to have been discussed at length, though they have received more than passing mention. As pointed out before, this is not literary history. Selection of material is intended to illuminate the marchland or common frontier shared by literature and history, each defined in broad terms and hence including some items that might be left out of studies in one dis-cipline or the other. By the same token, accounts of a political or diplomatic character have been omitted or severely pruned, for these may be studied in detail with the aid of standard reference works.

Treatment is not strictly chronological, though a general and inevitable chronological tendency may be noted in each chapter; in fact, after digesting the first chapter on historiography, the student may find it profitable to proceed to the penultimate chapter on Tudor history-plays. Some chapters, for example 3, 4, 5 and 6 incline to 'history', others, like 8, 9 and 10, to 'literature'. Chapter 7 is about language developments, which the two disciplines have in common. Quotations are fairly extensive, since the times ought to be allowed to speak for themselves—something they did very well indeed—but so far as possible, nothing has been allowed to go unexplained or without comment.

It should be said that it has not been found easy to cling to the outside limits of the historical period from the accession of Henry VII in 1485 to that of Elizabeth I in 1558. Such arbitrary lines of demarcation may suit the compilers of examination papers in Honours Schools of English, but we are for once going to rise above and beyond such barriers in the interests of accuracy of description and depth of comprehension. The *Paston Letters* span the fifteenth and sixteenth centuries, the medieval miracle cycles continued far into Elizabeth's reign and were seen by Chaucer and Shakespeare both; the Italian Renaissance had its first beginnings with Petrarch and the *Anglica Historia* of Polydore Vergil, which goes back to the earliest times recorded, was written, not in English, but in Latin, and by an expatriate Italian to boot. Malory's *Morte d'Arthur* was composed in the 1460s but did not reach its wider public until Caxton printed his version in 1485. Henryson's *Fables* were composed before 1480, in James III's reign, but he continued to live and write in Scotland until about 1505, and he is therefore included along with his fellow-*makar* Dunbar, the best-known poet of James IV's Court. *A Mirror For Magistrates* appeared in parts, written by various hands, between 1559 and 1583, but the first part was composed in the mid–1550s. Many of the items and movements referred to in the short chapter on the fine arts and in the specifically historical sections are of mid-fifteenth-century origin, and Giotto, like Petrarch, was a near-contemporary of Chaucer. Not even the scientists, far less the scientific historians, will deny that the order of precedence of chicken and egg still remain in doubt.

In a rule of democracy, where all are governors, all ought surely to have the education appropriate to a governor. Sir Thomas Elyot would have agreed, theoretically, in the manner of his time, had he been alive today to observe the modern caucus race, that for reasons of utility such a book as this one was necessary, hybrid though it undoubtedly is. Each one of its chapters may claim to treat fundamental matters so that in spite of earlier suggestions for rearrangement of the given order of reading, it is probably just as well to follow the logical advice of the King of Hearts in *Alice*, namely, to begin at the beginning, go on to the end, and then stop.

2 : The Writing of History in the Early Renaissance

HISTORY is recorded directly names, dates and statistics are added to a statement, and is mainly concerned with human actions and achievements. The original stimulus to its making was man's natural curiosity about the world and his desire to hand down information to his descendants and so preserve tribal pride in the deeds of their forbears. History could be presented in dramatic form, performed as regular ritual action, declaimed by reciters telling well-loved stories to eager audiences or preserved in cryptic illustrations, but for present purposes it is to be considered as a sophisticated activity, made possible by the survival of written material and itself written down for posterity to read. Manuscripts, miscellanies, journals, state papers and personal documents are the indispensable literary materials of the historian. Some of this material—drama, poetry, philosophical prose, intimate letters and social comment—is claimed also by the literary critic, though historians who believe that they themselves are practitioners of a 'science' made up only of verifiable facts prefer to place history and literature in separate compartments.

Are they to be isolated in this way because they have little or nothing in common, or united because the spirit of the human imagination gives impulse to both? If, as David Hume suggested, the historian's general aim is to trace the history of the human mind, as impelled by the humanly probable, even literature which does not deal with actual events is historical in the sense that it was written at a certain point in time and remains as a document of the language and the customs of that time—or of an earlier time should the writer himself happen to nurture a yearning for his own country's past, like Petrarch. The Old English poet's portrait of the hanging man, doomed to dangle from the gibbet, where

> the raven rips the eyes from the head,
> the dark-coated bird tears at the corpse;
> he cannot keep at bay the desecration of
> the hated winged enemy. His life has left
> him and without feeling or vital hope,
> pale on the gallows, he endures his fate,
> shrouded in the garment of death. Accursed
> is his name.
>
> *(The Fortunes of Men*, 33–43)

made it clear what the thief's destiny might be if the laws of his society ever caught up with him.

François Villon's *Epitaphe*, written about 1460, plays upon a very similar image of corpses hanging from a gallows, exposed to the elements and the birds, and since he may himself have been under sentence of death when he composed it, the poem suggests more than a conventional note of warning, directed at his 'human brothers who live after us'. The sentiments of these two poets, widely separated in time, seem similar, but this is not surprising in view of the context—the vision of the executed felons is powerful and independent of time's perspective. But although as embellishments to an historical account of life in Anglo-Saxon England or late medieval France these seemingly personal revelations from the imaginations of contemporaries may be attractive matter for modern readers, to an historian they are not strictly speaking, 'history' so far as their subject-matter is concerned.

Nursery-rhymes, too, often obscure references to actual personalities or events. Humpty-Dumpty and Little Jack Horner are both supposed to have contemporary fifteenth- and sixteenth-century originals and the verse

> Ring a Ring a Roses
> A pocket full of Posies
> A-tishoo! A-tishoo!
> And all fall down

to conceal a sinister reference to the symptoms and lethal character of one of the many medieval pestilences which started with a red rash, caused a fit of sneezing and choking succeeded by death, and in course of time inspired part of a child's playtime ritual. But nursery-rhymes, though they may be considered history, are not literature, and do not qualify for consideration in a work of this kind.

Yet, if history is to be roughly defined as an account in narrative form of some aspect or phase of human activity, inasmuch as human activity is enormous in scope, so is history. We may speak for example, of political history, constitutional history, economic history, church history, military history, diplomatic history, social history and even of the history of 'ideas', a recent offshoot of philosophy sometimes known as 'intellectual' history, and viewed dubiously by purists. However, no matter of what kind it may be, history must possess the triple virtues of accuracy, truth and freedom from bias or prejudiced distortion. Unless these conditions are met, one is dealing not with proper historical narrative but with legend, propaganda, or self-deception for political purposes, and unless the writer of history carefully sifts the evidence, separating truth from fiction without fear or favour, he may not be called an historian since he is not using proper historian's methods.

Nowadays these methods are quite well established and agreed upon by the majority of historians. For them accuracy, truth and impartiality are prime considerations and all else is secondary. This is the ideal. In practice absolute truth is not obtainable, even in science, and though accuracy and impartiality may be achieved theoretically, one never knows if some shred of evidence, essential to the completion of an account, may not be missing. *Humanum est errare.* No-one can claim infallibility.

Nor can bias be completely expunged. In *Iolanthe*, W. S. Gilbert has one of his characters say:

> . . . every boy and every gal,
> That's born into the world alive,
> Is either a little Liberal,
> Or else a little Conservative!

and although this may now be thought an over-simplified classification of personal political leanings which averts its ken from a

B

high proportion of the electorate, Gilbert's epigram hints at the prejudices inevitably found in each man's make-up which, if he should happen to be an historian, conspire to block him from his purpose to speak the truth. The truth becomes the truth as he sees it and in the ideal sense, not 'true' at all. Ranke, the nineteenth-century German historian, summed up his own way of writing history in words which have been repeatedly quoted ever since— 'I will merely state, how it actually happened' (*ich will blos sagen, wie es eigentlich gewesen ist*), a statement made in his *History of the Popes* (1834–36). He meant that documentary evidence and first-hand narrative were the best possible witnesses of past events, just as in a court of law.

More recent speculation has found this cryptic observation of Ranke's inadequate as a definition of how history ought to be written. May not the historian in fact be a seer trying to shed light on the mystery of human existence, predicting the outcome of man's strivings, using the past as a basis for deciding the future or even recording the march towards an inevitable destiny, implicit in the nature of man himself? A theory of history which sees it as the play of two opposing forces constantly reiterating their effects, or as the account of the various stages by which human society proceeds to evolve an ideal state by moving inexorably along a widening course (*i.e.*, Bergson/Toynbee and the Marxists respectively) subsumes all detailed examination of incidents under the one concept. David Hume answered eighteenth-century adherents to 'ascent' and 'decline' theories by saying that historical change is not predictable and that one cannot depend on past events as guides to those of the future. Neither optimism nor pessimism can provide a satisfactory basis for a 'universal' history of man's activities from the beginnings to whatever end may lie in store for him.

It should be added that historians are neither philosophers nor are they theologians, but recorders, solely concerned with describing the nature of the past. Nor are they scientists, as J. B. Bury suggested. History and science are of different worlds. The world of science is governed by inflexible laws; wherein events constantly repeat themselves, the operation of cause and effect may be precisely studied as observable phenomena checked by results and experience. In the historian's realm there are no inflexible laws, no repetitions, no uniformity, no seasonal changes, no regular cycles, predictable eclipses or fiery comets. Social movements and the incidents which they include are each unique, and there has been but one Norman Conquest, one Peasants' Revolt, one Reformation, one French Revolution, one Waterloo, one Charge of the Light Brigade, one Gallipoli, one Battle of Britain. The Time Machine cannot on any account be reversed, or at least there is until now no evidence that it can, so that for practical purposes it may be boldly stated that history does not repeat itself and that the moving finger, having writ, does indeed move on. No war or movement bears more than a superficial resemblance to another war or movement, nor is it fruitful to compare social institutions of different ages or geographical locations—Greek slavery, Eastern European slavery and Caribbean slavery are only crudely comparable. The 'communism' advocated by Plato and More is not that of Marx and Engels. No really sound analogies are to be drawn between the decline of the Roman and that of the British Empire. The historian cannot be assured of the value of his judgments or his descriptions of past events, nor is he able to test his conclusions. In these respects he is handicapped as the scientist is not. He certainly cannot recreate incidents, as the dramatist or novelist can, though in recent times, with the help of the cine-film, he has been enabled to compile historical documentaries which claim to 'reconstruct' the past. Widely different interpretations may be put on the selections of material for such documentaries, which are obviously liable to excessive distortion.

Another imponderable confronting the historian is chance. Voltaire, a contemporary of Hume, went so far as to call history little more than a succession of chances. If so, the world is irrational and man is but a plaything of the gods. Martin Luther was converted from the Roman to the Protestant faith by a lightning storm, or so it may be argued. After a bolt had narrowly missed him he entered an Augustinian monastery at Erfurt to do penance for his sins and remained in retreat for five years. During this period of meditation he arrived at the conclusion that the Roman doctrine of good works was wrong and that the just man lives by faith. This brought him into conflict with the Papacy and accelerated the process of Reformation. By a similarly biased selection of facts the length of Cleopatra's nose may be said to have caused the fall of the Roman Empire. Some principle of cause and effect seems to hold good but the effects may not always be judged from the causes, and an element of caprice is usually present. The murder of the Archduke Ferdinand at Sarajevo by a member of a group of fanatics who had strongly personal reasons for offering himself as the instrument of assassination was the spark which ignited the conflagration of World War I. In some respects such an assassin may be considered a romantic hero, of the type who takes chances and creates a situation which encourages others to do the same, but he is hardly a prime cause. Perhaps a prime cause can never be found. The seasons melt imperceptibly one into the next, youth is succeeded by maturity or at least by a maturing process the origins of which are difficult to establish. Change is continuous.

Nevertheless, there must be some exact time when an actual transition is made, for although the historical process is unbroken, it moves from phase to phase. Calendar changes are arrived at by astronomical calculation and physiological ageing may be accurately measured. For the sake of convenience, if for no other reason, an historical account must have some jumping-off point, like 1066, when William of Normandy defeated Harold at Senlac or Hastings and his compatriots introduced Norman-French language and customs into an Anglo-Saxon culture of long standing. At some point in time between 1130 and 1160, the written language used by the recorder in the *Peterborough Chronicle* may be described as changing from 'Old' to 'Early Middle' English. The prose of Malory (*c.* 1470) marked a transitional stage in the evolution of 'Modern' English; that of Elyot's *The Boke Named the Governour* (1531) is definitely 'Modern'.

So far as English history is concerned, 1485 offers itself as a convenient starting-place from which to examine relations between history and literature. A succession of events made 1485 the year when England's truly national history began; by the same token, it marked the end of the Middle Ages. In September the Wars of the Roses between the Lancastrians and the Yorkists ended with the

Battle of Bosworth Field, the death of Richard III and the immediate accession of Henry Tudor, Duke of Richmond, as Henry VII, who reigned as supreme monarch for twenty-four years. Since the death of Edward I in 1307 no English king had enjoyed such power. 1485 and the Tudors brought the beginnings of a different kind of world for the English, for the Scots and in the end for the whole of Europe. A new system, based on the triple rocks of order, peace and prosperity developed under Henry and his successors, who promoted that rule of law under stable government which has characterised the English way of life ever since.

In July of 1485 William Caxton issued Malory's *Morte d'Arthur* from his printing house at the Sign of the Red Pale (in Tothill Street), Westminster Abbey precincts, near the dwelling-houses of many of the rich wool merchants who were his patrons. Until the mid-nineteenth century he was held in some contempt as a populariser who made poor use of the new art of printing by issuing trivial books and pandering to philistine tastes. More recent biographers have seen him as a capable translator from three languages, French, Latin and Dutch, who printed all the English poetry, romances and chronicles as well as the significant devotional works then extant. In addition, he is credited with the establishment of modern English prose almost as a second classical language, eventually to supersede Latin completely as the literary medium of the new nation. Caxton helped to popularise English literature, as it then was, and to create a reading public. Between 1475 and 1491 he issued ninety-three works, some in two or three editions. Wynkyn de Worde and Richard Pynson, neither of whom were English, carried on the craft which Caxton had been the first to introduce into the country and printed over fourteen hundred books. They had many rivals, not so well known, John Lettou, William Machlinia, Julian Notary, Jean Barbier or Barbour, all contemporaries of Wynkyn de Worde, and at least sixteen other printers, some probably his apprentices, who formed a second generation. They flourished between 1501 and 1535. The only one of these who has a solid claim to inclusion in this present volume is John Rastell, Sir Thomas More's brother-in-law, who, besides being a printer, led an unsuccessful attempt to sail to the Americas and wrote a play called *The Four Elements* in which this venture is reflected. But Henry VII, who collected books and whose library contained works by Continental printers as well as by Caxton, de Worde and Pynson, Henry VIII, whose own work *The Assertion of the Seven Sacraments* (1521) was an orthodox answer to Luther, John Skelton, harshly critical of Wolsey, and Sir Thomas Elyot, who helped to establish a standard English prose, were each in their various ways connected with the rise of the printed book.

When Caxton died in 1491 the first signs of a split from Rome were evident, the influence of the Italian Renaissance was beginning to touch England and a hunger for book-learning was soon to develop among a small but influential class inspired by enquiring men such as Linacre, Grocyn, Lilly, Colet and More, and their friend Erasmus, who came to London for the first time in 1499. An Act regulating the book trade had been passed in 1484 and a later proviso to this Act stated that any foreign bookseller or printer might import books into the country, bound or unbound, and that they or any foreign scrivener, illuminator or bookbinder might live and work in England. This encouraged Continental stationers and printers to enter the country and enabled the number of books imported to be greatly increased. Between 1500 and 1520 scores of them settled in and around London. In 1523 a contrary Act was passed, forbidding any alien to take apprentices other than Englishmen and limiting them to two foreign journeymen. In 1534 another Act forbade importation altogether and dealt the death blow to foreign competition in the printing trade, which had not surprisingly led to a great deal of jealousy among the English printers who, without doubt, were with a few exceptions far less skilful than their European colleagues.

· · · · · ·

One way to gain an inroad into the complicated mass of material facing the student of literary-historical relations is to approach the subject by way of 'historiography', or the writing of history as it was practised at the time. To perceive trends in Renaissance historiography in something like their proper perspective, one ought first to know what medieval scholars understood by 'history', if only for the reason that nothing really significant was added to their definitions and distinctions before the early part of the sixteenth century.

A twelfth-century Benedictine monk, Gervase of Canterbury, said in his *Chronica* that there were two kinds of historical writing, both having the same aim, namely, the pursuit of truth. One was the history proper, conceived as a narrative and founded upon a personal selection of facts and opinions which by its cunning presentation persuaded its audience into accepting the composer's version. This was superior history, produced by masters of the 'grand style', like Bede, William of Malmesbury, Florence of Worcester, Henry of Huntingdon and other authorities pre-eminent in their craft, whose talent for 'bombast and swelling words' (*ampullas et sesquipedalia verba*, as Horace called them in his *Art of Poetry*,) convinced the learned that such skill in writing Latin partook of truth. The second and more common form taken by historical writing was described by Gervase as 'chronicles' or 'annals'. The chronicler was a humbler aspirant to the historian's office than the imaginative narrator; like Amyclas of old, he sat in contented poverty on his bed of seaweed, his attention directed towards facts and dates, portents and miracles. Most annalists were anonymous monks, disciplined by living in monastic seclusion under strict 'rules' and engaged for years in making records for a monastery or cathedral church, sometimes at royal command without reference to a wider lay audience, in a 'humble style' fit only for pedestrian descriptions of limited scope.

Gervase's theory is over-simplified and conventional. He did not admit of any 'middle style' and his sharp division into un-compromising opposite categories is but a very rough and ready guide to the assessment of actual writers. Most historians employ a variety of styles, according to the subject treated; sometimes imaginative narration is needed to bridge gaps in evidence or to suggest the drama of great actions in a manner which rings true emotionally; at other times the emphasis has to be on facts and dates. Nowadays we tend to distrust an over-polished style of delivery in speaking or in writing, on the grounds that it is full of tricks designed to persuade the audience into accepting statements which are open to question—the verb 'persuade' has degenerated in meaning since it was used by Renaissance rhetoricians and the art of persuasion has become a synonym for the subterfuges of the propagandist or the salesman. It often suggests insincerity, not, as formerly, successful communication of information genuinely believed to be true.

Narrative accounts of history emphasised violent action, battles and heroes, sieges and river-crossings, for medieval audiences were fascinated by tales of war and slaughter. Lively first-hand accounts of the Crusades, like the *Anonimalle Chronicle* (1333–81) and the French chronicles of Ambroise and Robert de Clari, are packed with personal details, graphically narrated. After a century or more, incidents acquired a veil of remoteness. Fact was easily blended with fiction in order to present a continuous story. Most medieval documents, though compiled in good faith, mingled truth with falsehood, and modern research prefers to look back at the Middle Ages through records rather than through contemporary narratives or chronicles. Prejudice was inevitable and selection of material lacked control since one writer reported another. Medieval audiences were fascinated by tales of the marvellous and romances, which spoke of fighting, love, strange happenings and the capricious turns of fortune, appealed to them as being close to truth, *i.e.* to life as they knew it could be. Supernatural visitants and widely exaggerated odds were the stock in trade of the romance writer but they also turned up in narratives which claimed to be history.

By the time of the Norman Conquest a medieval theologian's conception of 'universal history' had been established, originating in the thesis of St. Augustine's *De Civitate Dei*, in its turn inspired by the Book of Revelation. Works written in this tradition, of which Bishop Bossuet's *Discourse on Universal History* (1681) is a late example, were inclined to be long-drawn-out narratives, interpreting facts according to Christian doctrine and assuming that the march of history was divinely ordained. All human events were thought to be the results of God's direct intervention and the Old and New Testaments historical and prophetic. Man's destiny could be predicted and his ultimate goal, the Celestial City, the New

Jerusalem, was clearly forecast in *Revelation*, XXI, 10–27. As C. V. Wedgwood remarks:

> Much can be said against the romantic approach to history. It tended too easily to the theatrical and the fanciful; also it came into being at an epoch when the conviction that human life was a constant forward progress towards an unattainable perfection was very strong.
>
> (*Truth and Opinion: Historical Essays* [1960], p. 30)

In romantic history the creative imagination found wings. The great epics of Homer and Virgil, the Song of Roland, the emergence of the legend of King Arthur and the two long poems about the Scottish war of independence, Barbour's *Bruce* and Hary's *Wallace*, all share a common ground, that of history and literature. Miss Wedgwood points out later in the same volume that

> From the fusion of a little that was historic with much that was poetic sprang many of the great epics.
>
> (*ibid.* p. 98.)

for the creative imagination of the romantic historian and of the writer of epic were stimulated to drive towards the same end, to improve, to instruct and to please. Of Barbour's story about Robert the Bruce G. W. S. Barrow observes that

> If it were cast in the form of a romance it would possess at least one of romance's essential requirements, incredibility.
>
> (*Robert Bruce and the Community of the Realm of Scotland* [1965] p. 234.)

Bruce is, in fact, cast in the form of classical epic, which presented a combination of some fact with a great deal of fancy and it is written in a contemporary (late fourteenth-century) form of English, thus emphasising its popular literary character. The poem is still accepted as the main authority for the events of Bruce's campaign and for biographers of King Robert to draw upon. Other sources do nothing to upset or even seriously to challenge that authority for, whichever way the student may turn, he finds himself unable to dispense with Barbour as a primary source of information about Bruce, Scotland and her troubled times during the first half of the fourteenth century.

But this is a rare coincidence. Generally speaking, history and literature stand apart, because the historian's chief object is to make true record, not to embellish human experience. Macaulay, writing in the *Edinburgh Review* about Henry Hallam's *Constitutional History of England*, observed:

> History, at least in its state of ideal perfection, is a compound of poetry and philosophy. It impresses general truths on the mind by a vivid representation of particular characters and incidents. But in fact the two hostile elements of which it consists have never been known to form a perfect amalgamation; and at length, in our own time, they have been completely and professedly separated. Good histories, in the proper sense of the word, we have not. But we have good historical romances, and good historical essays. The imagination and the reason, if we may use a legal metaphor, have made partition of a province of literature of which they were formerly seized *per my et per tout*; and now they hold their respective portions in severalty, instead of holding the lot in common.   (September, 1828)

In other words, when a creative writer makes an historical statement he is chasing two hares and stands in danger of losing one if not both. The one he is more likely to lose is the historical hare, for very rarely is it that a poem, or a play or a novel, which takes as its subject real characters and events known to have taken place, is able to stand up to anything like a rigorous examination on present-day standards of historical accuracy. Real life lacks the neat and tidy qualities which a literary artefact usually aims to exhibit. Classical standards of symmetry in composition, the ideal of 'the beginning, middle and end' insisted upon by Aristotle in his *Poetics*, are hard to find in the everyday world. Hero-kings were not really consistently and continuously heroic when faced by overwhelming odds—they must have had their fainter moments, their doubts and fears, but the writer of romance nearly always presents them as full-dress stereotypes of the heroic character. Achilles, Hector, Alexander the Great, Hannibal, Julius Caesar, Charlemagne, King Arthur, Edward I, William Wallace, Robert Bruce and Henry V all partake of the same magnificence and all are cast in the same fundamental mould. Occasionally, they are given striking individual qualities—both Hector and Edward I were said to have a lisp, Achilles had his heel—but such distinguishing features were either legendary or traditional. These heroes, as presented by late medieval historians, are compounds, made up from romance sources, classical literature and myth and anecdotal traditions, handed down from one generation to another, usually within containable family circles.

· · · · · ·

We need not expect, therefore, to find that literature and history necessarily coincide even in 'biographies' in which the hero is central to the narrative, and even when the hero is a real person, known to have lived and participated in some of the deeds ascribed to him. In *Bruce* Barbour conceived a national hero mirroring the unadorned virtues of Scottish resistance to the English and he created this figure out of ready-made epic material. As an individual the glorious warrior king or prince does not exist above and beyond these, for no medieval historian tried to probe below the surface of outward behaviour and analyse personal motives or moral attributes. A hero's heroism could be summed up in half a dozen adjectives, extracted from textbooks on rhetoric such as Matthew of Vendôme's *Ars Versificatio* (1175) which was influenced by Cicero and Horace. Matthew based personal description on two formulas, which he called *effictio*, or outward appearance, and *notatio*, or moral qualities. Thus Barbour, writing of Sir James of Douglas, Bruce's second-in-command, says that

> All men lufyt him for his bounte;
> For he wes off full fayr effer,
> Wyss, curtaiss, and deboner;
> Larg and luffand als wes he,
> And our all thing luffyt lawte . . .
> He wes in all his dedis lele;
> For him dedeynyeit nocht to dele

With trechery, na with falset,
His hart on hey honour wes set:
And him contenyt on sic maner,
That all him luffyt that war him ner.
Bot he wes nocht sa fayr, that we
Suld spek gretly off his beaute:
In vysage was he sumdeill gray,
And had blak har, as ic hard say;
Bot of limmys he wes weill maid,
With banys gret and schuldrys braid.
His body wes weyll maid and lenye,
As thai that saw him said to me.
Quhen he wes blyth, he wes lufly,
And meyk and sweyt in cumpany:
Bot quha in battaill mycht him se,
All othir contenance had he.
And in spek wlispyt he sum deill;
Bot that sat him rycht wondre weill.
Till gud Ector of Troy mycht he
In mony thingis liknyt be.

(*Bruce*, I, 360–96)

[All men loved him for his excellence, for he was of a most
handsome demeanour, sensible, well-mannered and debonair;
he was generous and kind too, and above all else admired standards of noble conduct. In every action he showed his loyalty
. . . With treachery or falsehood he would have nothing to do.
His heart was always set on winning high renown. He conducted
himself in such a way that all who were near him loved him.
But he was not so handsome that we should dwell overmuch on
his good looks. In complexion he was rather on the pale side,
and I heard tell that his hair was black. But he had well-formed
limbs, big bones and broad shoulders. His body was of good
proportion and lean, as those who saw him told me. When he
was in a happy frame of mind, he was charming and modest,
easy to get on with in company; but whoever had the chance of
seeing him in battle met a very different side of his character.

In speech he lisped somewhat, but this suited him very well. He might be compared in many respects to good Hector of Troy].

Edward I's and Hector's lisp turns up here as well. It may be that the author of this description, written some forty-five years after Douglas' death in the Holy Land, had picked up a few stray items of information from old men who had known the original warrior, but there is still little to distinguish this valiant Douglas from any other fictional hero of romances. Like the latter, he betrays a few clear-cut primary emotions such as anger and sorrow, and, in the presence of women, behaves chivalrously according to the courtly code, though without the over-refinement of some of the Frenchified romances. These Scots warriors are so well occupied with their campaigns that their 'courtesy' is inclined to be rough and ready.

Loyalty to such champions as these is loyalty to nation, or patriotism. No second-hand knowledge of the intimacies of a hero's personal life is needed for the creation of such a character in a literary work. His virtues, prowess and the goals to which he aspires are constructed according to a formula, that of the chivalric romance. In his personality are summed up popular sentiments associated with success in war and particularly with the struggle against a foreign oppressor. Just as Arthur of Albion was the type of a successful British king so did Bruce become his Scottish counterpart. By 1350 the various streams of Arthurian tradition had fused into one broad legend, mingling fact and fiction, including the *Brut* narratives of Geoffrey of Monmouth, Wace and Layamon, the romances of Chrétien de Troyes and the *lais* of Marie de France. From this emerged the chivalrous figure of King Arthur. In Layamon's hands he became an actual English monarch conquering his enemies, who included the Scots. In the fourteenth century, under Edward III, Arthurian chivalry came to stand for a high ideal of soldierly conduct and contemporary historians, such as Froissart, wrote of Edward with Arthur, and occasionally Hector and Alexander the Great, in mind. The author of the alliterative *Morte Arthure* drew his portraits of the valiant king from Plantagenet history and Malory probably depicted Arthur with Henry V in mind.

The literary creations of Bruce, Wallace and Arthur, each cast in the same mould or moulds, were all products of the poetic imagination and even though Bruce was a near contemporary, he is not really any more solid than Arthur, who never existed. His creator's aim was to make the nation, as it then was, conscious of a clear destiny and in 1375, when the poem was being composed, Scotland needed a modern history. The only accounts available, about Celtic battles, feuds and intrigues, were concerned with building myths of doubtful origin into a universal structure, as in the *Brut* tradition. Barbour's unusual concern for chronological and statistical accuracy pulls away from romance and a realistic Scotland, possessed of an authentic topography, becomes in his hands the background for a solidly rooted narrative of heroic action shot through with the glamour of an apparent verisimilitude no less strange in its way than the romance of Troy. The hero is a real knight on a real liberating quest and the work is endowed with a moral as well as an historical unity. He and his army are on the side of right, though the 'rights' are political and territorial rather than moral. Bruce is one of the last medieval kings, a projection of nationalist feeling, portrayed as an exile who succeeds against overwhelming odds. He is no demi-god endowed with superhuman qualities, no chivalrous cavalier chasing any phantom honour, but a flesh-and-blood man liable to failure. The gap between romance and fact is bridged by this verisimilitude and the whole made much more plausible as an historical account by a constant assertion that the writer is resolved never to lose sight of the *verus historiae* and to speak the truth as he believed it to be.

Like most medieval personalities, Barbour is ill-defined owing to a lack of reliable factual information. Born in about 1320, he became Archdeacon of Aberdeen while still a young man. This title is usually attached to his name in contemporary records. He served three kings of Scotland, David II and Robert II and III, holding appointments as clerk of audit in the Royal Household and later becoming one of the auditors of the Exchequer. He was granted safe conduct by Edward III to travel through England, probably to study in Oxford, and he made several journeys to France. In 1388 he was awarded an annual pension of £10 for 'faithful service'. These payments ceased early in 1395, presumably on the death of the recipient.

Barbour is supposed to have been responsible for at least two other works, a poem in the Layamon tradition called *Brut*, and a genealogy of the Stewards or Stuarts which claimed to trace the royal line from Robert II, Barbour's patron, to Ninus, the founder of Nineveh. Neither of these compositions is extant, and Barbour's reputation as 'father of Scots poetry' rests solely on his *Bruce*, written in twenty books of octosyllabic couplets. From this statement volunteered in Book XII scholars have learned that he was working on it in 1375:

> The Kingis douchter, that wes fair,
> And wes als his apperand air[1]
> With Walter Steward can he[2] wed;
> And thai weill soyne[3] gat of thar bed
> Ane knaiff[4] child, throu our Lordis grace,
> That eftir his gude eld-fadir[5] was
> Callit Robert, and syne[6] wes king,
> And had the land in governyng
> Eftir his worthy eyme,[7] Davy,
> That regnyt twa yer and fourty;
> And in tyme of the compyling
> Of this buk, this Robert wes king,
> And of his kynrik[8] passit was
> Fiffe yeir; and was the yer of grace
> Ane thousand thre hundreth and sevinty
> And fiffe and of his elde[9] sexty.

.   .   .   .   .   .

Dr. Samuel Johnson declared that

> ... in historical composition, all the greatest powers of the human mind are quiescent ... there is no exercise of invention ... Imagination is not required in any high degree (Boswell, *Life*, 6 July, 1763; ed. G. B. Hill [1934], I, 424).

[1] heir apparent	[2] did she	[3] very soon	[4] male	[5] grandfather
[6] later	[7] uncle	[8] reign	[9] age	

a statement which is typical of many scholars and literary critics, who believe that the intoxication sometimes induced by fine phrases lures the mind away from its path towards historical truth. Yet an alliance between history and literature has always been apparent in English tradition since Lord Berners made his translation of Froissart's *Chronicles of France, Flanders, England, Scotland and Spain* (1524 and 1525), a Tudor translator's version of a fourteenth-century work which came, with the original, very close to Gervase of Canterbury's ideal of history-writing.

In the preface to his *Froissart*, Berners (John Bourchier), a leading man of letters at Henry VIII's Court during the first half of his reign, summed up the Tudor view of history as possessing a politically useful function as propaganda in the cause of the new nationalism:

> The most profitable thing in this world for the institution of the human life is history. One, the continual reading thereof maketh young men equal in prudence to old men, and to old fathers stricken in age it ministereth experience of things. More, it yieldeth private persons worthy of dignity, rule and governance: it compelleth the emperors, high rulers and governors to do noble deeds to the end they may obtain immortal glory: it exciteth, moveth and stirreth the strong, hardy warriors for the great laud that they have after they be dead, promptly to go in hand with great and hard perils in defence of their country. And it prohibiteth reprovable persons to do mischievous deeds for fear of infamy and shame .... But above all things whereby man's wealth riseth, special laud and cause ought to be given to history: it is the keeper of things as have been virtuously done, and the witness of evil deeds; and by the benefit of history all noble, high and virtuous acts be immortal .... What pleasure shall it be to the noble gentlemen of England to see, behold and read the high enterprises, famous acts and glorious deeds done and achieved by their valiant ancestors? (*Op. cit.*, preface; Everyman ed. [1906])

Froissart's characters and scenes are colourful and stirring, and they uphold fading standards of chivalry in an era when they were really very much on the wane. Froissart himself was no cloistered author. He accompanied King David Bruce on his tour of Scotland and collected his facts by interview but what he achieved was not an historical method but a seductive verisimilitude. His 'truth' was not that of real life, but of the *chanson de geste*, the chivalric romance, for he wrote lyrically to please his patrons. His tastes were not those of a clerical historian like Barbour, though he could at times write with considerable economy, as his bald account (frequently quoted as an example of graphic sixteenth-century prose writing) of Wat Tyler's march on London demonstrates. Here it is in Berners' translation from the original French:

In the morning on Corpus Christi day, King Richard heard mass in the Tower of London, and all his lords, and then he took his barge with the Earl of Salisbury, the Earl of Warwick, the Earl of Oxford and certain knights, and so rowed down along the Thames to Rotherhithe whereat was descended down the hill a ten thousand men to see the king and to speak with him. And when they saw the king's barge coming they began to shout and make such a cry, as though all the devils of hell had been among them . . .

And when the king and his lords saw the demeanour of the people the best assured of them were in dread; and so the king was counselled by his barons not to take any landing there but so rowed up and down the river. And the king demanded of them what they would, and said how he was come thither to speak with them, and they said all with one voice: 'We would that you should come a-land and then we shall show you what we lack'. Then the Earl of Salisbury answered for the king and said: 'Sirs, be ye not in such order and array that the king ought to speak with you'. And then the king was counselled to return again to the Tower of London and so he did.

And when these people saw that, they were inflamed with ire and returned to the hill where the great band was, and there showed them what answer they had and how the king was returned to the Tower of London. Then they cried all with one voice, 'Let us go to London' and so they took their way thither; and in their

c

going they beat down abbeys, and houses of advocates and men of the court, and so came into the suburbs of London which were great and fair and there beat down diverse fair houses . . . There were many within the city of their accord, and so they drew together and said, 'Why do we not let these good people enter into the city? They are our fellows and that they do is for us'. So therewith the gates were opened and then these people entered into the city and went into houses and sat down to eat and drink. They desired nothing but it was incontinent brought to them, for every man was ready to make good cheer and to give them meat and drink to appease them. (*ed. cit.*)

Froissart's philosophy of history is akin to that of Boethius, the author of *De Consolatione Philosophiae*, who so much influenced Chaucer. Froissart sees the governance of the external world as lying in the hands of Fortune, outside the control of men, and most of his characters, fictional and historical alike, are concerned only with wordly ambitions, a desire for fame and social approval, a love of shows and glittering armour and with longings for military success. His *Chronicles* describe the turn of the wheel of fortune in the House of Plantagenet from Edward II's murder until Richard II's and provide the main contemporary account of the Hundred Years' War which, as it happened, was a very appropriate example for Froissart's purposes, since it was a period filled with notable instances of change of fortune. Boethius had stated that men whose concerns were entirely of this world need not count on direct intervention by God and Froissart absorbed this belief. He thought that wordly success or failure was the result of accident, and wrote in one of his love poems

> . . . elle met un homme en haut
> Ne l'en chaut
> Comment voist, puis le renverse
> Et le berse
> A un trop villain bersaut (4*ème lai.*)

[I feel that she (Fortune) is so wicked, full of malevolence, that she should raise a man up and not care how things go with him, then cast him down and bring him to grief]

This attitude to human action sets Froissart apart from the clerical historians, who adopted the position that history was grounded in the persistent action of a just Providence which judged the actions of individuals. Universal history saw God as the punisher of evil and the rewarder of good. God aided the brave and the righteous, but left the individual to take his own chance. Shakespeare expressed the same idea in the words of Brutus before Philippi:

> There is a tide in the affairs of men,
> Which, taken at the flood, leads on to fortune;
> Omitted, all the voyage of their life
> Is bound in shallows and in miseries,
> On such a full sea are we now afloat,
> And we must take the current when it serves,
> Or lose our ventures. (*Julius Caesar* IV, iii, 217–23)

What Shakespeare was thinking about when he composed these lines cannot be known—he had Philippi in mind, certainly, but his thoughts were undoubtedly fixed upon men and situations of his own time, on personalities like Sir Philip Sidney, or Walter Raleigh, who grasped opportunities when they were offered, or like himself, who sought fame and fortune in London rather than abide in country obscurity as most of his fellows chose to do. Although he was consciously writing a 'history play' purporting to record incidents over fifteen centuries earlier, the 'psychology' by which he tried to explain the motives of his protagonists is Elizabethan (or modern for that matter), and could be easily understood by contemporaries. Caesar, or Brutus, or any of Shakespeare's historical kings, act in a recognisable way, as they might be expected to do in the present, and all history-writing cast in literary form tends to simplify or over-simplify its records in the interest of a non-expert audience. The subjects chosen for treatment are easily understood by intelligent men and the incidents of the action are made dramatic and exciting, so as to appeal to the 'groundlings'. The lasting impression made is of living characters and living issues confronting them and the kind of 'truth' which emerges is truth of feeling, not really truth of fact. Shakespeare's Roman and history plays are not history. They partake of propaganda, trumpet-blowing nationalism, thinly-disguised lessons in statecraft, a subject of which his age was inordinately fond, political idealism trying to work itself out in practice, strained human relations, particularly when they are affected and modified by the desire for or the possession of power, either directly exercised, as by a king or governor, or indirectly, as by an adviser. In such an atmosphere, the role of chance is important. Men poised on the tight-rope must believe in some source of guidance, whether it be God, their own consciences or Fortune—very often they draw strength from all three, according to the exigencies of the situation.

Romantic historians ask their audiences to admire great men and to follow their examples with the help of God, or Fortune or both. The individual conscience counted for little during the Middle Ages. It was fallible, always open to correction, and although it was one of the Seven Gifts of the Holy Ghost, it had only a negative balancing character, urging men to remember their duties to God. Human problems were not the concern of conscience. When faced with difficulties, man appealed to God and to Fate, the old Germanic 'Wyrd' which decided his lot in battle.

References to Fate or Destiny are generally qualified by allusion to God's power to assist the valiant warrior. When Bruce sees his men fleeing at the Battle of Methven he rallies them, exclaiming:

> Lordingis, sen it is swa
> That ure rynnys agane us her,
> Gud is we pass off thar daunger,
> Till God us send eftsonys grace

[Fellows, since it is the case that our luck is against us here, it is a good thing that we avoid trouble till God sends us his blessing in the future]. (*Bruce*, II, 433–6.)

The writer's point of view is that God is on the side of Bruce and his men because they are righteous, and so that they will live to fight again another day, they beat a retreat on this occasion. The word 'ure' implied *good* luck and the impression given by the words of the leader is that whatever happens is out of his hands. The only obligation of the soldier is to fight doughtily in a good cause and to leave the outcome to the hidden powers, the God of battles.

·   ·   ·   ·   ·   ·

As has been noted earlier, Froissart was first translated by Lord Berners. Berners was a scholar-courtier-soldier like Wyatt, Surrey, Sidney and Raleigh after him and his translation of Froissart marks the high water mark of English narrative prose to this time. He wrote in a compound of Saxon and Romance diction which blends without the strain apparent in earlier authors trying to communicate fully in English sentences. C. S. Lewis refers to Berners as 'the last of the great medieval translators'. His professed motives are the characteristically medieval ones of eschewing idleness and promoting the spirit of chivalry. Apologising for a lack of ability in the art of rhetoric, Berners says that he will reduce Froissart into 'fresh ornate polished English'. However, he does make conscious use of rhetorical tricks, such as multiplying synonyms and parallel phrases, especially in the prefaces to his works. His preface to Froissart recommends histories because they

> show, open, manifest and declare to the reader by example of old antiquity what we should enquire, desire and follow and also what we should eschew, avoid and utterly flee.

and in the words of Emile Legouis his translation is 'as animated, lively and highly-coloured as his original, yet represents a return to the fourteenth century'. The spirit is late medieval and his descriptions, such as the famous one of the Battle of Otterbourne (1388), are done with a knightly relish. The account stressed the chivalric aspects of real life, love and war and to a background of honour in amatory pursuits is added a narrative glorifying military prowess and the glamour of knightliness. The historical period covered by the *Chronicles* is 1326–1400, embracing the reigns of Edward III, Richard II and Henry IV, a colourful period of great conflict in Europe and in Scotland. The accounts of these actions and the swaggering personalities involved in them were probably quite inaccurate but they fascinated later generations and Berners' labours placed the *Chronicles* in the hands of a wide public who found his English less trouble to read than Froissart's Old French.

Froissart set up a novel standard of historical writing, quite different from that of the more prosaic annalists. A century and a half
later, Berners made the Frenchman's narratives a part of English
literature. His history was the only one written in English which
tried to achieve a literary style and could therefore be recommended
along with classical and Italian vernacular works as suitable for
young noblemen to study. Elyot, for example, had obviously read
it, as his statement concerning the value of history (ch. xi) echoes
that made in Berners' preface.

By 1550 it could be said that a second kind of history-making
had established itself in addition to the narrative or chronicle,
which was heavily weighted in favour of military exploits. This was
the precise study of laws and government and the examination of
the whole basis for ruling a modern state. Some of the works written around this theme have a distinctively literary character—
Elyot's *Book Named the Governor* (1531) and Ascham's *The Schoolmaster* (printed 1570) were about education and the kind of
training which a ruler, a scion of the élite, ought to be given by way
of preparation for his life's work. More's *Utopia* (c. 1516 but not
translated until 1551) was more fanciful and apparently 'progressive', though it was really a restatement of some of Plato's ideas as
laid out in his *Republic*. Written originally in Latin, *Utopia* touched
political thought, satire and social criticism at various levels of
seriousness; in fact, it was mostly not serious at all. It was the first
of several such works in English—Bacon's *New Atlantis* and
Swift's *Gulliver's Travels*, for example. Unlike Berners, More used
a battery of rhetorical devices and his works in Latin and English
are full of the couplings of synonyms, repetitions, alliterations and
cross-alliteration (in *Utopia* apparent only in translation), and
lively dialogue. It is this dramatic temper which makes *Utopia*
so attractive to the modern reader, for More let his characters
speak in their own personalities, as Shakespeare did. Its 'historical'
quality is more elusive than that of Shakespeare, as it is indirect
and reflective of contemporary or recent developments in exploration by Amerigo Vespucci and others. The work may be said to
mark the end of 'medievalism' for it rejected war and the chivalric
spirit, tolerated all religions, according no special privileges to

Christianity, attacked the penal laws of England by showing how they could be made unnecessary, and protested against asceticism and that contempt for the world which characterised the gloomy monastic attitude to material being. His ideal state provided an easy life for an ideal community wherein all men pulled together. *Utopia* reflected many of the impractical ideas current at the time, but not the country as it really was, or was likely to become, or, strangely enough, its author's actual conduct, since, as Lord Chancellor, devout Catholic and ascetic, More persecuted the early Protestants and was eventually executed by Henry VIII for his refusal to recognise him as Head of the Church. Considered as a mirror of the age, therefore, *Utopia* presents an immediate image only of a certain contemporary reality, namely, the escape into realms of intellectual fancy.

More's humanist friends, of whom Erasmus was the most brilliant, included Grocyn, Linacre, Colet, Fisher, Warham and Elyot, men who pursued new intellectual interests, each in his different way, but all starting with certain assumptions deriving from personal knowledge of Italian culture or from the direct influence of Erasmus, or from both. Though *Utopia* might signify an escape, the work of these English scholars, which helped to make the Reformation possible, was extremely practical in intention and effects even though it partook of that high idealism which all humanists shared.

.   .   .   .   .   .

Historical writing in England changed its character during the fifteenth and sixteenth centuries. The revival of classical scholarship in Italy had a powerful influence on the scope and form of histories. The authors of histories from the twelfth century onwards were usually monks and in no European country can the rise of historical composition be separated from monasticism. The monk-historian's ideas about chronology and his twin functions as moralist and recorder were governed by his faith in the significance of two historical facts, the Creation and the Incarnation. Although he frequently digressed, or was compelled by economic or personal enthusiasms to concentrate upon other and more mundane concerns, the monastic historian, writing in Latin for others like himself, was always ultimately inspired by a belief in the working out of God's purpose. This permitted him to write 'universal' history and yet to believe in his own reliability as a purveyor of historical truth.

The changing face of society during the period 1350–1500 also changed the approach to historiography. The old monastic outlook was too narrow, concentrated as it was on ecclesiastical affairs in this world and the hope of Paradise in the next, for the monk knew little of the countries across the English Channel. The Renaissance spirit demanded a fresher and more practical approach to historical compilations, and the fifteenth century saw the emergence of a great number of histories written in English and of multiplications, continuations and translations of the *Brut* and the *Polychronicon*. Caxton printed *Brut* and, in John of Trevisa's English rendering, continued the original *Polychronicon* to 1461. By 1500 there were six editions of *Brut* and two of *Polychronicon*.

During the fifteenth century at least 25 chroniclers were working in London making civic histories. Others concentrated on towns other than than the capital, but the *Chronicles* of London are the most significant historical authorities of the fifteenth century. Copies were numerous and of these about thirty remain extant, no two being quite alike. The tradition of keeping civic records in London goes back to the mid-thirteenth century and it continued into Elizabethan times. Apart from giving later historians information about the administrative affairs of the capital, the London *Chronicles* shed light on what the citizens were thinking about events in other places and the fact that they were in part written in diary fashion gives some of them a personal quality of spontaneity absent from accounts produced after long delay. These accounts are useful mainly because they are contemporary and lay some claim to accurate representation of current popular opinion among the London mercantile classes. Robert Fabyan's *New Chronicles of England and of France* was being edited about 1502 and is regarded as one of the last of the fifteenth-century *Chronicles*. It was printed by Richard Pynson in 1516 under that title and, with some additions, by John Rastell, author of *The Four Elements*, in 1533. The work of Fabyan ends with the year 1485 though the continuation in the latter edition extended to 1509.

Fabyan's *Chronicle* is divided into seven parts. The first is an account from Brut to Molmutius, the second takes the reader to the Roman invasion, the third to the death of Lucius, the fourth to the fall of Rome, the fifth to Cadwallader, the sixth to Harold and the last from the Conquest to 1485. Four-fifths of the work is taken up by the last two parts and by far the greatest space is devoted to the 1066–1485 period. Independent sections, treating of French affairs, appear in and after part five. Thus although Fabyan's book starts, according to monastic tradition, with the Creation and has a groundwork of faith, it shows clear tendencies towards lay or secular history-writing. The evolution of the urban chronicle and of the non-clerical historian are parallel developments, and occurred in Italy, Germany and France before they came to England. In England historiography at this period is most completely represented by the contributions of Caxton and of Fabyan, who between them show the culmination of historiographical developments to that time. Caxton and Fabyan are worth comparing in respect of their views on the study of history.

In his prologue to *Polychronicon* (1482), Caxton explains that the study of history is morally profitable. The experiences of other times are, he claims, useful in the education of youth and in the training of a governor. History encourages martial enthusiasm, discourages infamous acts by recording them and inspires virtuous acts by recording them in elegant language, or, as he says:

> the fruytes of vertue ben Immortal specyally whanne they ben wrapped in the benifyce of hystories. (*op. cit.*)

Caxton disregards the problems associated with historical accuracy and with the actual recording of events, as well as with the selection of those to be noted. His interests, he admits, are linguistic, and connected with translating old authors and his aim, above all, is one of pious edification. He looks at the past as a medieval man did, as though it were out of this world, except as an example which rulers might do well to regard.

Fabyan, in a verse *Prologue* (1516), is more down to earth. His aim, he informs his readers, is to gather a collection of historical narratives for information, not to reconcile divergent legends or to wax eloquent about the past. Such information as he proposed to offer would, he said, be confined to three main subjects, England, France and the City of London. He was not interested in moral content or in debating the historical accuracy or reliability of sources, but in writing an account of recent events and especially of local history which would satisfy popular wants. Fabyan expressed a solid admiration for English traditions and institutions and was one of the first patriotic historians of the sixteenth century, prefiguring the far more resonant tub-thumping of Edward Hall's *Chronicle* of 1548, though the character of his work places him more comfortably among fifteenth-century recorders. John Stow, the foremost antiquary of the Elizabethan age, depended a great deal on the fifteenth-century *Chronicles*, for he was the first historian to draw on public records systematically and to adopt methods of research which one may call modern, stating sources and authorities and not trying to embellish originals to suit his own purposes. Led to history from poetry, he produced a succession of works during the second half of the sixteenth century, culminating in the *Annales of England*, first published as a whole in 1592. He drew liberally on a score of annalists and on the work of more scholarly historians like More and Hall but comes too late for consideration here.

Thomas More is thought to have written a *History of King Richard III* in 1513, eventually printed by his nephew William Rastell in 1557. Two versions exist, in Latin and English, and authorship is doubtful. The Latin version ends with Richard's coronation in 1483; the English with the conspiracy of his follower the Duke of Buckingham and John Morton, Bishop of Ely, to overthrow the King. Morton, into whose household More was admitted as a boy, is believed to have supplied the material on which the book is based. The nineteenth-century historian Hallam describes the *History* as 'the first example of good English language; pure and perspicuous, well-chosen, without vulgarisms or pedantry' (*Introduction to the Literature of Europe* [1837–9], I. 454). As an illustration of 'More's' prose in this *History*, take his lively physical description of Jane Shore, Edward IV's mistress, in her old age:

Whose jugement semeth me somewhat like as though men should gesse the beauty of one longe before departed, by her scalpe taken out of the charnel-house; for now is she old, lene, withered and dried up, nothing left but ryvilde (*wrinkled*) skin and hard bone. And yet being even such, whoso wel advise (*may look closely at*) her visage, might gesse and devise whiche partes how filled wold make it a faire face. Yet delited not men so much in her beauty, as in her plesant behaviour. For a proper wit had she, and could both rede wel and write, mery in company, redy and quick of aunswer, neither mute nor full of bable, some-time taunting without displeasure and not without disport.

(*op. cit.*, ed. J. Rawson Lumby [1883], p. 54.)

A contributor to the account of scholars and scholarship in England given in the third volume of the *Cambridge History of English Literature* (1908), Mr. Charles Whibley, held that from the date of the composition of the English version 'our art of history must date its beginning', an exaggeration, but based on the obser-vation that the work possessed organisation and symmetry and was not simply a factual record. More refers to Morton, who later became Archbishop of Canterbury, as a man not more honourable for his authority than for his prudence and virtue, gifted with a polished and effective utterance (*sermo politus et efficax*). The tone is, as might be expected, totally hostile to Richard, from whose ven-geance Morton escaped by taking ship to Flanders, and the continuing note of apparently personal spite has been cited as evidence that the urbane More could not have written it.

The earliest English life of Henry V, presenting the King as an example of a fine Christian prince, was also written in 1513 by a shadowy figure known as the 'Translator of Livius', quoted as an authority in Holinshed's *Chronicles*, a compilation of 1578 and 1587 from which Shakespeare derived much of his historical information. The 'Translator' based his own statements on the accounts of the fourth Earl of Ormonde, who was on the field at Agincourt and other campaigns and died in 1452. The legends telling of the relations of Prince Hal and his father, Henry IV, of his camaraderie with ruffians, of his brush with the law and of his change from dissolute to virtuous habits of life, all have their roots in fifteenth-century *Chronicles* or cycles of anecdotes such as Ormonde's, as told by the 'Translator of Livius'. Their original sources are hard to trace—the tale of Hal's brush with the law first turns up in Elyot's *Book Named the Governor* (Bk II, vi; see chap. 4) and probably came from a London *Chronicle*, to be narrated by Stow, himself a main source for Holinshed and ultimately for Shakespeare. In most legends there is a substratum of truth, and these stories cannot be dismissed, though they cannot be corroborated either.

The 'Translator's' work is more interesting from the literary point of view, for in his preface he says that he has translated and reduced his originals into rude and homely English from which all skill and ornament is a long way removed. His aim is largely propagandist and he addresses Henry VIII in a number of moralistic statements; Henry VIII's French campaign was going on at the time of composition, and the didactic intention is plain.

. . . . . .

An influential Italian, Polydore Vergil (1470–1555), who spent most of his life in England, wrote in Latin an important work of history called *Anglica Historia* (printed in 1534) which went into three editions during his lifetime. The last of these included a section on the period 1509–37. Vergil was a friend of Colet, Linacre, Grocyn, More, Lilly, Ridley, Richard Pace and other English humanists, as well as of Erasmus, Budé and Aleandro. He had previously published *De Inventoribus Rerum* (1499), later expanded by five books and frequently revised by the author. It described the origins of human invention, such as the gods, the Creation, language, marriage and divorce, religion, learning, science, law, books, military tactics, athletics, money, art, agriculture, architecture, towns, navigation, commerce and prostitution. He considered the value of the historical approach to science and the scientific approach to comparative religion in a manner far in advance of his time.

Anglica Historia, first written in 1512–13, is divided into twenty-six books. The first seven deal with English history to Harold, book eight with William I and II, and the books from nine to twenty-five are given over to successive reigns from that of Henry I to Henry VIII's. It was first printed in Basle in a revised form in 1534, and translated into English about 1550. For present purposes, the important part of the *Historia* lies in its treatment of contemporary events from 1461, which depended on oral and documentary sources and for latter years on personal observation of events. Vergil is regarded as the principal narrative authority for the period 1485–1509, although his account was first read in English only in the form presented by Edward Hall, who reproduced him in his *Chronicle* in 1548. Vergil is a less reliable authority on Henry VIII's reign than Hall himself but for the reigns of Richard III and Henry VII he is to be looked upon as an original source.

The reign of Henry VIII is the first period in English history which can be approached by way of state records and papers. Archive material is for the first time available to the historian in abundance and old-fashioned narrative accounts thus begin to take second place in order of reliability. Vergil's account is coloured by the very fact of his own participation in the events of the times he tries to describe and by his desire to satisfy a contemporary audience. Its value lies in its contemporaneity, and, for the literary historian, in the parallel passages connecting Vergil with More. Vergil's description of English economic distress may well have been based directly on More's account which was also written in Latin. The choice of words certainly suggests that Vergil had *Utopia* before him when he was composing his statement about Henry's attempts to check the agricultural abuses of the sheep-farming nobles in 1517–21.

Compare this passage of Vergil's:

For half a century or more previously, the sheep-farming nobles had tried to find devices whereby they might increase the annual income of their lands. As a result the yeomen had incurred very considerable losses. The sheep farmers, cultivating pasturage (after the manner of Arabs) rather than arable, began everywhere to employ far fewer agricultural labourers, to destroy rural dwelling-houses, to create vast deserts, to allow the land to waste while filling it up with herds, flocks and a multitude of beasts; in like fashion they fenced off all those pastures to keep them private, thus establishing in their own right a monopoly of sheep and cattle. From this three evil consequences ensued for the state. First, the number of peasants, upon which the prince chiefly relies for waging war, was reduced. Second, a larger number of villages and towns, many stripped of inhabitants, were ruined. Third, the wool and cloth which was thus reduced, as well as the flesh of all kinds of animals which is fit for human consumption, began to sell much more dearly than it used to do, so that the price has not really dropped even to this day. Since in the past these abuses were not checked early in their development, they were afterwards hardened and became much more durable, so that later they could not be easily remedied. It was with this situation in view that the king in a proclamation to the whole of England ordered the magistrates (commissioners) to report how much of this type of evil practice had been permitted during the last fifty years. (*Anglica Historia*, 1517–21; ed. and trans. Denys Hay, Camden series LXXIV.)

with the corresponding passage of *Utopia*, from the second and revised edition, translated by Ralph Robinson and published in 1556:

. . . your sheep that were wont to be so meek and tame, and so small eaters, now, as I hear say, be become so great devourers and so wild, that they eat up, and swallow down the very men themselves. They consume, destroy, and devour whole fields, houses, and cities. For look in what parts of the realm doth grow the finest and therefore dearest wool, there noblemen and gentlemen, yea and certain abbots, holy men no doubt, not contenting themselves with the yearly revenues and profits, that were wont to grow to their forefathers and predecessors of their lands, nor being content that they live in rest and pleasure nothing profiting, yea much annoying the weal public, leave no ground for tillage, they inclose all into pastures; they throw down houses; they pluck down towns, and leave nothing standing, but only the church to be made a sheep-house. And as though you lost no small quantity of ground by forests, chases, lawns and parks, those good holy men turn all dwelling-places and all glebeland into desolation and wilderness. Therefore that one covetous and insatiable cormorant and a very plague of his native country may compass about and enclose many thousand acres of ground together within one pale or hedge, the husbandmen be thrust out of their own, or else either by cunning or by fraud, or by violent oppression they be put besides it, or by wrongs and injuries they be so wearied, that they be compelled to sell all: by one means therefore or by another, either by hook or crook they must needs depart away . . . out of their known and accustomed houses, finding no place to rest in . . . and though the number of sheep increase never so fast, yet the price falleth not one mite, because there be so few sellers. For they be almost all come into a few rich men's hands, whom no need forceth to sell before they lust (pleased), and they lust not before they may sell as dear as they lust. (*Utopia* [1556 ed.], I)

It is important to note, as its recent editor and translator does, that the first humanist history of England (and of France also) was written by an Italian. In a letter to the historiographer to the court at Rimini written in 1446, Guarino of Verona, a famed Latinist, distinguished between *history*, concerned with contemporary affairs, and *annals*, concerned with events of the past. His standards are Ciceronian, but although he thought that beautiful language contributed to the reader's belief that what is being presented is the absolute truth, he insisted on scholarly detachment, implying dependence upon fact alone, an attitude which was not always appreciated by diplomatic patrons in the Italian city states, who were more concerned with how the reader received the facts and considered that a grand style was more conducive to persuasion when the facts were awkward. What usually happened was that a compromise was struck between facts and style.

This influence was a happy one for later history-writing, since Polydore Vergil, educated in two Italian universities, Padua and Bologna, inherited an academic desire for detachment and, writing in Latin, appealed to an international audience imbued with the spirit of humanism. While vernacular historians at this time went on singing the praises of Arthur and his knights and fitting their accounts of England's past into the established mould of 'universal history', Latin writers, encouraged by royal patrons, sought to join English to Continental humanism by rejecting myth in favour of facts. In another work, *Gildas . . . de calamitate, excidio et conquestu Britanniae* (1525), Vergil provides the first critical edition of an English historical text. Gildas, a sixth-century Romano-British historian, was the forerunner of other early narrators, and provided Polydore Vergil with a good example of the unreliability which he needed in order to support his own rejection of legendary and mythical material disguised as history.

In his dedication to Henry VIII, Vergil described history as

> the only unique, certain and faithful witness of times and things, redounding as much to the glory of the author as to the usefulness of posterity . . . not only useful and enriching, but positively essential . . . it displays eternally to the living those events which should be an example and those which should be a warning

and proceeded to attack the old historians (with the exceptions of Bede, William of Malmesbury and Matthew Paris) for their baldness, uncouthness, chaotic presentation, and deceitfulness. He explained that he himself perused the chronicles such as were available to him and then consulted 'those who had often been employed in the highest business of state'. He also kept a diary.

He claimed that such an account as he had to offer demanded a fine style, but that he would rather spoil the Latin than the sense of what he stated was to be an *English* not a *British* history. His dedication to the King included the hope that 'even the wisest of men will be able to derive from it evidences of past action by which to guide his public and private affairs'. Vergil succeeded in interpreting the rise of the House of Tudor favourably and in this section alone, as we have noted earlier, does he become caught up in the horns of the dilemma of the humanist historian and indulge in the prejudices of his time at the expense of objectivity. He is violently critical of Wolsey, for example, and has nothing to say

in his favour, not surprisingly, since in 1515 the latter had had
Vergil put in prison:

> . . . 'be ye perfect even as your father in heaven is perfect'. Not
> even a spark of this perfection seemed to shine in Wolsey, who
> not only did not do good to his enemies (even those who were so
> involuntarily and without damage to him), but flaming with
> hatred and lusting to sate it with human blood, he began to
> contrive the destruction, upon which he had already resolved as
> we said above, of Edward Duke of Buckingham. (*Anglica
> Historia*, 1521.)

and elsewhere, announcing Wolsey's election to the archbishopric
of York and Lord Chancellor of the Realm;

> The enjoyment of such an abundance of good fortune is to be
> reckoned most praiseworthy if it is showered upon sober,
> moderate and self-controlled men, who are not proud in their
> power, nor are made arrogant with their money, nor vaunt them-
> selves in other fortunate circumstances. None of these charac-
> teristics could be described in Wolsey, who, acquiring so many
> offices at almost the same time, became so proud that he con-
> sidered himself the peer of kings. He soon began to use a
> golden chair, a golden cushion, a golden cloth on his table, and,
> when he was walking, to have the hat, symbol of the rank of
> cardinal, carried before him like a servant, raised up like some
> holy idol or other; and to have it put upon the very altar in the
> king's chapel for the duration of the service. Thus Wolsey, with
> his arrogance and ambition, raised against himself the hatred of
> the whole people and, in his hostility towards nobles and
> common folk, procured their great irritation at his vainglory. His
> own odiousness was truly complete, because he claimed he could
> undertake himself almost all public duties. It was indeed signi-
> ficant to see this fellow, ignorant of law, sitting in court and
> pronouncing judgment . . . (*Ibid*, 1514-5).

This portrait, or rather caricature, may well have contributed to
Skelton's representation of 'Magnificence', which bears some
resemblance to Wolsey, and even more to its morality-play figures,

D

Deadly Sins like Pride, Avarice or their material relation Luxury or Riches. In some of the street pageants and interludes of the period after Wolsey's fall the Cardinal himself occasionally appeared as a symbol of papal authority, as he does in Shakespeare's *Henry VIII*. The most direct representation of Wolsey's powers in contemporary poetry is to be found in the poetical works of Skelton, however, who, in *Colin Cloute, Speke Parrat* and *Why Come Ye Not to Courte?* leaves an impression of Wolsey that is as one-sided as Vergil's.

> To tell the truth plainly
> He is so ambitious,
> So shameless and so vicious,
> And so superstitious
> And so much oblivious
> From whence that he came
> That he falleth into a *caeciam*
> Which, truly to express,
> Is a forgetfulness,
> Or wilful blindness . . .
> But this mad Amaleck,
> Like to a Mamelek
> He regardeth lordés
> No more than potsherdés
> He is in such elation
> Of his exaltation
> And the supportation
> Of his sovereign lordé
> That, God to recordé
> He ruleth all at will
> Without reason or skill.
> Howbeit the primordial
> Of his wretched original
> And his base progeny
> And his greasy genealogy
> He came of the sang royall
> That was cast out of a butcher's stall . . .

Such is a kinges power
To make within an hour
And work such a miracle
That shall be a spectacle
Of renown and wordly fame.
In likewise now the same
Cardinal is promoted,
Yet with lewd conditions coated
As hereafter ben noted,
Presumption and vainglory,
Envy, wrath, and lechery,

Couvetise and gluttony,
Slothful to do good,
Now frantic, now starke wood.[1]

Should this man of suche mood
Rule the sword of might?
How can he do right?
For he will as soon smite
His friende as his foe—
A proverb long ago.

Set up a wretch on high
In a throne triumphantly,
Make him a great estate
And he will play checkmate
With royal majesty.

(*Why Come ye Not to Courte?* ed. P. Henderson [1931].)

No other historical personage is pilloried so openly by any Tudor poet. Wolsey is seen as the summation of all corruptions, ecclesiastical and political, and is described in *Colin Clout* as the ordinary man might have spoken of him. Later, Skelton was to make his peace with Wolsey and apologised, probably for his own security, and in *A Replication Against Certain Young Scholars Abjured of Late*, an anti-heretical poem written about 1526, he addressed the Cardinal in a Latin dedication as follows:

[1] mad.

To the most honourable, most mighty, and by far the most reverend father in Christ and in the Lord, Lord Thomas, etc. etc. . . . the most deserving Cardinal, Legate of the Apostolic See and the most illustrious legate *a latere*, etc. Skelton Laureate, *ora. reg.* declares humble allegiance with all fit reverence due to such a great and magnificent Chief of Priests, most equitable moderator of all justice . . .

and ended the poem with an envoy

> Go, little quaire, apace,
> In most humble wise,
> Before his noble grace,
>   That caused you to devise
>   This little enterprise;
> And him most lowly pray,
>   In his mind to comprise
> Those words his grace did say
> Of an amice gray.
> Je foy enterment en sa bone grace.[1]
>
> *(ed. cit.)*

which, in the light of what we know of Skelton's poetical nature, could hardly have been indicative of his true feelings in the matter. One can scarcely blame him for taking out insurance against Wolsey's likely vengeance, which he had only escaped by living in sanctuary at Westminster and by maintaining a deserved reputation as a strongly orthodox opponent of heresy.

This treatment of Wolsey, like Shakespeare's of John or of Richard III, indicates how misleading poets' or dramatists' accounts of historical figures may be, even when the latter are contemporary. After the mid-sixteenth century, narrative history developed through compilations or digests of chronicles put together, not by original explorers of the past, but by editors, some of whom were 'scissors-and-paste' hacks. Neither Hall nor Holinshed, main sources for Shakespeare and Spenser's patriotic presentations of history, were creators of 'literature' nor were they

[1] I trust entirely in his good grace.

masters of the English language. Polydore Vergil dealt narrative history a severe blow when he rejected the legends of Brutus and Arthur. This went against the patriotic tide of the times, since the Tudors, with some slight justification, liked to think that their dynasty was historically of ancient standing, resting their claim on the lineal descent of Owen Tudor, Henry VII's grandfather, from Cadwallader, last of the old border kings, and Vergil was many times attacked for his 'anti-Englishness'. Parochialism of this kind, summed up in John Leland's *Assertio Inclytissimi Arturii* (1544) and John Bale's *Scriptores* (1548), was closely associated with hostility to Rome. Vergil provided a convenient target for this kind of unscholarly abuse. A contemporary called him

> that most rascall dogge knave in the worlde, and Englyshman by byrth, but he had Italian parents: he had the randsackinge of all the Englishe lybraryes and when he had extracted what he pleased he burnt those famous velome manuscripts, and made himself father to other mens workes—felony in the highest degree; he deserved not heaven, for that was too good for him, neither will I be so uncharitable to judge him to hell, yet I think that he deserved to be hanged between both. (Quoted by Hay, *ed. cit.*, xxxv)

and it was not until the nineteenth century that his bespotted reputation was shown to be the result of xenophobia and quite undeserved. Although Leland, Bale, Foxe and others condemned Vergil, they did not scruple to use *Anglica Historia* as a main source for their own writings.

· · · · · ·

Edward Hall's Dedication to his *Chronicle* (1548) considered the nature of history and concluded that it is the record of the past set out in a form designed to keep fame and glory alive:

> so that evidently it appereth that Fame is the triumphe of glory, and memory by litterature is the verie dilator and setter furth of Fame.

He approached his task of recording events critically, systematically and logically and considered that the truth of history was best arrived at by dealing with specific themes. His *Chronicle* traced the struggle of Lancaster and York in the Wars of the Roses and their ultimate reconciliation from Henry IV to Henry VIII and its title claims to describe 'the union of the two noble and illustre famelies of Lancastre and Yorke'.

The standards which Hall proposed to uphold were similar to those of Vergil, though their effects would surely not have pleased the author of *Anglica Historia*. However, the latter did influence the character of Elizabethan drama from *Gorboduc* onwards. History plays were thenceforth always to be conceived as dramatised contests or conflicts between powerful personalities or factions, notwithstanding the time in which they were placed. Human character and human weakness governed the past and Julius Caesar, Henry IV, Macbeth and Antony were all types of men who 'made' history. Their faults (and virtues) were nearly always in themselves and not in their stars and in Shakespeare's ideal king, Henry V, a modern Arthurian figure emerged, only indirectly related to the real monarch. Poets, who according to classical dicta were gifted with the ability to enshrine heroes of the past in magnificent language and thus to be instruments of public and private morality, took precedence over historians in the view of many important writers of the later sixteenth century, notably Sir Philip Sidney, himself a poet, who endows the men of his profession with almost holy qualities.

Shakespeare took most of his historical information directly from the second edition of Holinshed's *Chronicle* of 1586. This, in turn, depended on Hall and Stow, and on staunch Tudor sympathisers like Fabyan, Berners and Vergil. Samuel Daniel's *Civil Wars*, a verse history in eight cantos, covered the same ground as Shakespeare's history plays. Daniel claimed, with some justice to himself:

> I versify the truth, not poetize.

For *The Civil Wars* is not poetry and its recital of facts is really a selection from those presented in the nationalistic chronicles, spiced by some incursions into supernatural origins. The fall of

Richard II, the unrest under Henry IV, the coming of the ideal monarch, Henry V, the Lancaster and York conflict ending in the happy union of the two houses as depicted in the three parts of *Henry VI* and the pageant of *Henry VIII* (the last two not completely of Shakespeare's authorship) made up the matter of Daniel's 'versification' of the truth.

The action of Shakespeare's *Richard III* owes its character to the narrative of Polydore Vergil and the history of that king attributed to More; its opening speech leaves an audience in no doubt as to its bias against the then Duke of Gloucester, a deformed pervert 'not shap'd for sportive tricks' who announces, in the manner of a morality-play vice:

> I am determined to prove a villain,
> And hate the idle pleasures of those days.
> Plots have I laid, inductions dangerous,
> By drunken prophecies, libels and dreams,
> To set my brother Clarence and the king
> In deadly hate the one against the other:
> And if King Edward be as true and just
> As I am subtle, false and treacherous . . .
>
> (I, i, 30–7)

and maintains to the end the character of an evil product of civil conflict. Compare 'More's' description:

Richard Duke of Gloucester . . . was little of stature, evil featured of limbs, crook-backed, the left shoulder much higher than the right, hard-favoured of visage, such as in estates is called a warlike visage, and among common persons a crabbed face. He was malicious, wrathful, and envious; . . . close and secret, a deep dissembler, lowly of countenance, arrogant of heart, outwardly familiar where he inwardly hated, not letting to kiss whom he thought to kill, spiteful and cruel, not always for ill-will, but oftener for ambition and to serve his purpose; friend and foe were all indifferent; where his advantage grew, he spared no man's death whose life withstood his purpose.

·   ·   ·   ·   ·   ·

When the 1st Duke of Marlborough said that his source for an item of historical information was 'Shakespeare, the only History of England I ever read' he would have been taken more seriously then than he would nowadays. Shakespeare's version of English history, the chroniclers' history, was true in essence, and had a kind of accuracy, the kind which appeals to patriotic feeling and encourages the Englishman to say that even if it is not true, it ought to have been. But it is not history according to the standards set in the nineteenth century. Poetry and history therefore parted company completely with the Elizabethans, who could see events only in terms of personalities, divisions of duty and motives, in other words between the 'fell incensèd points of mighty opposites'. This tendency is readily perceptible in the four great tragedies, two of which have an 'historical' setting, as well as in all the Roman plays.

The great increase of available information in the sixteenth century of which we have spoken, together with the mastering of new techniques for dealing with it, drove a wedge between the academic historian and the imaginative writer of narrative which could not be removed by the 'popular' chronicler. Inevitably, academic historians adopted an uncompromising position regarding the crude editorial or paraphrasing accounts and the imaginative literary creations or recreations of past events. Both were suspect. The simple two-term dichotomy of Gervase respecting the narrator and the annalist, with their appropriate styles, has its counterpart nowadays when the terms 'literary' and 'popular' are equated and both associated with amateurism, imprecision and lack of that specialisation indispensable to the historian proper. C. V. Wedgwood puts it succinctly:

The close relationship between clear thinking and good writing is illustrated time and time again by the work of the great scholars. This fact has been obscured by the common confusion between literary history and popular history. Properly speaking, all history which is written with style and distinction belongs to English literature; it need not necessarily be 'popular' in the sense that millions can read and understand it . . . In history alone the term 'literary' has associations with the idea of popularity.

It is assumed that good writing in history will occur most often, if not exclusively, in history which is directed towards a large public. But this does not follow. Much of the best historical writings of the last fifty years ... has come from scholarly specialists, with little or no interest in reaching a large public or being acclaimed as literary figures ... The practice of the finest scholars bears out the thesis that literature and scholarship, so far from being radically opposed to each other, are natural allies. Literary sensibility and literary technique are something more than pleasing additional graces to be cultivated by the historian if and when he has time ... they will guide, help, and illuminate the whole process of historical enquiry.

('Literature and the Historian' in *Truth and Opinion* [1960], p. 75.)

C. V. Wedgwood is talking here from the historian's point of view, not the poet's. She is considering tonal and narrative embellishments, figurative language, verbal sound-effects and the whole technique of style. How far does this technique add to, or detract from, the historian's concept of truth? How far may a historian work from his imagination without perverting the facts and distorting his explanation of their causes and effects? What may a historian eliminate in the interests of art in order to improve the form of what he is recreating? Must all history be verifiable, grounded in documentary evidence?

Benedetto Croce answered these questions as follows:

The partition of the sources (of history) into narratives and documents, and the superiority attributed to documents over narratives, and the alleged necessity of narrative as a subordinate but ineradicable element, almost form a mythology or allegory, which represents in an imaginative manner the relation between life and thought, between document and criticism in historical thought.

And document and criticism, life and thought, are the true *sources* of history—that is to say, the two elements of historical synthesis. ('History and Chronicle' in *History, Its Theory and Practice*, tr. Douglas Ainslie [1960].)

In other words, a historian proper works from documents,

records and verifiable facts, which he is not entitled to modify. The imaginative writers with whom the literary critic is concerned, and with whom this book is concerned, are not historians, but poets and dramatists, and as such, when they write on a historical theme, about a once living or still living personage, like Wallace or Wolsey, about a military campaign, like the Scottish War of Independence, about a conflict between opposing forces, each representing fundamental traits in human nature, like Richard III and Henry IV, they are creating not history, but hybrids. Croce called these hybrids 'poetical' histories and said that they were governed not by thought, but by sentiment:

> In order to turn poetical biography into truly historical bio- graphy we must repress our loves, our tears, our scorn, and seek what function the individual has fulfilled in social activity or civilisation; and we must do the same for national history as for that of humanity, and for every group of facts, small or great, as for every order of events. ('Pseudo-Histories', *ibid.*)

and went on to distinguish the imaginative reconstruction of the past, indispensable to the historian, from the free poetic imagina- tion. Poetry and history, for Croce, are contradictions in terms and their mingling is an illusion. He and Macaulay would not have disagreed.

To quote from a further paragraph of Macaulay's review of Hallam's *Constitutional History* (1828):

> To make the past present, to bring the distant near, to place us in the society of a great man or on the eminence which overlooks the field of a mighty battle, to invest with the reality of human flesh and blood beings whom we are too much inclined to consider as personified qualities in an allegory, to call up our ancestors before us with all their peculiarities of language, manners and garb, to show us over their houses, to seat us at their tables, to rummage their old-fashioned wardrobes, to explain the uses of their ponderous furniture, these parts of the duty which properly belongs to the historian have been ap- propriated by the historical novelist. On the other hand, to

extract the philosophy of history, to direct our judgment of events and men, to trace the connection of causes and effects, and to draw from the occurrences of former times general lessons of moral and political wisdom, has become the business of a distinct class of writers. (*op. cit.*)

What one takes for 'history' in medieval or Renaissance times is usually not really history at all but instead poetic fiction, intended, usually, to educate, edify and persuade a society in a progressive stage of development that it has a long tradition, or that it has been built by heroes who won noble victories over villains, and deserves the sort of affection which we call 'patriotic'. Much of it was propaganda, designed to promote certain moral feelings, and not simply to entertain, like the fictitious romances, and it took its character from the national myth which grew during the fifteenth and sixteenth centuries and reached a fuller development in Elizabeth's reign.

Relations between history and literature, studied in connection with the Renaissance in England, are thus not particularly evident if one is to take up specific works having obvious 'historical' content or interest and examine their usefulness as guides to the past. By modern historiographical standards, they are not very useful. The survival of the compulsion to write 'universal' history and to make moral education the end of literature pulled towards romance and away from true history. Nearly all the authors so far discussed in this book did this and, with the single exception of Barbour's *Bruce*, itself the sole authority for the events it records, no modern history student would find any of their works valuable as a primary source of information. From first to last, he would be dealing with legend, propaganda and the unverifiable fact. At best, he is getting good second-hand information about personalities and events and, even if Shakespeare's kings were more or less as the poet-playwright depicted them, his sources are suspect and unacceptable to later generations who do not see political developments in the naive way that the Tudors saw them.

.   .   .   .   .   .

If it be of no essential importance to seek historical facts in literary works, nor to hunt for literary qualities in history writing what, then, are the connections between history and literature? What *do* the two have in common? We have discussed what keeps them separate and have arrived at the conclusion that in many ways they are incompatible; in fact, from the historian's point of view, the process of invention, the fundamental literary process, is one that he must suppress. He gropes towards the truth but can never be sure how close he gets to it. His disciplines are stricter than those of the creative writer and he may not invent characters to suit his conceptions; although he draws his material from human experience and tries to illuminate that experience he cannot be so certain as the poet that he is telling the truth. Poetical truth is truth to the poet's own intuition concerning human nature and man's emotions and passions and he can create an infinite number of possible versions of such truth, from a complex intellect like Hamlet to a near-grotesque like Caliban. Or he can people his stage with simpler creations, cut to a conventional pattern and given vestigial human qualities to distinguish them from one another, like Malory's knights, the Seven Deadly Sins of the morality play, or the Roman comedy 'types' of classical English drama.

Therefore, although the poet shares with the historian (and also the philosopher) the claim that he is equipped to seek truth, poetic 'truth' is of a different kind, truth of feeling, and the implication of all later attempts to define poetry is that its concern lies with emotional states and objects. Behind the former lurks the assumption that some quality exists in poetry that is not to be accounted for on a wholly intellectual level. Aristotle, whose *Poetics* were rediscovered for the modern world about 1500, said that poetry was 'imitation'. Renaissance discussions of its nature and functions generally rejected medieval definitions, which regarded the art as at best a handmaid of philosophy or of theology, at worst a vain trifle, almost a sinful indulgence. The accepted notion in 1500 was that poetry was a mask for hidden meanings, conveyed through allegory and understood only by the initiated. Aristotle's *Poetics* encouraged people to think of poets, especially dramatic poets and above all tragedians, as talented men in whom those truths rest which a historian or a philosopher, toiling with reason in the shape of documents, records or systems of logic, may fail to elicit in a lifetime of contemplation.

For example, a philosopher may try to define the quality of jealousy by making abstract statements, or a historian may conclude from the facts at his disposal that King John was jealous of Richard I, but the poet will present a picture of a man being jealous,—not any man, but a creation of the poetic imagination embodying the idea of jealousy gleaned from the poet's own personal and intuitive experience of life. Hence Shakespeare created Othello. Even Plato, who was hostile to poets and banished them from his ideal Republic because he thought they told lies, came to admit this towards the end of his life. Aristotle, Plato's pupil, allied himself with poetry, since he conceived the poet as an illustrator of the universal (*e.g.* jealousy) by means of the particular (a jealous man) and in this respect he differed from his teacher. Aristotle's influence, together with that of Cicero and Quintilian, greatly affected discussions of the nature of poetry during the first half of the sixteenth century; Plato's is seen in the condemnation, by most humanists, of medieval romances, including the Arthurian cycle and of medieval love poetry. A good example of this attitude in England will later be noted in Ascham's *Schoolmaster*, although Tyndale and the followers of Erasmus had been equally explicit in their condemnation of such writings on moral grounds, half a century earlier.

The quarrel between the Platonic and the Aristotelian traditions is fundamental in the history of literary criticism. Should the poet's incursions into the realms of unguarded fancy be controlled, or not? Is poetry which pleases to be considered of a lower order than that which pleases *and* instructs? Has the poet a moral responsibility? Does a better man write a better poem and, if so, 'better' in what sense? (How could a ruffian like the historical Malory have written a noble romance?) Milton's observation to the effect that the didactic poet ought himself to be 'a true poem' was a felicitous way of summing up this humanist ideal, anticipated more prosaically by Erasmus. By Milton's time what critics sometimes call 'the Puritan dilemma' had fully evolved, without ever being acceptably resolved. The problem of reconciling humanism with theology was ever present in the writings of seventeenth-century poets, particularly Donne and Milton, both of whom seized on man-centred humanism as their Tudor predecessors' main error. Spenser's art reveals a maturing Renaissance reaction against medieval asceticism of the *De Contemptu Mundi* school, which asserted that this world is but a bridge to the next and that man is set on earth to purify himself and be tested for entry into heaven. *The Faerie Queene* sets out to sanctify worldliness, yet, in the name of the poetic art, it lays heavy emphasis on the impoverishment of man when cut off from his divine source. The classical Greek spirit was alien to those who believed that scorning the world's beauties made one virtuous. Hamlet's 'What a piece of work is a man!' summed up a more extreme view, the view which the writers of history and of historical plays found more in keeping with their political enthusiasms.

The focus on man suggested by words like 'humanism' and 'Renaissance' had its factual origins in man's achievements, for, although this period was one of violence and persecution, bitter quarrels over territorial rights and threats to the individual life, which might be snuffed out in its prime on the battlefield or by the official decree of a powerful state or monarchy, it was truly a golden age of artistic creation, in building, painting, sculpture, and music. The effect of this new flowering on England and Scotland will be the subject of the next chapter.

3 : Architecture, the Graphic Arts and Music

ALTHOUGH it has now become a very general term of description, the word 'Renaissance' was first used precisely only about a century ago in connection with architecture. In 1452 Léon Alberti's treatise *De Re Aedificatoria* appeared, a work regarded as the first serious study of architectural theory and practice to be based on examples given by the ancient world. Alberti's book was preceded by Flavio Biondo's *Roma Instaurata* (Rome Restored), of 1446, an important pioneer study of the topography of ancient Rome which inspired Alberti. The influence of Greek architecture affected the period known as the *cinquecento* hardly at all, but Romanesque structures, displaying the classical 'orders', retaining round arches, domes and a horizontal style, as distinct from the pointed arches, conical towers and vertical style of medieval Gothic buildings, started to appear in England as early as the fourteenth century. Lincoln Cathedral is one example of the transition from Gothic to Romanesque but such structural features as link it with the genuine Roman remains were less a result of 'Renaissance' influences than of the direct copying of actual buildings still standing as monuments to the olden grandeur. The cathedrals at Caen, Pompierre and Richmond in Yorkshire are not 'Renaissance' in the historical sense of the term and exhibit no new spirit of emancipated design.

College buildings at Oxford and Cambridge erected during the Tudor period were decorated in the ornate style of the Gothic. The towering spires and arched fenesters symbolic of man's reaching up at the eternal and the sense of community of artistic effort which marked the planning and construction of medieval cathedrals were to dominate English domestic building for many years to come and it was the seventeenth century before the real English Renaissance in structural composition came with

Wren. During the sixteenth, slight touches of Italian and Flemish influence left their mark on what was predominantly Gothic design. Foreign example was slow to make an impression, as St George's Chapel at Windsor, Henry VII's Chapel at Westminster and Wolsey's Palace at Hampton Court indicate. A few Italianate details and modifications of Gothic styles do not conceal the fact that these buildings are of medieval descent. Smaller houses were still being built of brick and wood and it was unusual to find instances of innovation outside the predictable limits set by the Court circle. However, as time went by, Italian craftsmen or Englishmen trained in Italy, commissioned by the king and other important personages to design mansions, gradually established a new standard of domestic building and so it was in domestic rather than public architecture that the Italian Renaissance gained a place on the sixteenth-century English scene. Most of these houses were built during the second half of the century and may be called 'Elizabethan'. Nigel Nicolson's beautifully illustrated *Great Houses of Britain* (1965) describes examples of transitional and early Renaissance mansions of which Oxburgh Hall, Norfolk, The Vyne, Hampshire and Longleat House, Wiltshire, especially recommend themselves to students of the period. Longleat, commenced in the 1550s by Sir John Thynne, knighted on the field of Pinkie by the Duke of Somerset in 1547 and later incarcerated in the Tower for two years after Somerset's execution in 1552, is described by Nicolson as 'the most classical house of the English Renaissance' (*op. cit.*, 62). The Duke of Somerset, who reconstructed Syon House in Middlesex and gave his name to Somerset House, probably influenced Thynne a great deal, since the Duke had a predilection for French design, but Thynne was the possessor of an original architectural flair. Longleat, like Syon, was raised on the site of a medieval building but, apart from the Great Hall, the design is not medieval.

Architecture influenced the theatre in the design of stage sets. In the first decade of the sixteenth century performances of Plautus and Terence were given in Italy and what is to be understood as a recognisable stage set, with an urban or rural background such as Shakespeare imagined when he set a scene in 'Venice, a street', or

'The Forest of Arden', was first recorded in Rome in 1514. By 1560 the architectural set had achieved a certain sophistication, gradually developing from the static backgrounds of the early period to the dynamic realism of the seventeenth and eighteenth centuries, which invited the audience to walk right in to the background in the belief that the designer's combination of painted canvas and solid structures was real. Less and less was left to the imagination. However, outside Italy Italian perspective scenery was not seen much in the sixteenth century, except on isolated occasions; in England there was no sign of it before the 1560s, and even then it would have been considered a departure from tradition. Sebastiano Serlio's *Second Book of Perspective* was first published in Paris in 1545 but these detailed instructions on how sets ought to be built were largely theoretical so far as the contemporary English theatre was concerned. Shakespeare's backdrops were conventional, and their lack of realism made the audience concentrate on the mental images conjured up by the spoken poetry, justifying Samuel Johnson's dictum that 'he who imagines this, may imagine more'.

Under Henry VII, economies began to be practised in stage production and design, casting and accessories. Account books of his reign show that interludes cost only about one-tenth of what a ceremonial disguising did, and the rise of travelling companies of actors, who had to be paid, together with the need for playwrights to compose plays which would please patrons and make a profit, meant that financial considerations for the first time came to dictate the terms of play production in England. Little is known about the history of the public theatre before the construction of the four London theatres towards the end of the century but it is reckoned that by James I's reign 21,000 Londoners out of a population of 160,000 were attending a play each week, truly a high proportion.

In Scotland, royal interest in architecture dated from James III's reign, and one of his favourites, Robert Cochrane, was a noted builder and designer. James added extensions to his residences at Stirling, Falkland, Lochmaben, Dingwall and Linlithgow. James IV continued his example by rebuilding and repairing old castles, both for military and for domestic purposes. He spent a

E

great deal of money on his various projects. The tower of the new palace of Holyroodhouse, which had been partially completed before James's marriage, was finished in 1505. Additions to Linlithgow were begun as early as 1490; the new palace at Falkland and the extensions to Stirling were started in 1501. Rich burghers followed his example. Not much survives today of the original building work, though the Holyroodhouse tower may still be seen and the skeleton of Linlithgow remains without its roof. James V, who employed a French master-mason, ordered him to turn Falkland into a French-style château, the only genuinely successful example of such a transplant, though there were other, cruder attempts to recreate the kind of domestic architecture represented by the châteaux of the Loire valley. England has no examples of this and indeed French architectural influence in the south was negligible, even though a few scattered creations by Frenchmen may be seen as, for example, in the monument in the Oxenbrigge Chapel in Brede Church, Sussex, dated 1537 and made, like Henry VII's Chapel at Westminster, from Caen stone.

As artillery improved, the castles of England and Scotland ceased to have real military value and by the 1520s fortifications had lost their strategic significance as symbols of the power of the nobles as opposed to that of the king. One of the last instances of serious resistance to a monarch in which a castle was the bulwark took place in 1528, when the Earl of Angus, Margaret Tudor's second husband and Chancellor of the Realm during the minority of James V, held out for a short time at Tantallon before being driven into exile. Besiegements later in the century were nominal, and none of the defenders had any illusions about the outcome. The towers built by rich men during the reigns of James IV and V were not strongholds in the military sense, but were instead mainly erected to secure persons and their movable possessions against the depredations of violent men and thieves who might at any time descend upon a lonely house, force entry and despoil the property without much fear of interruption or effective legal penalty.

·   ·   ·   ·   ·   ·

Turning to art, one finds that the influence of Greek and Roman models was felt directly by Renaissance painting and sculpture only after a long delay. Before 1400 very few examples of classical art were available to the practitioner, for the remains of 'the grandeur that was Rome' lay buried and had to be excavated. Even in 1450 all that Rome could produce consisted of a handful of bronzes, two imposing statues of Castor and Pollux and effigies of pagan river gods. Elsewhere in Italy sepulchres, like that at Pisa, were to be found, as were the bronze horses of St Mark's Square in Venice and a number of damaged busts and torsos. Specimens of genuine 'Golden Age' sculpture were rare, for the Apollo Belvedere, the famous Vatican Venus, the Laocoön statue and the torso of Cleopatra were not unearthed until the late fifteenth century. So far as the immediate example of the work of the ancients was concerned, therefore, the *cinquecento* was scarcely affected at all.

In painting, the first notable influence was the fourteenth-century Florentine monk Giotto, who also designed the *campanile* tower of the city. He is to pictorial art what Dante is to literature—a Janus who looked backward and forward, with one part of his creative being in the cloister, while the other yearned for greater freedom of expression. His frescoes at Assisi and Padua marked a change in visual representation from medieval convention to an increased realism, but he founded no school and his influence was slight. Leonardo da Vinci held that Tomaso of Florence, who executed the famous frescoes in the Carmelite Church there, was the real founder of the Italian artistic Renaissance. A race of painters was sown in numerous cities, Florence, Siena, Mantua, Ferrara, Verona, Venice, Brescia, each with his circle of adherents and disciples. Each of these 'schools' had its own style, and could be distinguished from the others. This period is known as the *quattrocento* and includes Fra Angelico, Fra Lippo Lippi, Botticelli and Perugino.

Their subject-matter was predominantly religious, but the old stereotypes had disappeared, for the painter was learning to work with one eye on the world around him, so that it was not long before religious subjects had become pegs on which to hang portraits of contemporary life. The life of the times asserted itself more and more and painting, whatever its nominal subject might be, became in motive 'secular'. Raphael, Michelangelo, Titian, Leonardo, the Ghirlandajos and del Sarto dominated the *cinquecento*. As his mastery of technique increased, the artist widened his range of subjects and looked for patronage beyond the Church. He found it in the Sforzas, the Medicis and the enlightened Popes, especially Julius II, whose enthusiasm for the fine arts was no less notable than his love of military action. The pictorial artist roamed over a whole field of classical myths and legends and copied their human subjects from live models. The same buxom peasant girls sat for paintings of both the Madonna and Venus, fresh-faced shepherd boys for Christ and Apollo. Gradually the religious motive sank into the background and art, with increasing intensity, became, like literature, a vehicle for expressing the individual artist's interpretation of life.

If the historian claims, as he sometimes does, that the Renaissance marks a revolutionary change-over from a religious to a secular presentation of life he is exaggerating. The art of the Renaissance was not intensely 'secular' as opposed to medieval art which was 'religious', nor did the Renaissance artist owe his inspiration to classical examples. The trend admittedly moved, as conventional argument has it, from religious to secular, but it was relatively slow in its positive effects. Later fifteenth-century artists like Raphael, Michelangelo and Ghiberti show that for them the fine arts remained predominantly religious in sentiment and for every 'classical' picture conceived during the *cinquecento* a score of religious subjects were painted. As a handmaiden to religion, medieval art persisted for a longer time than is often supposed, and to separate medieval from Renaissance by appending the terms 'sacred' and 'profane', or some like distinction, is to mislead.

However, differences between them are historically clear. Medieval art was primarily didactic and those who practised it did not consider their activity to be an end in itself or as something to be enjoyed independently—its function was rather to intensify the meaning of human existence in one of its nobler forms and the artist's aim was of greater importance than the aesthetic value of what he created. He sought to deepen devotion by representing

Christ's sufferings pictorially or by stressing the importance of good works, by recording the piety of generous benefactors in stained glass or church fabrics, by embellishing religious festivals, and so increasing their splendour and solemnity, or by building sepulchres and sarcophagi to express family affection and commemorate the virtues of the departed. Medieval art had a didactic purpose and its increasing purity and separation from other pursuits came to imply that it copied from life rather than merely decorated it. It was this change in technique that marked the transition period, for artists then sought to imitate nature or, as Michelangelo put it: 'to be true to Nature, the mistress of all masters'. He and his contemporaries studied anatomy, perspective and the effects of light and shade (*chiaroscuro*), which gave their pictures an illusion of depth. An artist could thenceforth be judged by the accuracy with which he gave his pictures such an illusion. In life-drawings Leonardo has never been excelled and names like Bellini, del Sarto and Titian conjure up visions of the superhuman in artistic attainment. The medieval painter of religious works had no name and was content to take his place as an anonymous, individually unimportant contributor to Christ's holy labour. One sign of the new spirit was the disappearance of this anonymity and the establishment of personal reputations. The Greek emphasis on *areté*, the skill of a champion, the outstanding quality that raised a man above others and made him a genius, a hero like Tamburlaine or even an outstanding villain, like Iago, put no value on the self-effacing virtues extolled by Christian teaching.

In painting this is to be seen in Tudor portraits wherein Tudor England followed the example of Germany and the Low Countries. Holbein painted three pictures of Erasmus, the More family, Elyot and others of their circle between 1526–8. Returning in 1532, when More had fallen into disgrace, he sought other subjects among the mercantile class, and collected several commissions, including that of the title-page design for Coverdale's Bible. Henry VIII provided Holbein with influential patronage, enabling him to execute a series of well-known portraits of Tudor courtiers, including the famous one of Henry himself which made that monarch's appearance known to succeeding generations, Wyatt and a life-drawing of Surrey. Holbein was a 'photographic' painter and the first major artist working in England to pass on life-likenesses rather than the stylised representations of famous people made by medieval artists.

He had many imitators. Most Tudor painting of note was portrait painting but the majority of the artists were foreign-born, and no native school as such existed. The family of Hornbout, three miniaturists for whom Henry VIII sat, came from Ghent. 'Johannes Corvus' (Jan Raf) hailed from Bruges—he painted John Foxe and Mary Tudor when she was Duchess of Suffolk (1532). Antonio Toto was Italian, Guillim Stretes and Antonis Mor were Dutch. Holbein's assistants were nearly all compatriots of his own, like Gerlach Flicke, although he did employ a handful of Englishmen, including Shute and Betts, later well-known miniaturists. This preference for foreigners excluded the French School, which continued to be neglected throughout Elizabeth's reign.

A connection between the fine arts and historical change is easy to demonstrate since the artistic revival was exported from Italy largely by Charles VIII's returning army, which left Naples in 1494 loaded with plunder, including paintings, statues, busts and tapestries. They were followed by Italian artists who stayed to practise their skills in France. The reconstruction of historic châteaux like Chambord on the Loire, or of buildings like the Louvre in Paris, were undertaken by native Frenchmen but inevitably the Italian influence is noticeable in these and in many other famous French buildings of the sixteenth century. In England the severity of the Gothic was made less obvious by a diluted Italianism. The rash of portraits and life-likenesses dating from Henry VII's reign was part of the ethos of the Court; Henry VIII's generation emphasised personality more and more, and the individual portrait represented the beginnings of ancestor-worship. The proliferation of new titles awarded by Henry VIII for political services, which did much to create a new class of aristocratic *parvenus* (much resented by the older hereditary peers and powerful Catholic families) was to exercise a beneficial influence on the fine arts, on the general level of education, on standards of domestic living and on public entertainment. A growing audience interested in the arts, in the theatre, in book-buying and in reading emerged from the ranks of the new nobility, of the rich mercantile class, of superior tradesman and later from what were to be known in the Elizabethan theatre as the 'groundlings'. Art was coming to be a profession, and the exercise of it a recognised form of making a respectable living. The full-time professional actor, writer, painter and poet began to come into his own under the Tudors—literature and the fine arts were soon to lose their heavy courtly veneer and also some of their popular undertones and to aspire to essentially 'bourgeois' or well-to-do middle-class standards, a movement which was to reach its fullest expression in the eighteenth and nineteenth centuries.

. . . . . .

Tudor music and Tudor poetry are associated. Wyatt, Surrey and Henry VIII's Court are important in the history of English poetry, and both the musical and the poetical repertory of the Court became popular in high society and eventually among the upper middle classes. In brief, national music in England dates from the beginning of the fifteenth century. Its development was largely due to the institution of royal chapels in imitation of the Papal Choir in Rome, so that the position of musicians in society was gradually elevated. From being considered as near-undesirables on the fringes of respectability and as such constantly in need of absolution as a shield against ecclesiastical disapproval, instrumentalists and composers became in course of time admired members of the royal retinue. Henry V had a Chapel Royal which followed him to France and he himself was a composer of songs. After the Wars of the Roses and the long period of stability associated with Henry VII, foreign musicians, mostly Flemings, came to England and joined Henry VIII's household chapel, to which foreign visitors in the first half of Henry's reign made reference. Musicians like Robert Fayrfax, William Cornyshe, Richard Sampson, Richard Davy, Hugh Aston and John Taverner all flourished during the halcyon days of the King's Court. Most of their work was concerned with sacred music—masses, antiphons or anthems and magnificats, full of expressive passages and free vocalisation in the style of the medieval trope. About the Court song of sixteenth-century Scotland, however, little is known before James VI's reign, though James V was musical and a number of Franco-Scottish love songs are preserved from the period 1528–42. Helena M. Shire's *Song, Dance and Poetry of the Court of Scotland under James VI* (1969) contains a full account of the subject and promises a future study of the songs of James VI's reign.

Like Henry V, Henry VIII was a composer of mild accomplishment, and from all accounts a skilful executant on various instruments who could read musical notation at sight, at that time quite a rare talent. A songbook known as *Henry VIII's MS* contains thirty-four of his pieces, all competent enough. One of them, 'Quam pulchra es' is a three-part motet which is by far his best work. Another song-book, called *The Fayrfax MS*, is earlier, and includes forty-nine songs of Henry's Court (two missing). A third collection, *Ritson's MS*, of Devonshire origin, contains forty-four carols in the medieval style, love songs and some ecclesiastical music. The first collection of English polyphonic song to be printed was issued by Wynken de Worde about 1530.

Henry, James IV of Scotland and his wife Margaret, as well as Mary Tudor, were all capable solo performers on keyboard instruments. Both Sir Thomas More's wives learned to play and most noble houses had their consorts of semi-professional performers. The lute became popular and replaced the harp, which had been the main musical instrument in domestic circles during the fifteenth century—Henry V and his French wife are known to have played it. However, singing rather than playing was the conventional musical pastime of the Tudor upper classes and both Barclay and Skelton refer to it. Outside the Court, musical activity was not widespread and it is likely that only a small circle were really competent musicians, capable of sight-reading, though many more could play by ear or pick up a tune. Most treatises on education refer to music as a necessary recreation for the children of noblemen and as the century advanced the talents first confined to Henry's immediate presence were more widely commanded; lute- or viol-playing became popular with the richer bourgeoisie, and books were printed which described the construction and techniques of various instruments.

The most obvious meeting-place for music and poetry is in opera, but although medieval liturgical drama was musical the first composers of opera, true to contemporary prejudices against anything monastic, despised the old traditions and resolved to copy Greek drama. They composed musical settings for poetry in such a manner as to preserve both the metrical patterns and the meaning of the words. However, opera as we know it did not originate until the end of the sixteenth century, when Italian composers, like Monteverdi and Jacopi, created *Orfeo* and *Euridice*, two operas based upon the ancient legend, long a favourite subject of authors from Ovid and Virgil to Poliziano and Henryson.

The majority of early humanist references to music and especially to the desirability of learning to play instruments were qualified by the suggestion that this was an art which had to be practised in moderation lest it lead to the weakening of resolution, the loss of self-control and the arousing of too much passion. The tradition of Orpheus was to be cultivated by princes, but only to refresh their spirits, to compensate them for hardship and to fulfil the harmony of their lives.

4 : The Influence of European Learning in England

So far as enthusiasm for humanism went, the most intense follower of Italy was France. For centuries the University of Paris had stood as the main bulwark of scholasticism in Europe, attracting the best minds from other countries, so that progress of the new movement was retarded by entrenched disciples of the old order. However, in 1458, the study of Greek began there and by 1508, when the Italian scholar Aleandro was lecturing to large audiences on Greek, Latin and Hebrew, the new learning was soundly rooted in Paris. Aleandro left for his native country in 1516 to take up the post of Vatican Librarian, and the leadership of French humanism fell to a Frenchman, a Parisian named Guillaume Budé, and a Belgian scholar-printer, Jodocus Badius Ascensius, the author of a valuable commentary on Virgil's *Aeneid*.

Budé, or Budaeus as he was known, was a near-contemporary of Erasmus. Originally a law student, he developed an interest in Greek in the 1490s and learned the language from an elderly tutor. In 1502 he started an exhaustive investigation into the *Pandects* of Justinian, the basic text-book of Roman law, corrected the text, added an explanatory commentary and published the whole in 1508. He then wrote a treatise on classical numismatics, which was published in 1515 under the title *De Asse*. These were both very learned works. The annotations to the *Pandects* referred not only to the law, but also to the language, literature and society of the ancients, while the treatise on their currency shed light upon a dense and at that time unknown subject. Budé was hailed as the most erudite scholar of the Renaissance, Erasmus not excepted— in fact, in 1515 Erasmus wrote to him, saying

You have preferred to be understood by the learned, I, if I can, by the many; your aim is to conquer, mine to teach or persuade. (*Epistles*, trans. and ed. F. M. Nicholas [1901–8].)

Because he was a brilliant Latin stylist, Erasmus is remembered whereas Budé is not. The Frenchman's formidable scholarship has melted into the common stock of classical erudition and his name is significant now chiefly to legal historians.

Badius Ascensius (Josse Bade), a pupil of Guarino of Verona, came from Ghent. His life's work was to make classical studies known by issuing cheap and well printed texts. He said himself that it was his object to collect everything that might show the virtuous character of learning and give pleasure to the noblest minds, thus joining the tradition of Renaissance tutorship viewed as a duty compelled by faith which marked the writers of didactic treatises during this time. His commentary on Virgil was used by Gavin Douglas and among his other productions were the works of two Scottish historians, Major and Boece, to whom later reference will be made. Badius was a man of broad interests and a stream of grammar books, dictionaries, encyclopaedias and other aids to language study flowed from his press until his death in 1535. He was a far more academic printer than Caxton and did not seek to please the readers of popular literature.

The French considered the English to be a barbarous people, discourteous, ignorant and wanting in all desirable human qualities save physical courage and doggedness of purpose. The legend, first stated explicitly by Polydore Vergil, that the men of Kent had tails had long persisted in France and there are many references in French literature to the boorishness of the lower-class English citizenry. Shakespeare catches the temper of Gallic contempt for his countrymen in *Henry V*, when the French lords awaiting Agincourt sneer at their adversaries' love of beef and lack of 'any intellectual armour'. Many Tudor commentators writing in the 1540s and 1550s speak of the insults directed at French visitors on the streets of London and the common practice of spitting in the face of a 'French dog'. This kind of behaviour stood in contrast to the polite reception given to Englishmen in France.

However, the prejudices of the insular and intensely nationalistic

English vulgarian have little connection with cultural relations, and French influences on language, literature and fashions were exceptionally strong during the Tudor period. The antipathy towards foreigners, given a fresh lease of life by the vaunting nationalism of Henry VIII, was essentially a manifestation of lower-class assertiveness and was not shared by the educated classes of England. Knowledge of French became a sign of good breeding in the early years of Henry's reign and the publication of manuals of instruction in that language by John Palsgrave, Alexander Barclay and others helped to make it accessible to a wide circle of young English men and women. With the language went an uncritical admiration of the Gallic style. Thomas More wrote a Latin poem about the English gallant:

> He struts about
> In cloaks of fashion French. His girdle, purse,
> And sword are French. His hat is French.
> His nether limbs are cased in French costume.
> His shoes are French. In short, from top to toe
> He stands the Frenchman.
> (*Epigrammatica* [c. 1518], 'In Anglum Gallicae
> linguae affectatorem'; tr. [1878] J. H. Marsden)

and Edward Hall describes in his *Chronicle* how a group of young English noblemen, newly returned from the French Court in 1518, were completely Frenchified and derisive when anything English was discussed—possibly the same crowd lampooned by More. More had a low opinion of their actual knowledge of French, however, and wrote:

> With accent French he speaks the Latin tongue
> With accent French the tongue of Lombardy,
> To Spanish words he gives an accent French,
> German he speaks with his same accent French,
> In truth he seems to speak with accent French,
> All but the French itself. The French he speaks
> With accent British.   (*Ibid.*)

while Nashe's *The Unfortunate Traveller* (1587) suggests that one could tell a long sojourner in France by his strange manner of speaking English. The returning Francophile formed a distinct class and brought back with him unmistakable characteristics of speech and social habits. By 1550 French was spoken by all courtiers, a tradition begun by Henry VIII who had a versatile French tutor, and there was by that year hardly any aspect of social life in Tudor England which French taste did not govern—dress, cooking, wines, deportment, dancing and even the Italian art of fencing, for, although Italians had perfected it, the technique reached England largely through the offices of French masters. The same may be said for equestrian pursuits. Shakespeare refers to the Norman Lamord's skill at both arts in *Hamlet* (IV, vii, 81–92).

Turning to Spain, it is not difficult to discern that although the new learning was well received at first, it soon began to be regarded as a danger to established religion. Possession of a Greek Testament rendered a man liable to interrogation by the Inquisition (though a Latin one was acceptable). In consequence, Spanish humanists were forced to work under threat to life and liberty and so the reactionary powers of medievalism lingered on in strength long after they had waned elsewhere in Europe. No humanist could flourish in such an atmosphere and until Mary Tudor married Philip II of Spain in 1554 Anglo-Spanish cultural relations were negligible. The kind of enthusiasm for Spanish fashions which the English Court showed for French ones was not to develop until the end of the century.

Before 1530 no Spanish literature was available in English translation and even by 1559, only fourteen separate works were available. The first example, an adaptation by John Rastell of the *Celestina* tragedy (1530), came through an Italian translation made twenty-five years earlier. The anonymous English play *Calisto and Meliboëa* which appeared in the same year was inspired by *Celestina*, but in the hands of the Englishman it emerged as a tragi-comedy, with a happy conclusion. A second example, *The Golden Book of Marcus Aurelius* (1534), was translated by Lord Berners from de Guevara's *Libro Dureo* (1520), not directly, but through a French version of 1531. All but one of the others were versions of Latin works by Spanish writers like Vives, who spent over a decade in England as Fellow of an Oxford college. Vives' best-known translator was Sir Richard Morison, whose *Introduction to Wysdome* (1540) was a version of the Spaniard's *Introductio ad Sapientiam*, originally printed at Bruges in 1524.

Berners served as Ambassador to Spain in 1518–19 but was ill much of the time and hardly left his Embassy. He knew no Spanish. Not many Englishmen did. Until 1543, when a direct sea service between England and Spain was started by Henry VIII and Philip, then Regent of Castile, travel from London to Madrid had to be arranged by road through French territory. Dissemination of Spanish culture depended upon political and commercial exigencies and the market for Spanish books of any kind—grammars, dictionaries, didactic and learned works, scientific treatises, narratives of exploration—and religious matter (such as the writings of the Sevillean Reformers) was slight until the last quarter of the sixteenth century. The marriage of Mary and Philip certainly gave some impetus to this demand but, even so, its immediate effect was to encourage the reading of chronicles recording Spanish history and navigational feats, not of Spanish poetry and prose.

Portuguese influence was also slight, in spite of the ancient treaty between that country and England, made in 1387 and renewed by Henry VII in 1489 as one of several agreements made to increase English trading privileges in opposition to the merchants of Venice and the Hansa. Portugal was a more distant and remote country than Spain, and practically no cultural link between her and England existed. The first translation from a Portuguese original was made by More's son John and printed by Rastell's son William in 1533, a good example of how this family worked together to spread the new learning. The book in question had a Latin original, printed in Antwerp the year before—the English translation was called *The Legacy or Embassate of the Great Emperour of Inde Prester John, unto Emanuell Kynge of Portyngale.* The author was Damião de Goes and the work, as its title implies, was patriotic in character.

Portuguese navigators were the first to explore the sea route to the Indian Ocean by way of the Cape of Good Hope and they followed hard in the wake of the Spaniards in the latter's search for a sea passage to the New World and round South America to the Orient. These two nations were acknowledged pioneers in navigation and accounts of their exploits and impressions of strange new lands were authoritative. Richard Eden's translation of the Spanish works (two from Spanish, one from Latin) published in London in 1555 under the title of *Decades of the New World* was the first Spanish book of this kind to appear in English and Eden included in the volume translations of official Portuguese documents. However, no major Portuguese translation into English was available until 1582, and the first English polyglot dictionary to include the Portuguese language appeared in 1617. Compared even with Spanish books the number of Portuguese translations into English is disproportionately small—before Elizabeth's death only about a dozen, of which more than half are concerned with exploration. Of literary Portuguese nothing came to England before the 1580s and even then most of it was rendered from Spanish originals.

German humanism, Erasmus and Brant excepted, is summed up in the personalities of Johannes Reuchlin and Philip Melancthon. Reuchlin, a Bavarian born in 1485, started as a Greek scholar but developed mainly as a student of Hebrew. His aims were to open up the Old Testament to criticism and by so doing to balance what he and Erasmus considered excessive absorption by humanists in pagan (*i.e.* Latin) literature. He produced the first Hebrew grammar to appear in Western Europe and became the foremost Hebrew scholar of his day, the founder of New Testament criticism and an authority on medieval Jewish philosophy. Reuchlin published two treatises, *De Verbo Mirifico* (1494) and *De Arte Cabbalistica* (1517), and came to be a spokesman of the Jews in their struggle against religious persecution. His Latin dictionary was a mainstay for early translators, such as Skelton, who used it extensively in making his version of Diodorus Siculus's *Bibliotheca Historica* (see chapter 7).

Melancthon was appointed Professor of Greek at the new University of Wittenberg in 1518 and formed a friendship and alliance with Luther, fourteen years his senior, who was Professor of Divinity there. Melancthon's knowledge of Greek enabled Luther to translate the New Testament into vernacular German and his textbooks took the place of the antiquated ones formerly used in schools and seminaries. *Institutions of Greek Language* (1518) and a Latin grammar (1523) earned him the imposing title of 'Preceptor Germaniae' (Teacher of Germany). Neither he nor Reuchlin could be said to have had many affinities with the Italian Renaissance, however; the German humanist was a nationalist and an austere moralist who aimed to reform German schools and imbue humanism with a Germanic spirit which, under Luther's influence, was also a Protestant spirit. Like Piccolomini, Bruni and Budé, Melancthon produced a tract on the education of a prince, following the Italian pattern but dogged by a heavy Teutonic seriousness.

One German author must be taken into account in any discussion of the Renaissance. This is Sebastian Brant (1457–1521) who in 1494 published a seminal work called *Das Narrenschiff* or Ship of Fools. Brant was a scholar-printer, like the Italian Aldo and the Belgian Bade. He was born in Strasbourg, an important humanist centre, and knew both Erasmus and Reuchlin. *Das Narrenschiff* was translated into Latin by his pupil Jacob Locher in 1497 and it was on this Latin version that all the translations made in the sixteenth century depended. Locher's *Stultifera Navis* was greatly different in character and content from its original, so that the vernacular versions, in turn free renderings of Locher, were all a long way removed from Brant. Only a Low German translation, *Dat Narren Schiff*, made before Locher's, preserved the original in anything like a literal form.

Written originally in the Swabian dialect of German, *Das Narrenschiff* contains 113 sections of iambic pentameter, each dealing with a different class of fool, summed up in a 'type'. Brant even included himself as captain of the vessel, which was supposed to be sailing for Narragonia, the Fools' Paradise. The work was the first one printed in German to deal with current affairs and to probe the behaviour of the contemporary bourgeoisie. Its author did not make much effort to sustain the ship allegory, contenting himself with periodic references to it as he unfolded the human comedy as it appeared to him.

Pierre Rivière's French *Nef des Folles* (1497) and Badius Ascensius' curtailed version of 1505 were probably sources for Alexander Barclay's *Ship of Fools*, discussed elsewhere in this book. Indeed, Barclay refers to Locher and Rivière (but not Badius) as his models, the former as though he, and not Brant, were the original author. Brant's *Ship* was reprinted many times in various languages. Much of its popularity was due to the woodcuts which Bergman, the Basle printer who first issued *Das Narrenschiff*, caused to be executed as illustrations to each chapter. Brant probably made a number of them himself and a team of engravers assisted in cutting the remainder. They are of uneven quality.

The idea of the ship packed with fools was an old one and Brant had several earlier precedents, such as Nigel Wireker's *Speculum Stultorum* of *c.* 1180, a poem on the adventures of the donkey Brunellus in search of his tail. Like the pilgrimage, the ship was a useful literary device that enabled a writer to bring different kinds of people together; Brant used it for satirical purposes and it was with similar aims that Barclay and, more significantly, Erasmus presented their versions of the questing vessel and its crew of diverse types. The anonymous *Cock Lorell's Bote* (1510), Skelton's *Bouge of Court* and *Colin Cloute* and the stream of low-life satires which appeared throughout the sixteenth century, like Copland's *High Way to the Spital House*, Andrew Borde's *First Book of the Introduction of Knowledge* and John Awdelay's *Fraternitye of Vagabonds*, all owe something to Brant's example. Dekker's *Gull's Horn Book* (1609) is a late example of the trend, which combined irony, complaint and a genuine interest in the miseries of the poor.

Germany's most positive contribution to the Renaissance has been left to the last—the invention of printing with movable type. The credit for this goes to Johannes Gutenberg of Mainz, of whom very little is known save that in 1456 he printed a beautiful edition of the Vulgate, known as the Gutenberg Bible, in 150 copies. From Germany the new craft spread to Holland, Italy, France and, as already described, to England with Caxton. Germany retained her leadership in the printing trade for most of the fifteenth century and held the principal book market of Europe, but Italy was not far behind. Thanks to the scholar-printer Aldo, more than 150 presses were at work in Venice before the close of the century,

F

producing compact volumes to supersede the ponderous tomes of bound MSS with which scholars had hitherto been forced to grapple.

Italian cultural influences permeated the upper levels of English society and Italian economic power made itself felt in Henry VII's reign through the Italian import of wool and export of general merchandise of a kind then unknown in England. Moreover, the Florentine Medicis' methods of banking and finance were adopted in England, and it is well known that early Italian bankers were called 'Lombards' and gave their name to Lombard Street in the City of London. During the fifteenth century the Medicis founded two banks in London and a French commentator, Etienne Perlin, writing in 1558, was able to observe that 'the Italians frequent this country much on account of the bank'. Articles of luxury started to enter England from Italy as a result of Henry VII's trade policy and this trend increased in volume under Henry VIII. Henry VII was also responsible for initiating the employment of Italian diplomats, for the Italians were the first nation to look upon diplomacy as a career. Silvestro Gigli served both Henrys as ambassador to Rome and became one of Wolsey's principal agents in the latter's dealings with the Holy See. It became the fashion for well-born young men to travel to Italy in order to finish their education and equally fashionable among their elders to express horror at the results of this civilising and/or corrupting process. Ascham's observations on the subject, made in *The Schoolmaster*, are referred to later in this chapter. In *As You Like It*, Shakespeare makes Rosalind mock Jacques's melancholy, which he accounts for in part by his experiences as a traveller (*op. cit.*, IV, i, 17–31).

Bacon's essay *Of Travel* is concerned with the serious visitor, not the dilettante sojourner in other countries, and indeed much of the objection to Italianisation came from scholars concerned with education, who thought that the benefits of Italy could be obtained largely from books, the *novelle* excepted. As we have noted, the Italian Renaissance represented not only Italy, but the whole of European culture. Only a very few people actually travelled out of England and only a handful of diplomats and scholars knew the Italian language, though Elizabeth when a young girl of twelve, was said by an Italian poet, Pietro Bizari, to be 'a perfect mistress of the Italian tongue, in the learning of which Signor Castiglione was her principal master'. Ascham confirms her ability in Italian, as well as in French, Spanish and Latin, and she is recorded as having said (in French) that she was herself 'half Italian' (*me semble que je suis demie Italienne*).

Of translations from Italian into English there was no dearth during her reign; Spenser published a translation from Petrarch in 1569, when he was only seventeen. Versions of Italian romances poured forth in the 1560s and the works of Petrarch, Boccaccio, Tasso and Ariosto were revered almost as much as those of Homer and Virgil. In the first half of the century, however, the dissemination of Italian literature in English versions had not properly begun and in fact the seventeenth century was the real epoch of the Italian-English translators. Hoby's version of Castiglione's *Il Cortegiano* (The Courtier), printed originally in 1528, did not appear until 1561, though its content was known to upper-class Englishmen, like Wyatt and Surrey, soon after it appeared. The real 'courtiers' in the Italianate tradition were Sidney and Raleigh, and the most powerful imitators of Italian poetry and music were late Elizabethans. One should be on guard against attributing too much to Italian example in Henry VIII's reign, at least so far as the arts are concerned.

One reputed effect of Italian writing on English literature needs some detailed discussion, if only to demonstrate that its effect in the sixteenth century was negligible. Niccolò Machiavelli's *The Prince*, written about 1517, was not published until 1537. By 1557, it had passed through twenty-five editions but, in spite of comments, references and attacks made on the book by numerous writers in English, like Ascham, who considered him pagan, opportunist and immoral, like all things Italian, no translation into that language appeared until 1636. Like Marx, Machiavelli was a writer familiar to all by reputation, but actually read by relatively few, and of those who did read him, most misinterpreted what he had to say in *Il Principe*. Statesmen devoured it because of its practical utility, men of the world were entertained by it because of its cynicism and philosophers studied it because of its original slant on things. But its effects on literary characterisation were negligible, and the few references to Machiavelli by name, in Marlowe, Shakespeare and elsewhere, and the signs of 'Machiavellianism' in Bacon's *Novum Organum*, together with the creation of villains like Iago or Milton's Satan, constitute a subject outside the scope of this book. (Felix Raab's *The English Face of Machiavelli* [1964] is the most up-to-date study of it.) Suffice to say that the association of Machiavelli with diabolical motives was inherited by the Elizabethans chiefly from a French Huguenot denunciation translated into English in 1577. If people read *Il Principe* at all, they read it in French, divorced from its background, for the work itself was a product of current events and its author intended it to be read in conjunction with those events. When it was written, Italy was the most disunited country in Europe, Germany excepted, and was threatened with political disaster following attacks by France and Spain. Although the Italians were intellectually pre-eminent in Europe, their factional divisions and unwarlike nature left them an easy prey for greedy, bellicose nations. No country was more defenceless, nor more attractive to the would-be conqueror.

By choosing Cesare Borgia, an unscrupulous power-seeker, as hero, Machiavelli unknowingly damaged his own reputation. Cesare's example, which Machiavelli suggested should 'be imitated by all who with fortune and the arms of others have risen to power' was scarcely acceptable even in the context of late fifteenth-century Italy. Fifty years later, the glorification of such qualities as Borgia possessed—cunning, deceit, cruelty and the love of violence—was not fashionable. *Il Principe* was placed on the Index of Prohibited Books in 1559, the Inquisition ordered all Machiavelli's writings to be destroyed and the Council of Trent confirmed this decision.

The intellectual climate of England between 1485 and 1558 was increasingly affected by the growth of humanism in Italy, France and the Low Countries. The word 'Renaissance' describes the rediscovery of classical (especially Latin) literature and a consequent admiration of the societies of ancient Greece and Rome which produced it. This movement began in fourteenth-century Italy for, as Macaulay put it: 'the dawn came before the last streaks of the Roman sunset had faded', and the Italians regarded themselves as the direct heirs of the ancients. Roman remains, temples, aqueducts, theatres, triumphal arches, baths, colonnades and public buildings lay around in astonishing profusion and, despite their ruined condition, survived to confirm the sophistication and skill of those who had conceived them. Consciousness of this rich inheritance from their own past undoubtedly spurred on Italian patrons and scholars to champion its revival and, although Rome had been ravaged by barbarians, it had suffered less than other old cities. Medieval writers accepted ruins left over from earlier civilisations, but did not seem curious as to how they came to be there. Like Holy Writ and the Code of Law, the ruins of Rome existed, and, so far as living men were concerned, they symbolised the eternal. It seemed that such magnificent creations were the work, not of men, but of giants.

The economic basis for the Renaissance was provided by Italy's material wealth. Italian seaports were situated in the very centre of the Mediterranean and through them traffic passed from Asia to Rome. The merchants of Venice and Genoa became very rich and such wealth as theirs supplied the means and the opportunity for prolonged intellectual activity, from actual ex-cavation to the criticism of documents. In other parts of Europe the fifteenth century witnessed the rise of nationalism and we have described how related emotions, such as reverence for the patriotic hero and dislike of the foreigner, were encouraged by poets and historians writing under influential patronage. In Italy this did not happen, for the Italians were not a united people, but a conglomera-tion of peoples, Tuscans, Calabrians, Venetians, Lombards, Romans, each with their own loyalties and traditions, frequently at war with one another and held together only by the ancient heritage which they all shared.

Another word, 'humanism', refers to the learning and training of men in virtue (*virtù*) which, supposedly brought about by book-learning, distinguished the educated ruler from the untutored subject. This was how the humanists themselves understood it. Such learning produced an inquiring mind and set afoot a new 'Renaissance' spirit, guided by a knowledge of the classics, first Latin and, much later, Greek. These languages were the keys to knowledge of the world, and a large proportion of every humanist's time was devoted to learning and teaching them. Humanism became a new gospel of deliverance from what came to be regarded as scholastic ignorance, blind acceptance of written authority or unwritten legend and the treatment of Scripture as an oracle, not as an historical document capable of literal interpretation. Man was to be understood, not pessimistically, as a creature originally created in God's image but freed to commit sin, but optimistically, as a unique entity in whom rational faculties resided. Greece and Rome showed man's creative capacity, long dormant, but ready to be reawakened and 'born again'.

. . . . . .

The first leader of the new movement was Petrarch (1304–74), who is supposed to have died at his desk annotating a Latin translation of Homer. He was an antiquary with a powerful love for ancient Rome, where he said he would have lived had he been given the choice, and possessed a sense of historical change which he considered represented a decline in standards of civilisation. Petrarch wrote to an imaginary Livy:

> Often I am filled with bitter indignation against the morals of today, when men value nothing except gold and silver, and desire nothing except sensual, physical pleasures. If these are to be considered the goal of mankind, then not only the dumb beasts of the field, but even insensible and inert matter has a richer, a higher goal than that proposed to itself by thinking man.
>
> (*Familiar Letters*, XXIV, 8; tr. M. E. Cosenze, *Petrarch's Letters to Classical Authors* [1910].)

Petrarch learned the secret of a fine Latin style from his beloved Roman authors, but knew little Greek, a fact which he himself bewailed. His epic about Scipio, called *Africa*, included a description of what he thought ancient Rome was like, presented as a guided tour offered to visitors. Near the end of his life he asked rhetorically, 'What else does history amount to other than the praise of Rome?' (*quid est enim aliud omnis historia quam Romana laus?*).

After Petrarch, a succession of antiquaries added to and corrected his work. Chrysoloras' pupil Poggio Bracciolini of Florence, Nicholas of Cusa, better known as Cardinal Cusanus, a German, Cyriaco of Pizzicolli and Guarino of Verona were among them. Patrons who subsidised this new exploratory movement included Cosimo de Medici and his grandchild Lorenzo the Magnificent, to whom we owe the foundation of the Great Medician book collection. Niccolò de Niccoli of Florence acquired the best private library of MSS in Italy. Niccolò's work on texts, excising corrupt passages and restoring the originals, gives him claim to be called the first textual critic. Between 1447 and 1521 the Popes Nicholas V, Pius II, known as a scholar-traveller under his own name of Aeneas Sylvius Piccolomini, Julius II, the soldier-Pope, and Leo X all rendered outstanding services to art and letters. The first-named, who founded Glasgow University in 1451, perceived that if the Church was to maintain its position in a rapidly changing world it must accept and assimilate contemporary developments. He tried to harness the whole humanist movement in the service of religion and the Vatican Library is a monument to his perspicacity.

The study of classical grammar in schools, the proliferation of texts, the compilation of dictionaries and manuals and the foundation of a sound basis for advanced scholarship resulted in the formation in the mid-fifteenth century of the Italian academies. Those outstanding were the Platonic Academy at Florence, inaugurated by the Medicis for the study of Plato's philosophy, and the Roman Academy, founded by Pomponius Laetus, a student of the plays of Plautus and Terence; this institution devoted itself to archaeological and topographical researches into Roman remains. With the Florentine Academy are associated Marsilio Ficino, Angelo Poliziano or Politian, Michelangelo, Leon Alberti and Leonardo da Vinci. The Roman Academy numbered among its scholars Baldassare Castiglione, whose *The Courtier* (1528) provided an abstract or epitome of the most significant moral and social ideas of the period, a period when individual relationships at the diplomatic level began for the first time to affect international relationships between countries and peoples as a whole. The rough-and-ready fighting knight was replaced by the new-style courtier, a term which applied to men in the service of the State, not just to any hanger-on at Court, though the latter's cynical and essentially pragmatic approach to personal intercourse was to become part of the stock-in-trade of this significant Renaissance type.

.   .   .   .   .   .

One important effect which Italian humanism had upon social evolution in other European countries was on education. In the medieval school, instruction had usually fallen into the hands of priests who themselves were only slightly more advanced than their pupils. Better schools existed, like the Cathedral schools at Chartres or Beauvais, or those founded by the Brethren of the Common Life in Holland and the Rhineland, where Thomas à Kempis, Nicholas of Cusa and Desiderius Erasmus were educated. But, however well taught, Latin was normally regarded only as a means to an end, a tool for learning law, theology or medicine, never as a language worth knowing for its own sake or because it was a key to classical literature. This attitude was characteristic of teachers in all the universities of northern Europe until 1550 or later.

Teaching was held in contempt as a base occupation, unfit for men of ability, an opportunity for sadists to indulge themselves at the expense of children and, traditionally, a brutal process. As Petrarch himself observed in 1351:

> Let those teach who like disorder, noise and dirt and the screams of the victim as the rod falls gaily, who are not happy unless they can flog and torture. How then can teaching be a fit occupation for an honourable age?

> (*Familiar Letters*, XII, 3.)

However, after 1400 a stream of treatises on education started to flow out of Italy, advocating a humanistic training imparted by means of gentler methods. Three of these are especially to be noted— *De Ingenuis Moribus* of Vergerius of Padua (1392) and Piccolomini's (Pius II's) letter to the young child Prince Ladislas of Hungary and Moravia (1444) and his *De Liberorum Educatione* (1449). Erasmus followed Vergerius, and the English educationists of the sixteenth century, in their turn, took example from Erasmus.

Vergerius saw the object of education as the production of the complete citizen, the man who applied his gifts as a member of a civilised community and he utterly rejected medieval asceticism. Particularly significant for our present purposes is his assertion that the study of history and philosophy deserved pride of place above all others, for history shed light upon what men have already done, philosophy upon what they ought to do in the future. From history man might draw lessons for the present, said Vergerius, calling it 'the storehouse of experience and wisdom of the race'. This stress on the finer cultivation of the mind was to be fundamental in the teachings of Vittorino da Feltre, Palmieri, and Erasmus. Like Erasmus, Vergerius was a Christian humanist, insisting that Latin literature be admitted into the curriculum but subordinated to the divine ordinances. Literature, he declared, ought to be the main instrument of education, since it is closely connected with life and people should learn to guard against the degeneration of the reverential attitude of mind into mere unreasoning superstition.

Following Aristotle's dictum that literary studies followed to the exclusion of all else were unhealthy, Vergerius argued that boys ought to be able to defend the state in time of war, so that gradual training, related to the physical development of the pupil, should build up a sound body at its physical peak, in early manhood. Physical power, a contempt for death and invincible courage go together and life ought to be regarded as of less moment than noble action—a version of Cicero's famous statement (*De Officiis*, I, 6): 'the praise of all virtue consists in action' (*laus omnis in actione consistit*).

Like Vergerius, Piccolomini emphasised history and philosophy and advised the young Ladislas to read history—not the history of his own country in contemporary Latin, but the history of the ancient world. His own words to the young prince were Ciceronian:

> History is the living witness of the past,
> the lamp of truth, our guide to days that
> are now, exhibiting those that are gone
> (*De Lib. Educ.*, Book I)

and this was a history that had to be read in the full dress of fine language. *De Liberorum Educatione* was one of the first of many works that sought to introduce a Greek spirit into the education of children. The ideas of Vergerius and Piccolomini brought great changes into the practice of pedagogy and a new type of schoolmaster came into being, revered for his many-sided accomplishments. Every princely house in Italy aimed to found a Court school wherein humanist doctrines were taught, and under influential patronage Vittorino da Feltre and Guarino of Verona opened such schools, offering a curriculum rooted in Latin, but containing Greek, mathematics, physical culture and music, designed to ally strength of character to love of book-learning. Vittorino named his school *'La Casa Giocosa'* (The House of Fun) a title indicative of his insistence upon the pleasures of education.

These theories and resulting practices were introduced into England by Erasmus (1466–1536), the man who brought the mainstream of humanism to England early in the sixteenth century. He was of Dutch ancestry and birth but German by adoption and hence claimed by German historians as a fellow-countryman though he was really a cosmopolitan and a wanderer, educated in Holland and Paris and at various times a sojourner in Italy, Switzerland and England. From 1510–13 he lectured at Cambridge on Greek and enjoyed the intimate friendship of Colet, More and their circle. He was the greatest man of letters of his time—the master of a flexible Latin style and unsurpassed north of the Alps in Greek—and his work was a strong instrument of Church reform. He spent 1506–9 in Italy and bequeathed to English scholars the considered results of what he had learned there. His influence on the English Renaissance cannot be overrated.

For Erasmus, the Renaissance meant far more than the revival of the classics or the liberation of the human spirit from the medieval schoolmen. He was a rebel who attacked medieval foundations root and branch and in *Encomium Moriae* (*In Praise of Folly*), his first work, written in England and published in 1512, he attacked the contemporary establishment, especially that of the clergy, whose scholastic theology and narrow intolerance he ridiculed unmercifully. Bishops, overdressed and eager for gold, monks, ignorant and dwelling in dirt, and even the Popes themselves, surrounded by pomp and plenty, are all thrashed in this book. Students of English literature may have their thoughts drawn to Langland's Fair Field of Folk but Erasmus's immediate model was Sebastian Brant's *Narrenschiff*, which has been mentioned already in this volume. *In Praise of Folly* was a *jeu d'ésprit* written by a bitter enemy of long-accepted practices and it voiced the unspoken thoughts of his own generation. Before he died it had passed through twenty-eight editions.

In 1516 Erasmus published a New Testament in Greek accompanied by a Latin translation correcting the errors of the Vulgate, and Latin paraphrases supplying the meaning of the text. The text itself was based on a minimum of versions and not, as was usually the case, upon the collations of a dozen. Erasmus' aim was to bring theology back to life-giving contact with the actual basis of the Christian faith, so that all men might know its import.

All the English writers on education who took their example from Erasmus shared a common conception of what its aims ought to be. Elyot, Cheke, Wilson, Gilbert, Cleland and Ascham all adopted similar arguments and to read one is to read all, at least so far as essential content is concerned. Although they professed concern for popular education they were humanists, individualists who provided for an intellectual *élite*, what More called 'the order of the learned'. The titles of their works, *e.g.*, *The Book Named the Governor*, *Queen Eizabeth's Academy*, *The Institution of a Nobleman*, denote their character. Erasmus's own works on educational practice, *De Pueris*, *De Rationii Studii* and *Colloquia*, emphasise his belief that men may be formed, and are not born complete (*homines, mihi crede, non nascuntur sed finguntur*). It was important, therefore, that the forming should be properly carried out.

One of the earliest and most typical English examples of this trend was Sir Thomas Elyot's *The Book Named the Governor* (1531). which, with Roger Ascham's *Schoolmaster* (1570), holds some claim to consideration as a work of literature. Elyot (1490–1546), the son of a landed gentleman who was a friend of More, learned Greek from Linacre and held a Crown appointment under Wolsey.

He read widely in classical and modern Italian literature and knew many of the leading humanists personally. Employed on diplomatic duties by Cromwell, he passed his leisure time writing, translating from Greek and making a Latin-English dictionary.

In *The Governor* he deliberately tried to increase the English vocabulary—indulging a yearning common to many English humanists to augment the language. The most successful producer of new words was Skelton in his translation of Diodorus Siculus, but all students of Greek, Latin and Hebrew tongues, as well as of French and Italian, perceived their advantages over English in the matter of expressing complicated philosophical ideas, communicating information of a scientific nature with precision and as vehicles for imaginative literature. The desire to make classical and modern authors known in England manifested itself in a spate of translations—especially during the second half of the century. Elyot himself made translations from Plutarch and Isocrates, and by training and interest was equipped with a formidable armament of classical authors such as Plato, Aristotle, Cicero and Quintilian as well as with a wide reading of recent Italians like Palmieri, Piccolomini, and the very recent Castiglione, whose *Il Libro del Cortegiano* had only just been published (1528).

Elyot set himself to write a manifesto of humanistic education for use in England and if the English Renaissance had to be represented by one author and one work, this man's *Book Named the Governor* ought to be chosen as the most representative of its time. He was the first to infuse the 'Renaissance spirit' into the English language, as distinct from Skelton and others of a more lexicographical turn of mind, who collected words as though they were old coins. Elyot developed a well, though not highly, polished prose style, a rival to Latin, so that although he and More shared a common purpose (that of elevating standards of public and private conduct), *The Governor*, written in English, was immediately seen to be a useful work of instruction, whereas *Utopia* was not known at all during the author's lifetime, except to a privileged few of his friends. Before 1600 at least nine editions of *The Governor* were printed.

The Governor is divided into three books, comprising the political, intellectual and moral education of a public official at a time when the English state service was young and flourishing as a healthy new growth. In Book I Elyot distinguishes a republic and a commonwealth, talks of degrees and order of precedence and describes the ideal state as being a monarchy having subordinate governors, for whom his book is designed. He enumerates in considerable detail the education of such a governor, stressing the values of Latin, ancient literature, legal studies, music, poetry, dancing, fishing, hunting, and, like Ascham after him, archery (all illustrated from the classics).

He is especially interested in dancing, and devotes four chapters to this art, which he discusses philosophically as a combination of recreation and meditation, a physical and mental activity leading, in a young man, to the exercise of prudence. Elyot explains the steps and figures of dancing symbolically, interpreting them as honour, maturity, providence and industry, circumspection, election, experience and modesty, all branches of prudence. He illustrates these qualities from ancient and modern history. As an example of circumspection he cites Henry VII and asks,

What incomparable circumspection was in hym alway founden, that nat withstandinge his longe absence out of this realme, the disturbance of the same by sondrye seditions amonge the nobilitie, Civile warres and batayles, wherin infinite people were slayne, besyde skirmisshis and slaughters in the private contentions and factions of divers gentilmen, the lawes layde in water (as is the proverbe), affection and avarice subduinge justice and equitie; yet by his most excellent witte, he in fewe yeres, nat onely broughte this realme in good ordre and under due obedience, revived the lawes, avaunced Justice, refurnisshed his dominions, and repayred his manours; but also with suche circumspection traited with other princes and realmes, of leages, of aliaunce, and amities, that during the more parte of his reigne, he was litle or nothyng inquieted with outwarde hostilitie or martiall businesse. And yet all other princes either feared hym or had hym in a fatherly reverence. Whiche praise, with the honour thereunto due, as inheritaunce discendeth by righte unto his most noble sonne, our most dere soveraigne lorde that nowe presently raigneth. For, as Tulli (i.e. *Cicero*) saithe, the best inheritance that the fathers leve to their children, excellynge all other patrimonie, is the glorie or praise of vertue and noble actis.   (*op. cit.*, I, xxiv.)

after which encomium he goes on to say that he will not speak of Henry's other virtues lest he might be accused of flattery, a habit of which he claims, rather unconvincingly, to disapprove especially.

The second book enumerates the various qualities which a governor ought to possess, how he should regulate his conduct, what he needs to avoid and even his wearing apparel. The qualities specified include majesty, nobility, affability, placability, mercy, humanity (divided into benevolence, beneficence, liberality and amity), that is to say, a combination of Graeco-Christian-chivalric ideals of behaviour, with a veneer of modern social or rather sociable qualities such as Castiglione's ideal courtier was expected to demonstrate. Elyot illustrates his argument by means of classical and historical anecdotes, including the dubious story about the young Henry V quoted below and, at greater length, the legend about Titus and Giseppus, taken from Boccaccio and used to illustrate perfect amity.

Book III continues the process of instruction with reference to other aspects of morality, such as justice and other Greek virtues—fortitude, magnanimity, abstinence, ambition, continence and experience, temperance, understanding and good counsel, which is (he says) the end of all study. He concludes by comparing the public weal to a garden and its counsellors and governors to gardeners who seek to destroy the moles ('vices and sundry enormities') that turn up the earth, and he instructs all the gardeners to care for all the garden and not just a section of it. The garden metaphor, inherited by Elyot from the Bible and used by Shakespeare in Richard II (and subsequently by a long line of writers on education down to the present day), is in Elyot's hands rather wordy. The author of *The Governor* is inclined to build up sentences ponderously, as though he were composing Latin. Of humour he has practically none, unlike More, whose spontaneity makes him far more readable—at least in translation.

In chapter XXV Elyot discusses 'Experience which have preceded our tyme, with a defence of histories' and defines knowledge or experience, the origin of wisdom, as 'example', expressed by history, called by Cicero 'the life of memory'. He goes on to explain what history is, *i.e.*:

> . . . a greke name, and commeth of a worde or verbe in greke *Historeo*, whiche doth signifie to knowe, to se, to enserche, to enquire, to here, to lerne, to tell, or expounde unto other. And than muste historie whiche commeth thereof be wonderfull profitable, whiche leaveth nothinge hydde from mannes knowlege, that unto hym may be eyther pleasaunt or necessarie. For it nat onely reporteth the gestes or actes of princes or capitaynes, their counsayles and attemptates, enterprises, affaires, maners in lyvinge good and bad, descriptions of regions and cities, with their inhabituantes, but also it bringeth to our knowlege the fourmes of sondry publike weales with augmentations and decayes and occasion therof; moreover preceptes, exhortations, counsayles, and good persuasions, comprehended in quicke sentences and eloquent orations. Finally so large is the compase of that whiche is named historie, that it comprehendeth all thynge that is necessary to be put in memorie. (*op. cit.*, III, xxv.)

He goes on to give examples of authors and works which he considers come under the general head of history—Aristotle, Theophrastus, Pliny the Elder and the Holy Scriptures, both Old and New Testaments. Hardly any books of the Bible may not be described as histories, states Elyot, from the Pentateuch to the Gospels, which contain the temporal life of Christ. This down-to-earth attitude to the Bible Elyot shared with Erasmus and other humanists whose researches were scholarly and not inhibited by the unintellectual awe of many medieval schoolmen when confronted by Holy Writ. Elyot's explanation of what history is and its value is a useful one, for it sums up the view of his humanist circle. Since *The Governor* was the first treatise on education to be published in English the prominence given to history as a subject for study in this influential book is especially worthy of notice. Literature was not so highly recommended—the antipathy towards poets as purveyors of lies, inherited from the Plato of the *Republic*, made the humanists hesitate to advance favourable pronouncements on imaginative works. 'Poets' were distinguished from 'authors' (*auctores*), who were models to be emulated in respect of style. Elyot refers to the 'lyes and fayninge of poetes'; and there is nothing in *The Governor* that deserves the name of literary criticism.

The succession of anecdotes with which he illustrates his argument saves Elyot's book from being considered tedious—in fact, on the whole *The Governor* is quite readable. Most of his stories are extracted from the classics, but English chronicle-history occasionally furnishes him with a useful example of how his precepts work in action. One such is this tale of the young prince Henry, afterwards Henry V, who fell foul of the law and was sent to prison by one of his father's justices. It is intended to illustrate placability, a quality much admired by Cicero, which emerges when a man is justifiably angry, yet does not seek revenge. Its opposite is ire, or wrath, which Elyot describes as though he were witnessing the antics of one of the Seven Deadly Sins in a morality play:

> a man . . . by furie chaunged in to an horrible figure, his face infarced with rancour, his mouthe foule and imbosed, his eien wyde starynge and sparklynge like fire, nat speakyng, but as a wylde bulle, rorying and brayienge out wordes despitefull and venomous; forgetynge his astate or condition, forgeting lernyng, ye forgetynge all reason, wyll nat have such a passion in extreme detestation? (Book II, vi.)

an expansion of Ovid's picture of the furious man in the *Ars Amatoria*, which Elyot cites as further illustration.

After calling up a succession of examples from ancient history, Elyot comes at length to his English embodiment of placability:

> The most renowned prince, Henry the fifth, late king of England, during the life of his father was noted to be fierce and

of wanton courage. It happened that one of his servants whom he well favoured, for felony by him committed, was arraigned at the king's bench; whereof he being advertised, and incensed by light persons about him, in furious rage came hastily to the bar, where his servant stood as a prisoner, and commanded him to be ungyved and set at liberty, whereat all men were abashed, reserved the chief justice, who humbly exhorted the prince to be contented that his servant might be ordered according to the ancient laws of this realm, or if he would have him saved from the rigour of the laws, that he should obtain, if he might, of the king, his father, his gracious pardon; whereby no law or justice should be derogate. With which answer the prince nothing appeased, but rather more inflamed, endeavoured himself to take away his servant. The judge considering the perilous example and inconvenience that might thereby ensue, with a valiant spirit and courage commanded the prince upon his allegiance to leave the prisoner and depart his way. With which commandment the prince, being set all in a fury, all chafed, and in a terrible manner, came up to the place of judgement—men thinking that he would have slain the judge, or have done to him some damage; but the judge sitting still, without moving, declaring the majesty of the king's place of judgement, and with an assured and bold countenance, had to the prince these words following:

'Sir, remember yourself; I keep here the place of the king, your sovereign lord and father, to whom ye owe double obedience, wherefore, after this in his name, I charge you desist from your wilfulness and unlawful enterprise, and from henceforth give good example to those which hereafter shall be your proper (*own*) subjects. And now for your contempt and disobedience, go you to the prison of the king's bench, whereunto I commit you; and remain you there prisoner until the pleasure of the king your father be further known.'

With which words being abashed, and also wondering at the marvellous gravity of that worshipful justice, the noble prince, laying his weapon apart (*aside*), doing reverence, departed and went to the king's bench as he was commanded.

G

Whereat his servants disdaining, came and showed to the king all the whole affair. Whereat he a whiles studying, after as a man all ravished with gladness, holding his eyes and hands up towards heaven, abraided (*started up*), saying with a loud voice: 'O merciful god, how much am I, above all other men, bound to your infinite goodness; specially for that you have given me a judge, who feareth not to minister justice, and also a son who can suffer semblably (*as is fitting*) and obey justice.

Now here a man may behold three persons worthy of excellent memory. First, a judge, who being a subject, feared not to execute justice on the eldest son of his sovereign lord, and by the order of nature his successor. Also a prince and son and heir of the king, in the midst of his fury, more considered his evil example, and the judge's conscience in justice, than his own estate or wilful appetite. Thirdly, a noble king and wise father, who contrary to the custom of parents, rejoiced to see his son and the heir of his crown to be for his disobedience by his subject corrected. Wherefore I conclude that nothing is more honourable or to be desired in a prince or noble man than placability. As contrary wise, nothing is so detestable, or to be feared in such a one, as wrath and cruel malignity. (*Ibid.*)

The historical facts of this incident are not authentic and the anecdote is part of the Henry V legend. The lesson emphasised in Elyot's concluding sentence may well have been conceived with Henry VIII in mind, for the king had a violent temper when opposed and was by no means unready to take out ruthless personal revenge, an unattractive trait which became more and more evident during the second half of his reign. When *The Governor* was being composed, the writing was already plain on the wall for Elyot's friend More, and the ideal state of Plato seemed to be far removed from actual conditions in England, as More himself had observed in *Utopia*. *The Governor* was in fact dedicated to Henry VIII and might be described as a compilation founded on Elyot's reading—the work was not about 'government' or 'civics' but dealt with personal morality in service to the 'state', itself a new concept. The standards of conduct appropriate to a feudal knight and summed up in the chivalric code were by Elyot softened and modified into the practical pursuit of fresh ideals of service in a different cause, a secular and abstract concept sanctioned by the King's Court. Although established in Italy, the 'state' was a novelty elsewhere in Europe at that time.

History is important to Elyot, for it is a guide to the methods of making war and the reasons for doing so and also to the condition of a body politic, its good and bad features, rulers, members and national health. He brings history and literature together when he remarks:

Admit that some histories be interlaced with lies; why should we therefore neglect them since the affairs there reported no thynge concern us, we being thereof no partners, nor thereby only may receive any damage. But if by reading the sage counsel of Nestor, the subtle persuasions of Ulysses, the compendious gravity of Menelaus, the imperial majesty of Agamemnon, the prowess of Achilles, and valiant courage of Hector, we may apprehend any thing whereby our wits may be amended and our personages be more apt to serve our public weal and our prince; what forces it us (*does it matter to us*) though Homer write lies? I suppose no man thinks that Aesop wrote gospels, yet who doubts but that in his fables the fox, the hare and the wolf, though they never spoke, do teach many good wise things? Which being well considered, men if they have not vowed to oppose reason shall confess with Quintilian that few and hardly one may be found out of ancient writers which shall not bring to the readers some thing commodious (*useful*); and specially that they do write matters historical, the lesson whereof is as it were the mirror of man's life, expressing actually and as it were in the eye, the beauty of nature and the deformity and lothliness of vice. Wherefore Lactantius says: you must needs perish if you do not know what is profitable to your life, so that you may seek for it, and what is dangerous, so that you may flee and eschew it. Which I dare affirm may come soonest to pass by reading histories and retaining them in continual remembrance. (Book III, xxv.)

but it is plain that he regards history as on a much higher plane than literature.

Elyot is very considerate of style in his recommended authors, so that although Lord Berners' *Froissart* translation, no doubt read by the author of *The Governor*, might have qualified as a sound text-book for the well-born young man to study, both in respect of its contents and its translator's similar view of the value of history (quoted previously), Elyot would not have dreamed of substituting it for ancient history. The dilemma of an Alexander, a Caesar or a Hannibal was, so far as Elyot was concerned, a far more useful source of information and instruction than that of any medieval or modern prince, mainly because Latin style was superior to any vernacular style whatsoever. Training in classical rhetoric was in the end a training in writing one's own language well. All the humanists agreed on this. They also agreed that what was worth knowing was written in Greek or Latin, according to certain criteria of stylistic attainment. None of them held that rhetoric for its own sake—what Hobbes later referred to as 'the windy blisters of a troubled water'—was valuable. Erasmus's *Institution of a Christian Prince*, dedicated to Charles V, however, is recommended by Elyot as a modern work which contained an abundance of good advice, elegantly put (in Latin).

Though it suffered from many of the shortcomings of its time—a blinkered view of the present, an uncritical worship of antiquity and an incapacity to perceive that the problems of ancient Rome, or modern Italy, were not those of Henry VIII's England, *The Governor* reveals its author's grasp of the essential fact of political evolution. Without understanding completely what he was advocating, Elyot could perceive that the old order which had so long been gifted with hereditary authority was not going to be able to maintain that authority unless it acquired new skills. The age of professionalism was about to begin, yet the landed classes of England despised book learning, specifically-directed training, the gathering of skills, and in fact expertise of any sort other than the military. Castiglione's *Courtier* sneered openly at the loutishness of the feudal knight, but English popular opinion still supported the aristocratic assurance that one mark of a gentleman was his academic ignorance and that clerkly abilities went hand in hand with lower rank. Since, however, good government was no longer accepted as being a matter of accident but as a skill which could be taught, Elyot insisted that the governor and, incidentally, many of the servants who aided him to rule, should be deliberately subjected to a 'civilising' process, based on Italian precepts adapted from the ancient classics.

Although only a theoretical treatise produced by a man with no children of his own who was not himself a teacher, *The Governor* is an indispensable guide to the changing attitudes of the sixteenth century. The aristocracy strengthened itself and its fortunes by marrying outside its ranks. Riches and titles came together in marriages of baron with *bourgeoise*, new peers of the realm were created by Henry VIII, accelerating a process begun in Chaucer's time, and the English law of primogeniture made certain that only the eldest son inherited a title. Younger sons were forced to depart from the estate and to make their own way in the world—the 'world' of the mid-sixteenth century so far as they were concerned meant the Church, the Law and, as in the case of the Pastons of an earlier generation, mercantile pursuits. Elyot was acquainted with many members of the new class and with families like the Johnsons who were not aristocratic, but highly respected in City business. It was in this changing society that his *Governor* held real significance and the kind of education it advocated was soon to be highly sought-after by the English upper middle classes. In fact, it was an education for the English upper middle classes rather than for the kind of remote aristocracy which one associates with Europe. Castiglione's *Courtier* was a handbook for 'gentleman-amateurs', of a species which did not exist in England at the time. In spite of Spenserian ideals, the psychology of the English gentleman did not develop fully until the period of the Whig aristocracy—the Romantic period of literature.

.   .   .   .   .   .

In much the same spirit Roger Ascham wrote *Toxophilus* (1545) and *The Schoolmaster* (1570). *Toxophilus* or 'Lover of the Bow' is a whimsical plea for the revival of archery, which its author claimed was essential to the physical and moral health of the country. Composed in dialogue form in the Platonic manner, it is a light-hearted piece of writing, full of enthusiastic prejudice in favour of the sport of shooting with the bow and against other pastimes, such as gaming, bowls and lute-playing. Ascham prefaced his work with a verse:

> Rejoyse Englande, be gladde and merie,
>> Trothe overcommeth thyne enemyes all.
>> The Scot, the Frencheman, the Pope and heresie,
> Overcommed by Trothe, have had a fall:
> Stick to the Trothe, and ever more thou shall
> Through Christ, King Henry, the Boke and the Bowe
> All maner of enemies, quite overthrowe,

lines which sum up the temper of mind of all the Protestant humanists of his generation—they saw England as a morally righteous champion doing battle with a succession of dragons and defeating them one by one—an allegory made prominent in Spenser's *Faerie Queene* and, more forcefully, in Shakespeare's *Henry V*.

It should be noted that Ascham was not writing about an obsolete or even markedly obsolescent article of military offence, although the use of the longbow had undoubtedly declined after Bosworth and Flodden. Its last appearance on the battlefield was at the battle of Pinkie in 1549, when it was opposed to the arquebus and the cannon. Henry VIII, to whom Ascham dedicated *Toxophilus*, was a keen archer and showed off his skill in person at the Field of the Cloth of Gold in 1520. Elyot concluded Book I of his *Governor* with a chapter claiming that 'shotyng in a longe bow is principall of all other exercises' and in 1549 Bishop Latimer preached a sermon extolling archery as a gift from God. The legal statutes relating to archery passed between 1503 and 1558 show how official efforts to maintain bowyers in England progressed:

1503   The use of crossbows is forbidden to all except lords and well-to-do freeholders (19 Hen VII).

1511-2 To encourage the diminishing exercise of archery, every man up to 60 years old, and every man child shall have and use longbows; and bowyers shall be compelled to reside in such localities as may require their services (3 Hen VIII).

1511–2 The Statute of 19 Hen VII is to be enforced (3 Hen VIII).

1514–5 Further legislation against crossbows (6 Hen VIII).

1523 The acts against crossbows are partially relaxed (14 Hen VIII.)

1533–4 The same are enforced again (25 Hen VIII.)

1541–2 As for 1533–4 (33 Hen VIII.)

1541–2 The Provisions of 3 Hen VIII are confirmed and rules for regular shooting practice laid down. Houses for 'unlawful games' played to the detriment of archery are prohibited (33 Hen VIII).

1557–8 Orders are issued for the keeping of bows and arrows by all the population (4 & 5 Philip and Mary.)

(Summarised from A. E. Hodgkin's *The Archer's Craft* [1951].)

The law of 1557–8 stood until 1662, when 'An Act for ordering the Forces in the Several Counties of the Kingdom' (14 Charles II) entered the statute book; it referred to swords, pistols, muskets and pikes but not to the bow. Henceforth archery survived only as a sport and Ascham, himself a man of delicate health who took it up as a means of keeping fit, left behind a standard textbook on the bowyer's art. He stands in the same relation to his beloved toxophily as Isaac Walton does to halieutics, or fishing.

Ascham wrote in English, not Latin, and studied to achieve a plain, undecorated style that does much to conceal the labour that went into its making. He was a purist, depending upon precision and balance to make up for his rejection of ornamental devices, particularly those borrowed from French and Italian. Carried to extremes, such purism can be as repellent as the other extreme represented by the excessive use of so-called 'inkhorn' terms from an unspoken literary language. However, Ascham was nowhere near reaching such an extreme in style, though he shows signs of it. *Toxophilus* is full of recollections of life in humanist circles when the author was younger and includes references to Erasmus,

Cheke and Elyot. C. S. Lewis compared it with Dorothy Words-
worth's *Journals* in its degree of loving observation. The book did
lead to the revival of archery as a sport in Cambridge and, inevitably, to a statute prohibiting it in St John's, Ascham's own
college. The superficially waggish character of the writing and the
remoteness of the main subject have tended to discourage later
generations from reading *Toxophilus* but in fact it is an excellent
piece of humanistic entertainment, in many ways more durable
than *The Schoolmaster*.

This latter work was written towards the end of Ascham's life
and published posthumously. It had an alternative title: 'a plain
and perfite way of teaching children to understand, write and
speake the Latin tong', but it also dealt with moral training and the
use of vernacular English as well as with current questions of
prosody, wherein the respective values of rhyme and no-rhyme
were debated. As a tutor to Princess Elizabeth and to Lady Jane
Grey, Ascham had some experience of instructing potential rulers
and though, in common with many of his contemporaries, he
pretended to an interest in 'popular' education, it is obvious from
The Schoolmaster that his ideal pupil is an aristocrat.

His methods of teaching, based upon a profound reverence for
the classics and a contempt for the moderns, are humane in the
tradition of Vergerius, Palmieri, Erasmus and Elyot, for Ascham
does not believe in beating book-learning into a child. In fact, he
starts by making remarks about Etonians who ran away from
school to escape the birch rod, and his protest against such methods
is one of the first recorded objections to corporal punishment to
be made in the English language. Like his pupil and his teacher,
Ascham's curriculum is an ideal one, though not of a kind likely
to find much favour nowadays. He adopts the position of the
extreme humanist, believing in subordination to models and the
handing on of original styles by imitation—what he refers to as
'a following of the best authors'. Erasmus had said that knowledge
was of two kinds—things and words—and Ascham quotes him in
support of his own view that the development of a good style was
central to learning.

He enters into a vehement digression on the Italian travel undertaken by contemporary scions of the nobility in order to obtain 'experience of life'. Reference has been made to his hatred of the Italian *novelle* as being more harmful than ten *Morte Arthures* and to the confusion of aesthetic and moral standards of literary judgement which affected Renaissance criticism. Ascham seems to have been hostile to poetry, like his severely academic contemporaries, and, though he generally finds a place in histories of literary criticism, he was not a critic.

Much more interesting than his 'schoolmasterly' arguments are the digressions and references to Court life—in particular his sketch of his tutorial pupil Elizabeth ten years before she became Queen and a similar one of the ill-starred 'Queen' Lady Jane Grey, later beheaded with her husband Dudley in 1554 after a rising led by Sir Thomas Wyatt, son of the poet, who himself met the same fate two months later. These accounts are at first hand, but, as one might expect of a courtier-usher, Ascham has made his royal charges ideal recipients of instruction. Elizabeth, for example

> who never took yet Greek nor Latin grammar in her hand, after the first declining of a noun and a verb, but onely by this double translating of Demosthenes and Isocrates daily without missing every forenoon, and likewise some part of Tullie (Cicero) every afternoon, for the space of a year or two, has attained to such a perfect understanding in both the tongues, and to such a ready utterance of the Latin, and that with such a judgment as they be few in number in both the universities or elsewhere in England that be in both tongues comparable with her Majesty   (Book II)

may have been as brilliant as the writer suggests, but she could hardly have been typical of the average child faced by the classics for the first time.

One must read *The Schoolmaster* carefully for examples of the writer's fine eye for realistic detail and for the occasional artist's observation which Elyot lacks:

> They be like trees, that show forth fair blossoms and broad leaves in spring time but bring out small and not long lasting fruit in harvest time; and that only such as fall and rot before

> they be ripe and so never or seldom come to any good at all
> (Book I)

is how Ascham describes men who live and die obscurely. Again, of the taking-up of crude and vulgar fashions or habits, he says:

> And if some Smithfield ruffian take up some strange going, some new mowing with the mouth, some wrinching with the shoulder, some brave proverb, some fresh new oath that is not stale but will run round in the mouth, some new disguised garment or desperate hat, fond in fashion or garish in colour, whatsoever it cost, how small soever his living be, by what shift soever it be gotten, gotten must it be, and used with the first or else the grace of it, is stale and gone. (*Ibid.*)

The Tudor humanists who wrote about education may all be said to have agreed that all children could profit from purely academic training, that what suited adults suited children, that learning from books surpassed experience and that theoretical instruction in moral conduct would prove itself in actual practice. All these idealistic assumptions fell short of the truth but they were characteristic of the head-in-air theorism indulged in by contemporary scholars—a trend later commented upon by Montaigne in his essay on pedantry. The fashioning of a 'gentleman' was an Italianate aim of education which may now seem narrow and ineffective but the English practice of these theories persisted for over three centuries and indeed has only recently been abandoned. The connection of 'gentlemen' with 'classical studies' has had an unfortunate effect on both. In Ascham's time the courtliness by which a gentleman was supposedly to be distinguished was not necessarily a mask for shams or insincerity but a refining influence on the traditional crudeness of the English nobility who, as Shakespeare makes clear in the wooing scene of *Henry V*, lacked the refinement of their French counterparts.

. . . . . .

The most striking and typical man of the early Renaissance in England was, however, not a scholar but a writer whose links with English literature are indirect because his best known imaginative work was composed in Latin. More wrote his *Utopia* between 1514–16 when he was in his thirties, 'in the middle of life's road', as Dante put it (*'nel mezzo del cammin di nostra vita'*), when a man may be expected to reach the summit of his intellectual and creative potential. *Utopia* is a prose romance about an ideal republic, similar to Plato's, in which More attacks the social evils of his own time. In content the work may be compared with Erasmus's *In Praise of Folly*, which undoubtedly inspired it, though its models were the real-life voyages of Amerigo Vespucci to the Americas, voyages which sought to discover a fresh world, symbolised in *The Tempest* by Shakespeare's enchanted island, where man might make a fresh beginning. In *Utopia* the past is represented by scholasticism, chivalry and the ownership of private property, all three of which More attacks. He hates war, praises communal ownership and, by discrediting gold, thinks to do away with theft. For him the end of existence is happiness in this world, not in the next, as the monastic doctrines advocated, and he has great faith in human goodness, loving nature almost in a Rousseauist manner.

More tries to counter dogmatic theology with an entirely new form of religion, free from dogma. He said once that the right prayer to the Creator consisted in thanking him for putting the divinely human soul in such a divinely beautiful body. The religion and ethics of the Utopians were grounded in this rule; it stood in absolute opposition to cloistered asceticism, which rejected the body as a corruptible thing and sought felicity in preparation for an after life. In Utopia self-indulgence was encouraged, though higher and lower degrees of enjoyment were recognised and More, following Plato in the *Philebus*, aimed to establish a standard of pleasure by which men might know the worth of their specific enjoyments.

This spirit was typical of the Renaissance in its least complicated form—the belief in life as a joyful gift and in the glory of man himself. In Elizabethan poetry, particularly Spenser's, it was a fundamental belief but in More's own time it was undeveloped. Like Erasmus and Colet, More attacked the shortcomings of his society. The unjust laws of England, harsh landlords evicting tenants, land enclosure, particularly the enclosure of commons for grazing purposes, and the inflicting of capital punishment for trivial offences involving property were all facts of which he had personal knowledge. The reality of war, divided authority, a scramble for wealth and position and harsh political discord were social evils each of which he shows up by picturing its opposite, namely, peace under one ruler, unity, security of status, the unimportance of gold and sound organisation. *Utopia* pleads for reason and order to be built up carefully, neither by royal absolutism, such as Henry VIII sought to establish, nor by the power of the 'estates'.

However, in principle and practice More himself seems to have done little to encourage the growth of a Utopia in England—indeed the word itself has a contemptuous connotation and is derived from two Greek words meaning 'no place'. His hero, called Raphael Hythloday, a philosopher, is nothing like himself and although More argued for the employment of philosophers in Utopian state affairs, a Hythloday living in England at that time would have been imprisoned by More himself in his capacity as Lord Chancellor. But Utopia is an authoritarian state, with inflexible laws, and the libertarian language which More and his circle use to advocate reform is not to be taken literally but rather as a means of emphasising their dislike of medieval institutions. The early humanists were not believers in the natural goodness of man nor were they free from medieval insistence on the importance of authority. In the name of one set of values they rebelled against another set and, far from being the forward-looking liberals which some historians have tried to make them, More, Elyot, Ascham and their friends were all extreme conservatives. Their zeal for looking back for a standard at a far-off past society and language suggests that they had little or no appreciation of social evolution and were satisfied that Athens and Rome were unquestionably the proper standards of urban excellence at which Tudor Londoners should aim. Change since the fall of Rome was but an unfortunate descent into barbarism. The replacement of Latin with vernaculars was considered as a development for the worse and the authority of learned men who had studied classical authors was to be established as society's only hope. As a practical solution to the ills of the body politic *Utopia* is not to be taken seriously. It was an

intellectual exercise, full of invention and intended for the edification of a sophisticated group of admirers—one reason why it was
written in Latin and why More would not permit translation. The
English version, by a Fellow of Corpus Christi, Cambridge, named
Ralph Robinson, appeared in 1551, and a second edition in 1556.
More's Platonic idea of pure pleasure, as Cassirer puts it, 'the token
of genuine humanity, a boundary between human and animal
being' entered English literature only at the very end of the century
and became a fundamental tenet of aesthetic theory in Shaftesbury's
Characteristics of 1711. More's influence on his own age is not to
be measured in terms of *Utopia* but rather in the example he gave
to his friends and disciples.

.　　.　　.　　.　　.　　.

One of the main manifestations of the new learning was the
spate of translations from Greek, Latin, French and other vernaculars into English. The translations vary in quality from utilitarian
renderings, designed to serve the barest descriptive purposes,
without embellishment, to imaginative recreations of their models
and, in one case only, a substitute for the original work, a definition
summing up the German poet Goethe's highest ideal of what a
translation ought to be. This was Gawain Douglas' Scots version
of Virgil's *Aeneid* which Ezra Pound actually claimed was better
than its original—no gross exaggeration, though Tillyard's statement (*The English Epic and its Background* [1954], p. 340) that
despite its weaknesses it 'is a very distinguished work, probably the
best translation of one of the great epics till Dryden and Pope' is
closer to the mark. C. S. Lewis's observation that 'time after time
Douglas is nearer to the original than any version could be which
kept within the limits of later classicism' was published in the same
year as Tillyard's. His general argument is that the conception of
classical writing as dignified and cold, representative of superhuman heroics and sophisticated emotions is false, in other words,
that the academic tradition of high seriousness as an inescapable
concomitant is blinkered. Douglas' Scots retained much of the
vitality and vivid freshness of Virgil's Latin as it must once have
impinged on Roman audiences. The formal English into which

Surrey, Phaer and Stanyhurst turned Virgil's *Aeneid* during the sixteenth century set the standard and the pattern for later translators, while Douglas' Scots version had no imitators. This is a fact of language history, which helps to explain the uniqueness of the latter. As a language of literature and of literary translation, Scots had no future after the Reformation, associated as it was with the old religion, for the widespread use of the Genevan Bible in English had a far-reaching effect on Scots. The language of Douglas and Lyndsay ceased to be written as a literary standard after about 1550 and from then until the end of James VI's lifetime manuscripts of Scottish origin show a decline in the number of Scots words used—in fact James VI's own writings, taken chronologically, show this trend towards anglicisation. The Union of the Crowns in 1603, which made James VI into James I of the United Kingdom, set an official mark on an accelerating movement. By the end of the seventeenth century little remained of Scots as a written medium, but its rugged strength as a colloquial tongue, in many dialects, continued to keep the two countries apart, culturally and politically, until comparatively recently.

Douglas' *Aeneid* is accepted as the most ambitious work written in Scots, and as the highest flight of imagination in that language. The underlying motive of much classical translation, certainly that of major works into a vernacular, was patriotic. If Virgil could be expressed in a vernacular, that vernacular was thereby enhanced. Douglas proved that Scots was adequate, or nearly adequate, for the purpose of rendering Latin, if it were augmented by borrowings from French and English and what he referred to as 'bastard Latyn'. He opened his Prologue to Book I with a prayer to Virgil, the prince of Latin poets, asking pardon for making this attempt and for his own presumption in thinking

> . . . that thy facund sentence mycht be song
> In our langage alsweill as Latyn tong (39–40)

a conventional sentiment concealing the real pride in language which Douglas shared with other sixteenth-century translators of Latin poetry. At that particular time, Scots was in many respects a more passionate and precise language than English and capable of producing emotional effects of great subtlety, as one may discern from reading Henryson and Dunbar. What Tillyard vaguely calls 'splendid things', run all through Douglas' poem, so that although the *Aeneid* in Scots is now something of a museum piece, cast in a language partially synthesised out of other languages, extremely 'literary' in character and deliberately experimental, historically it remains as the first work of the Scottish Renaissance. Since the Scottish Renaissance never really took flight, the *Aeneid* may also be described as its only major work, a repository of Scots words the linguistic value of which was not understood until the eighteenth century and the poetic worth unappreciated until the twentieth, when after the First World War attempts were made to bring about a second Scottish Renaissance by C. M. Grieve, Lewis Spence and the many disciples of the 'Lallans' movement.

Classical literature interested the sixteenth century for other reasons, and in most instances translation was only a means to an end, namely, that of making the writings of the ancients available in English or some other European language, notably French, Italian or 'Dutch' (which included German). Europe was at that time divided into powerful territories, each with its own autocratic ruler, and we have noted that Italy displayed all the vices of this system of government. Statecraft was seen to be an important object of study and the lesson which the translators of Greek and Roman history sought to inculcate was that rebellion against the Prince or ruler is evil—the same lesson, in fact, urged by all historians and authors of treatises on government, ecclesiastical or civil, during the Tudor period. Their main emphasis is on obedience, acceptance of rule, and the equation of God's law with King's law. Tyndale's *Obedience of a Christian Man* (1528) bears a title which is typical of many such works, and Baldwin's Preface to *A Mirror For Magistrates*, quoted elsewhere, is a forthright statement of the prevailing attitude to government.

Roman (and secondarily Greek) imperial history provided historical examples of civil conflict of a kind which the Tudors found appalling—and which their philosophy of government had not equipped them to understand. For this reason most translations from the classics are from late authors whom we should now consider second rate, rather than from, *e.g.*, Homer, Herodotus or Thucydides. The Greece which the early Tudors knew was the declining later Greece, sifted through Roman civilization, and not the land of Pericles, great drama, lyric and philosophy. Euripides and Sophocles were barely known, Aeschylus not at all. The Tudors' notion of serious classical drama was that of Seneca, an inferior Roman tragedian, who seemed to have something specific to say to them about the trials of great men which struck a chord and touched their own circumstances.

'The classics' provided scholars with norms of conduct, sources of instruction in the art of war, in medicine, gardening, personal conduct, education for civic responsibility, ethics and practical wisdom in general. From 1479 until about 1520 there was little translation into English—only thirteen printed books, all from Latin, of which six were translated indirectly from French. All of them are moralistic, some are narrative, but no drama, history, satire, lyric or rhetoric was included. The authors represented are Aesop, Boethius, Cato, Cicero, Frontinus, Lucian, Ovid, Sallust (by Alexander Barclay), Terence, Vegetius and Virgil; but Catullus, Horace, Juvenal, Livy, Lucan, Plautus, Seneca, Statius and Tacitus (to name the more obvious examples) are absent. The important authors were Boethius, an old war-horse, Cato and Aesop; the style of the translations themselves is poor and the quality of the English, Caxton and Barclay excepted, hesitating, marred by an inevitable tendency to multiply synonyms in order to blanket the precise meaning of the Latin and somehow to bear down ponderously on its subtler values.

Translations of classical historians from Latin into French had been dedicated to European princes, in the hope that they might profit from the advice thus given. Out of the study of history the prince-governor would be formed, according to the writers on education, and few scholars failed to subscribe explicitly to the notion that history was of prime importance in education for statecraft. The translations offered were annotated and augmented and in some cases paraphrased for the benefit of those whose duties gave them little opportunity to study the finer points of the original. Thomas Paynell's preface to Barclay's translation of Sallust's *Jugurtha* (1557), originally made in 1520, explains that this is the intention of the translator:

> The translation doth paraphrasticallie so open the hole matter, that no scruple remaineth to be douted upon. For Saluste the noble historiographe, doth in the laten tonge so compendiouslie and briefly but yet most eloquentlie and truely, knyt up the whole historie of Iugurth, that the reader in divers places (excepte he be very rype and perfecte in the eloquence and figures of the laten tonge, and phrases of the same) shal stumble and stagger in the conveyance and understandinge of the true meanyng and sence thereof

and Barclay's own English preface, which was aimed at Thomas Howard, 1st Earl of Surrey and the victor of Flodden, makes it clear that the Jugurthine war is to be taken as a piece of practical advice 'bothe plesaunt, profitable and right necessary unto every degre: but specially to gentlemen whiche coveyt to attayne to clere fame and honour: by glorious dedes of chivalry'. The moral is that wars in a right cause bring order and extirpate vice and evil. Barclay's admiration for James IV, mentioned elsewhere, did not prevent him from addressing this to the very commander who had left the Scots king dead on the battlefield.

In 1544, twenty-four years after the *Jugurtha* translation, Sir Anthony Cope published an account of Hannibal and Scipio, based largely on Livy's *History* and dedicated to Henry VIII. In the year 1544, Henry was embroiled in war with France and Scotland, and Cope points out that there is a time for everything and that this was a time for war, so that the martial acts of Hannibal and Scipio, the two worthy captains of Carthage and Rome respectively, would help men to

> learne bothe to dooe displeasure to theyr enemies, and to avoyde the crafty and daungerous baites, which shall be layde for theim

and strengthen Henry's resolve to meet aggression with aggression.

John Brende printed Quintus Curtius's *History of the Acts of Alexander* in 1553, dedicated to the Earl Marshal, John, Duke

H

of Northumberland. Made between 1551 and 1553 and reprinted four times before the end of the century, Brende's was the best translation of a classical historian to appear during the period, and its dedication, apart from containing the stock observations on the value of history to governors, insists on the Scriptures as the only rule of faith and as such speaks for the reign of Edward VI, when Protestantism was in the ascendancy:

> There is required in all magistrates both a fayth and feare in God, and also an outwarde policye in worldlye thynges, wherof as the one is to be learned by the scryptures, so the other must chiefly be gathered by readyng of histories

states Brende, who goes on to emphasise the importance of obedience, citing history as an example:

> In historyes it is apparent how daungerous it is to begyn *alteracions*[1] in a common welth. How envy & hatredes oft risyng upon smal causes, have ben the destruction of great kyngdomes. And that disobeyers of hygher powers, & suche as rebellyd agaynst magystrates, never escapyd punishment, nor came to good end . . . Seing histories be then so good and necessary, it were muche requisite for mens instruccion, they were translated into suche tounges as most men myght understand them; and specially the histories of antiquitye, whych both for the greatnes of the actes done in those daies, and for the excellencie of the writers have much maiestie and many ensamples of vertue. I therefore havyng alwaies desired that we englishmen might be founde as forwarde in that behalf as other nations which have brought all worthie histories into their naturall language, did a few yeares paste attempte the translacion of Quintus Curtius, and lately upon an occasion performed and accomplished the same.

Herodian's *History of the Roman Emperors*, dedicated to the Earl of Pembroke, was translated by Nicholas Smith from Politian's Latin version between 1554 and 1558. Herodian was a late Syrian-Greek writer of no great importance and the reasons for selecting his history as a subject for translation into English

[1] Altercations

are obscure—possibly his frequent observations concerning early Britain struck Smith as a patriotic qualification. The emphasis of this, as of other classical histories, was utilitarian and the post–1520 translators were little interested in literature as such, any more than were their predecessors of the post-Caxton school. Important portions of Thucydides, Livy, Caesar and the other historians mentioned were turned into competent English and used as guidebooks for governors. Cicero's *De Officiis*, translated in 1540 by Whytinton and more significantly by Grimald in 1553 (reprinted ten times during the century) was noted as a guide to social conduct. *De Officiis* was thought by Grimald to have influenced English prose style, and chapter 7 of this book contains two apposite quotations from the preface to his translation.

The translators of the 1520–60 period were better Latinists than most of the earlier ones and were all directly or indirectly influenced by Erasmus who, as we have seen, sought to resolve the apparent conflict between ancient philosophy and Christian teachings. More, Elyot, Rastell and Barclay all set out to refashion and reform the Englishman's way of life according to Greek ideals of rational conduct and they placed a premium on sound intellectual power, accompanied by a corresponding contempt for superstitions such as they believed medieval scholasticism fed upon. Plutarch and Lucian provided the school of Erasmus with valuable models on which to found their satirical and critical attacks on contemporary follies and More himself translated several of Lucian's dialogues, including the *Cynicus*, the *Necromantia* and the *Philopseudes*, dealing respectively with the austere life, the illusionists of society (magicians, poets and philosophers, treated satirically) and superstitions which make truth hard to attain. The spirit of *The Ship of Fools* was a classical spirit, though the form was medieval and the objects of attack contemporary. The figures of classical epic were treated as though they were modern Europeans and the fictitious characters of Virgil's *Aeneid*, the pseudo-historical heroes like Hannibal, Scipio and Alexander and their ancient problems of state were presented by the translators as though they were no different in motive, speech and action from those of known fifteenth- and sixteenth-century champions.

5 : New Movements : Exploration, Science and Religious Reformation

BY their rediscovery of Greek and Latin the humanists extended man's knowledge of the world in point of time, restoring for later historians a civilisation and a culture which had flourished long before Christ and, declining, had remained hidden for 1000 years. Parallel to this revival of interest in the ancients came a similar extension of man's knowledge of the world in point of space. This was achieved by navigators in the fifteenth century who opened up new sea routes, continents, lands and peoples for the Europeans and by doing so, revealed a creation of nature which was not known and hardly suspected. The humanist movement was both intellectual and literary in character, and smelled not a little 'of the lamp', but the exploratory movement was essentially practical, redolent of the wide-open sea and of brave men battling with the elements. Even so, they have a meeting point, namely, the enlightenment afforded by ancient documents written by Greek and Roman geographers, astronomers and mathematicians. These had much to communicate to fifteenth-century Europeans regarding heavenly bodies, tides, the calculation of distances and the finding of direction. Treatises by Aristotle, Ptolemy, Strabo and Pliny the Elder were as important to Renaissance geographers as were the works of Plato, Homer, Cicero and Isocrates to the humanists.

After the Roman Empire disintegrated, the geography of the ancients gradually faded from mens' minds. The cardinal belief of Plato and Aristotle, namely that the Earth was a sphere, was superseded by a naive assumption that it was flattened, like a disc. Pictorially, it was generally represented as a great land mass intersected by rivers and inland seas, flat and either circular or oblong, centred around Jerusalem in accordance with the medieval text:

> Thus saith the Lord: this is Jerusalem: I have placed her in the midst of the peoples and the circuit of her lands.

Around this central land mass lay the oceans, stretching out to the limits of the universe, the whole being covered by the dome of sky. Only a part of the land was thought to be habitable, for to the north lay the zone of eternal ice and to the south the torrid zone, neither capable of supporting life. So far as the medieval man was concerned, Europe and the Mediterranean represented all the known world. Africa and India were known as the dwelling-place of strange creatures and Cathay, or China, attracted many missionaries who followed in the footsteps of Marco Polo and reported on this marvellous land to the east. In the late fourteenth century 'world geography' was still a mixture of a few facts with a large amount of legendary matter, as the *Travels* of the fictitious 'Sir John Mandeville' (1377) indicate.

However, this fog of ignorance and superstition was not totally impenetrable, since many scientific ideas passed into the keeping of the Arabs, from whom many long dormant techniques were inherited through Spain and Sicily. In Columbus's time no intelligent and educated man really thought that the earth was flat. Knowledge of medicine, algebra, the magnetic needle essential to the compass (originally Chinese), the art of cartography, the astrolabe, a primitive sextant (on which Chaucer wrote a treatise), were all owed to the Arabs. Their maintenance of scientific facts served the Renaissance well, for without the main instruments of navigation, the map and the compass, trans-oceanic exploration would have been impossible. Map-making was one of the by-products of humanism.

The Portuguese were the first to avail themselves of these new technical devices and to launch out into the unknown waters of the South Atlantic. They were to become the foremost maritime nation and between 1420 and 1500 established the foundations of a great empire of sea power stretching from Lisbon to India and the China Sea. By the latter year the voyagers Bartholomew Diaz and Vasco da Gama had rounded the Cape of Good Hope, reached Indian waters and brought back a rich cargo of porcelain, spices, drugs, silk and precious stones to be sold at great profit in European markets. The campaigns of Almeida and Albuquerque in the first two decades of the sixteenth century consolidated Portuguese commercial power and gave Lisbon the first place in the world's markets, followed by the ports of Cadiz, Antwerp, London and Amsterdam. Economic leadership slipped from the once secure grasp of Venice and Genoa. Turkish pressure on Venetian colonies in the Levant and the Aegean broke up the old established sea routes of the Mediterranean and hit the city particularly hard. Italian intellectual leadership was affected by her economic losses and the fertilising stream of commercial enterprise swept past her to improve other lands to the north. By 1530 the Italian Renaissance was over, and Italy once again began to look back on past glories and to rest upon her now twice-won laurels as the repository of ancient civilisation, the benefactress of Europe.

Indirectly, the Portuguese triumphs in the East were beneficial to Europe as a whole, since the new diversity of economic wealth from India and Africa made possible by the discovery of the Atlantic route round the Cape weakened the potential resources available to the Turks in their drive westward. It remained for Spain to complete the Portuguese transformation of the known world and to make Cadiz one of the world's great seaports. The strength of the Spanish monarchy backed by treasure looted from the Americas eventually destroyed the Turkish menace to Europe in the sixteenth century.

.   .   .   .   .   .

Columbus, born in Genoa, was not of Italian origin, but was probably a Spanish Jew whose forbears had left Spain to escape persecution. He made four voyages in the last years of the fifteenth century, sailing westward in order to seek a new route to Cathay and the East. He discovered America, the West Indies, including the Bahamas, Cuba, Haiti, the Lesser Antilles, Jamaica, Puerto Rico and Trinidad, and founded the first Spanish colony in the New World at San Domingo. In 1497–8 John Cabot, a Venetian, sailed from Bristol and after fifty-two days at sea landed on the American continent at Cape Breton Island, then sailed north to Cape Race along the coast of Newfoundland, where he discovered rich fishing waters. Cabot did not return from a second voyage west and the evidence concerning what happened is purely circumstantial. Polydore Vergil refers to it ironically:

John set out in this same year and sailed first to Ireland. Then he set sail towards the west. In the event he is believed to have found the new lands nowhere but on the very bottom of the ocean, to which he is thought to have descended together with his boat, the victim of that self-same ocean; since after that voyage he was never seen again anywhere.   (*Anglica Historia*, 1499)

In 1509 his nephew Sebastian sailed to find the North-west passage to Asia and rounded the southern point of Greenland before heading north-westwards across Davis Strait, on the far side of which he discovered a channel leading west. He sailed round the northern coast of Labrador and found that the channel widened until he was finally in an open sea. Cabot thought he had circumnavigated the 'New Found Land' and that the ocean would eventually lead to Cathay but ice floes forced him to abandon his investigations and to sail along the American coast in search of an easier passage—which he did not find.

    ·   ·   ·   ·   ·   ·

One play of the period reflects exploration of the North-west passage directly. It was written by John Rastell, who in 1517 set out to explore the New Found Land and from there to sail to Cathay, which he thought was 1000 miles farther on. He fitted out his expedition in the Thames, obtained letters of recommendation to all Christian princes from Henry VIII and started his colonising voyage. Unfortunately, his crew mutinied and after wasting time in Channel ports, claiming that repairs were needed, they sailed to Ireland. This is as far as they were prepared to go and Rastell found himself put ashore in Waterford, County Down. It is likely that the mutiny was inspired by Thomas Howard, Earl of Surrey, Lord Admiral and the father of the poet, who needed ships and men for the war against France and thought Rastell's expedition unimportant in comparison.

Rastell crossed the Atlantic in his imagination if not in fact. He wrote *A New Interlude of the Four Elements* soon afterwards and published it himself. This was a play, in rhymed verse, which, better than any other drama of the time, reflects the interests of its day, so that, although it is not first rate of its kind, it deserves closer attention here than its purely literary merits warrant simply because it draws intellectual history and literature together. The interludes of the sixteenth century were short plays intended for performance, often by way of diversion, in noblemens' houses or at banquets and ceremonies. They dealt with some political, moral or intellectual matter, as a rule, and were usually topical. The predominantly secular drama grew up in the time of the Tudors alongside the religious miracle or morality play and had by 1520 shown its uses as a vehicle for the discussion of matters having topical attraction. The patronage of writing in Tudor interests which is apparent in the production of patriotic histories extended to that of plays and many interludes contained an obvious 'message' justifying the performance just as the moral plays had done, though the lesson of the interludes often deviated in numerous respects from the earlier moralities. In the Tudor drama one may savour the atmosphere of the times, since they are mostly topical, chatty and informative.

The characters of *The Four Elements* include a child, Humanity, the son of Natura Naturata, Studious Desire, Sensual Appetite, Experience, Ignorance and a Taverner, all depicted as abstractions in the style of the religious morality play. The action is introduced by a Messenger who in the course of his preamble hopes that scholarly works will in future be written in English rather than in Latin, since the native language is now adequate to support serious writing. He deplores man's ignorance of material phenomena, the elements, which are the creations of God. He asks

> How dare men presume to be called clerks,
> Disputing of high creatures celestial,
> As things invisible and God's high works,
> And know not these visible things inferial?

(Text from Charles W. Traylen's reprint of J. S. Farmer's edition for the Early English Drama Society.)

Natura Naturata, a Platonic concept of natural origins, an earthly reflection of the fountain of Creation,

> The immediate minister for the preservation
> Of everything in His kind to endure,

> And cause of generation and corruption
> Of that thing that is brought to destruction

describes the world as divided into two regions, the ethereal, containing the heavens and the constellations, and the elemental, containing fire, air, water and earth. The first region affects the second. The four elements are the fundamental nature of things on earth, and cannot be destroyed, though they may be altered. Natura Naturata has given birth to something new, namely man, a creature which, like everything else, is compounded of these selfsame four elements, though unique in respect of having 'soul intellective'. The speaker concludes with a moral stricture,

> So by reason of thine understanding,
> Thou hast dominion of other beasts all,
> And naturally thou shouldst desire cunning
> To know strange effects and causes natural;
> For he that studieth for the life bestial,
> As voluptuous pleasure and bodily rest,
> I account him never better than a beast.

This was a commonplace among the humanists, who subscribed to the Thomist view of the superiority of intellect over body and of human over animal life. The angels were said to be elevated above man on the scale and it was man's duty to aspire to higher rather than lower forms of activity. The so-called 'Great Chain of Being' takes its ultimate origin from Aristotle, and all this condensed information about the elements may be traced to the Greek's systematisation. The raw material for the latter came from certain of Aristotle's predecessors, like Empedocles and Heraclitus, who first conceived that four physical elements existed, but so far as the sixteenth-century humanists were concerned, these ideas were accepted as being 'Aristotelian'. Aristotle's system of physics had been preserved for the European Middle Ages by the Arabs, and given to St. Thomas Aquinas by his own teacher, Albertus Magnus, in the thirteenth century. Humanist physics thus inherited a predisposition to asceticism and, as applied to man, compelled a puritanical attitude to living which employed the Biblical symbol of the 'beast' as a ready reference to what a human being ought not to be. This is frequently used in Tudor drama; Shakespeare employs it extensively in his great tragedies and finally sums up the duality of man's nature in the figure of Caliban in *The Tempest*.

Natura Naturata then proceeds to give her offspring, Humanity, that is, man in his proper intellectual place, a course of instruction in elementary physics. According to a teacher called 'Studious Desire', entrusted with the task of instructing Humanity after Natura Naturata has given him some grounding, the earth is round, a fact proved by the motions of the sun, moon and stars which rise in the east and set in the west, also by the eclipse, observable at different times in different places. Humanity is hard to convince, however, and Studious Desire refers him to a man called Experience, who could demonstrate the truth of these points by the use of instruments. Humanity asks to see him.

Unfortunately, at this point the lesson is interpreted by Sensual Appetite, who distracts the pupil from his earnest contemplation with a quip:

> Well hit, quoth Hykman, when that he smote
> His wife on the buttocks with a beer-pot.

and says he would rather be dead than put off his time on serious mental pursuits. He slanders Studious Desire and describes himself:

> I am called Sensual Appetite,
> All creatures in me delight;
> I comfort the wits five,
> The tasting, smelling, and hearing;
> I refresh the sight and feeling
> To all creatures alive.
> For when the body waxeth hungry
> For lack of food, or else thirsty,
> Then with drinks pleasant
> I restore him out of pain,
> And oft refresh nature again
> With delicate viand.
> With pleasant sound of harmony

The hearing alway I satisfy,
I dare this well report;
The smelling with sweet odour,
And the sight with pleasant figure
And colours, I comfort;
The feeling, that is so pleasant,
Of every member, foot, or hand,
What pleasure therein can be
By the touching of soft and hard,
Of hot and cold, nought in regard,
Except it come by me.

Sensual Appetite scorns Studious Desire, who departs, and Humanity is soon persuaded to go to a tavern 'to make solace'. The tavern was a frequent symbol of corruption in medieval drama and continued to be used as a device for indicating the pleasures of the flesh by a succession of sixteenth-century playwrights including Shakespeare, whose Boar's Head Tavern in Eastcheap provided an appropriate background for Prince Hal's youthful indiscretions. In *The Four Elements* (and in an older play, Henry Medwall's *Nature*), there is no tavern scene, which is a pity, since this opportunity for livening up the drama, not missed by Shakespeare, is ignored by Rastell. However, the Taverner comes and recites a wine-list and takes part in a humorous dialogue with Sensual Appetite concerning the three courses to be served, as well as the female company to be provided.

When Sensual Appetite has led his charge off to the tavern, their places are taken by Studious Desire and Experience. The latter gives an account of the geographical world as the explorers knew it in the early years of the sixteenth century. This is where Rastell's personal enthusiasm for discovering the North-west passage is revealed. Pointing to a chart, Experience describes the various countries:

. . . and northward on this side
There lieth Iceland where man doth fish,
But beyond that so cold it is,
No man may there abide.

This sea is called the Great Ocean,
So great it is that never man
Could tell it, since the world began,
Till now, within these twenty years,
Westward be found new lands,
That we never heard tell of before this
By writing nor other means,
Yet many now have been there;
And that country is so large of room,
Much longer than all Christendom,
Without fable or guile;
For divers mariners had it tried,
And sailed straight by the coast side
About five thousand miles!
But what commodities be within,
No man can tell or well imagine;
But yet not long ago
Some men of this country went,
By the king's noble consent,
It for to search to that intent,
And could not be brought thereto;
But they that were the adventures
Have cause to curse their mariners,
False of promise and dissemblers,
That falsely them betrayed,
Which would take no pains to sail farther
Than their own list and pleasure;
Wherefore that voyage and divers other
Such caitiffs have destroyed.
Oh, what a thing had be then
If that they that be Englishmen
Might have been the first of all
That there should have taken possession,
And made first building and habitation,
A memory perpetual!
And also what an honourable thing,
Both to the realm and to the king,

To have had his dominion extending
There into so far a ground,
Which the noble king of late memory,
The most wise prince the seventh Henry,
Caused first for to be found.
And what a great meritious deed
It were to have the people instructed
To live more virtuously,
And to learn to know of men the manner,
And also to know God their Maker,
Which as yet live all beastly;
For they nother know God nor the devil,
Nor never heard tell of heaven nor hell,
Writing nor any other scripture;
But yet, in the stead of God Almighty,
They honour the sun for his great light,
For that doth them great pleasure;
Building nor house they have none at all,
But woods, cots, and caves small,
No marvel though it be so,
For they use no manner of iron,
Neither in took nor other weapon,
That should help them thereto;
Copper they have which is found
In divers places above the ground,
Yet they dig not therefor;
For as I said, they have none iron,
Whereby they should in the earth mine,
To search for any ore:
Great abundance of woods there be,
Most part fir and pine-apple tree
Great riches might come thereby,
Both pitch and tar, and soap ashes,
As they make in the east lands,
By brenning thereof only.
Fish they have so great plenty,
That in havens take and slain they be

> With staves, withouten fail,
> Now Frenchmen and others have found the trade,
> That yearly of fish there they lade
> Above a hundred sail;
> But in the south part of that country
> The people there go naked alway,
> The land is of so great heat:
> And in the north part all the clothes
> That they wear is but beasts' skins,
> They have no other fete;
> But how the people first began
> In that country, or whence they came,
> For clerks it is a question.

and ends by describing the inhabitants of this country as he imagined them to be.

Later, Experience explains the position of different lands in relation to the Mediterranean, which he says is two thousand miles long:

> The Soldan's country lieth hereby
> The great Turk on the north side doth lie,
> A man of marvellous strength,
> The said north part is called Europa,
> And this south part called Africa,
> This east part is called India,
> But these new lands found lately
> Been called America, because only
> Americus did first them find . . .
> But these new lands, by all cosmography,
> From the Can of Catowe's[1] land
>   cannot lie
> Little past a thousand miles:
> But from these new lands men may sail plain
> Eastward, and come to England again.

A personage named Ignorance, representing vice in general, then appears to aid Sensual Appetite in his corruption of Humanity

[1] Khan of Cathay's

and this provides Rastell with a chance to insert some lighter comic episodes, including singing and dancing, a feature of many Tudor entertainments from Court masques to interludes. Eventually Natura Naturata comes back to discover what her errant pupil has been doing and utters an uninspiring admonition:

> Though it be for thee full necessary
> For thy comfort sometime to satisfy
> Thy sensual appetite,
> Yet it is not convenient for thee
> To put therein thy felicity
> And all thy whole delight;
> For if thou wilt learn no science,
> Nother by study nor experience,
> I shall thee never advance;
> But in the world thou shalt dure[1] then
> Despised of every wise man,
> Like this rude beast Ignorance . . .

This is as far as the play's unique manuscript goes. Dramatically it is unexciting and the dialogue is flat, relieved only by the songs sung by Ignorance towards the end; these were insertions probably not by Rastell. (The musical notes and the horizontal stave were printed together in the original edition; this was the first example of this familiar convention to appear in England so that in this respect Rastell was a pioneer of music-printing.) Its first editor, J. O. Halliwell, writing in 1848, said of *The Four Elements* that

> it possesses an interest, beyond its connection with the history of the stage, as being the only dramatic piece extant in which science is attempted to be made popular through the medium of theatrical representation . . . (its) value . . . must be allowed to consist in the curious illustration it affords of the phraseology and popular scientific knowledge of the day.
>
> (*ed. cit.*, preface)

The 'science' is hardly new, for men of the thirteenth century knew as much as Rastell about the relative positions of the con-

[1] endure

tinents. His patriotic propaganda on the subject of colonising the territory beyond the North-west passage, which he himself wanted to do, is of more immediate interest to students of literary-historical relations because the author was himself a would-be follower of the Cabots. The play contains the first description of North America to be written in the English language, mentions its copper, lack of iron, fire and apple-trees and its rich fishing-fields, but Rastell is, to his own regret, not speaking at first hand.

It should be pointed out at this stage that the theories of Copernicus embodied in his great work *Concerning the Revolutions of the Heavenly Spheres* (1543) affected popular scientific thinking in England not at all during the period with which we are concerned. The first English Copernicans began to express diffident opinions in favour of the heliocentricity of the universe in the 1550s but poets and playwrights were not quick to replace the older Aristotelian and Ptolomaic geocentric systems with the new conception, though 'new' is hardly the proper adjective to apply to the heliocentric theory, which had been outlined by Aristarchus of Samos about 250 B.C. Copernicus himself explained that the proposition that the earth rotated every day had originated in the minds of a group of ancient Pythagoreans, long before Plato and Aristotle. However, the exciting debates concerning the 'Copernican Revolution', as historians have called it, did not take place until the late sixteenth and early seventeenth century, when they are associated with the name of Galileo, a far subtler genius than Copernicus. English literature is not affected by these incursions into celestial mechanics until after Milton's time; *Paradise Lost* still relied upon the Ptolemaic concept and for centuries the Roman Church officially resisted Galileo's denial of the Scriptures as a scientific authority. The works of Copernicus, Galileo and Kepler remained on the *Index of Prohibited Books* until 1835.

To explain the nature of the universe Catholic theologians relied upon the undeveloped ideas discovered in the Vulgate. When Aristotle's system of physics was rediscovered in the thirteenth century St. Thomas Aquinas reconciled it with Christian theology. Pythagoras and Plato were ignored until Copernicus adapted their ideas on the relativity of motion. The numerology of the Pythagoreans and the mysticism of Plato were incompatible in many important respects with the Judeo-Christian concepts of sin, redemption and faith in a Messiah, whereas the Aristotelian system, more intelligible to the layman since it seemed to have a common-sense basis, lent itself far more easily to union with Church doctrines. The conflict amounted to one between Paganism and Christianity, a conflict underlying the Italian Renaissance.

·   ·   ·   ·   ·   ·

The transition from medieval to modern times begun by the Renaissance was continued and completed by the Reformation, but the latter was not an effect of the former. The two movements were quite different. The Renaissance was an intellectual movement. Even when it turned its attention to the Scriptures and the writings of the Church Fathers its methods were textual and academic, just as, then the secular authors of Greece and Rome were in process of revival, Erasmus, Colet and Tyndale, men of the study and not of the market place, were using the same scholarly methods to plumb the mysteries of the Bible. What public utterances they made were directed by intellectual convictions, arrived at after long study. Colet translated the *Celestial Hierarchies* of Dionysius and by so doing established the neo-Platonic method of interpreting Scripture allegorically. Previously influential in Ficino's Florentine Academy, Colet had been inspired by the doctrines of this fifth-century Christian while he was in Italy, and Ficino's *Theologica Platonica* is one of the few authorities cited by Colet in his lectures on the Pauline Epistles.

Ernst Cassirer's *The Platonic Renaissance in England* (1932) lucidly explains the nature of this reconciliation of Platonic and Christian doctrines. Whereas Italian humanism was marshalling its forces against the traditional objects of faith,

> . . . in England humanism takes the opposite course from the first. Its criticism is directed against scholastic systems and against antiquated and 'barbaric' forms of theological learning, but never against religion. On the contrary, the forces of humanism work for the sake of religion. The humanist watch-

I

word *ad fontes* is applied primarily to further the discovery and interpretation of the sources of Christianity.

(*op. cit.*; tr. James P. Pettegrove [1953], p. 12.)

The early Tudor humanists tried to strike a balance between different kinds of meaning. The kinship between metaphor and religious allegory does not become clear in literature until the second half of the sixteenth century, but the new humanistic religion had its beginnings in England within the circle of Erasmus, Colet and More. Erasmus wrote *In Praise of Folly* in More's house. To quote from Cassirer again:

> In this work as in the *Enchiridion Militis Christiani*, the main ideas of religious humanism acquired new scope and substance along with a new literary form. They are not merely abstractly developed; they do not remain confined to the scholar's study, but venture to encroach upon the immediate problems of life and the important problems of the time. With this courageous spirit for the criticism and renewal of life, humanism became for the first time a truly intellectual and reforming force. In Italy it had never attained such force and depth. (*ibid.*, p. 18)

and later Tyndale's *Obedience of a Christian Man* explained the humanist method of interpreting the Bible by using its literal meaning to express its truth in extended metaphor or allegory:

> not the Scripture but an ensample or a similitude borrowed of the Scripture to declare a text or a conclusion of the Scripture more expressly and to root it and grave it in the heart. For a similitude or an ensample doth paint a thing much deeper in the wits of a man than doth a plain speaking. (*op. cit.*, Parker Soc. ed. [1894], p. 306)

a technique which half a century later was being regularly applied to the interpretation of classical myths, thereby accounted for as allegories of scientific processes.

On the other hand, the Reformation itself was primarily a practical movement, devoted to the correction of Church abuses and religious observances. It started with a rebellion against

Papal authority and resulted in the re-organisation of religion in what Luther described as 'the liberty of the Christian man'. But there is no necessary logical connection between the Renaissance and the Reformation. It was possible to be both a humanist and a devout Catholic and supporter of the Papacy. In fact, Erasmus and others were far from enthusiastic about the Reformation because it betokened a falling-off in the high standards of scholarship set by the early humanists.

The doctrines and practices, government and methods of administration of the late medieval Catholic church all invited reform. Transubstantiation, the celibacy of the priesthood, the power of giving absolution and of awarding indulgence gave the priest a status which the layman did not have and made of the priests a caste apart. The doctrine of purgatory, the efficacy of saying masses for the dead, the adoration of the Virgin, the worship of saints, the veneration of relics and the going on pilgrimages to holy places all combined to obscure the simplicity of Christian teaching and to hedge it in with rights, ceremonial and observances. Too much stress was being laid on outward forms, and the increasing knowledge of the Scriptures which the availability of a vernacular Bible made possible encouraged private judgment in the interpretation of texts. The decrees of Popes and Church Councils, the writings of the Church Fathers and the traditional authority of the apostle Peter seemed to be of no higher standing than that of the individual conscience. When the doctrines and practices recognised and maintained by the Church were subjected to the test of the Scriptures many of them fell short. The resulting attitude of discontent was felt by many members of both clergy and laity in the early part of the sixteenth century, especially in the leading urban centres of Europe, and a new consciousness of the inspirational character of the Christian religion as inculcated by the early Church Fathers spread slowly but surely. Luther and Calvin urged a revival of the spirit of St. Paul's Gospels and Epistles and the Anabaptists, a clique of German fanatics, demanded a society organised according to the communism of the early Christians. It was generally recognised that the Church had changed since its beginnings and needed to return to its primitive origins. The introduction to the Lutheran formula of Concord said that the Holy Scriptures alone remain the only judge, rule and guiding line by which all doctrines shall be tested and judged and that belief in the Bible as the word of God is the self-evident foundation of Reformation. The Westminster Confession declared the Bible to be the rule of faith and of life. From it may be deduced the whole counsel of God concerning things necessary for man's salvation, faith and life, for the latter are explicitly or implicitly set down in Scripture. These attitudes were fundamental to Protestantism, which really began in a revival of Biblical studies.

The more glaring abuses resided in Church administration, which called for immediate reform. Government by a hierarchy of officials directed by the Pope and regulated by a special code of law known as Canon Law, which was not subject to the jurisdiction of the civil law courts, gave priests a privileged status. Thus was the Church brought directly into conflict with the state, for ecclesiastical courts claimed jurisdiction not only over all cases involving members of the clergy but also over 'lay' cases where a moral issue was thought to be concerned. The definition of 'moral' was wide and moral offences included breaches of business contracts, disputes over wills, marriage settlements, payments of tithes and taxes and a whole host of other differences which might reasonably be thought civil. It was hard to draw a line between civil and ecclesiastical jurisdiction and many times the Church authorities, trying their strength, deliberately chose to encroach upon State rights. For the whole of Christendom the final court of appeal was the Papal Court at Rome, the Curia, involvement with which led to long delays and the payment of exorbitant fees to foreigners.

By the year 1500 the Roman Church owned about a quarter of the soil of Europe, possibly more, and was Europe's greatest landowner. Financing of Papal policy and undertakings and of the bureaucracy which carried it out depended mainly on taxes imposed on the laity. The Church was very wealthy and late fifteenth-century Popes like Paul II left behind enormous treasures in money, jewels and ornaments, a fact that did not seem to be consistent with monkish vows of poverty. In virtue of his position as Supreme

Pontiff, the Pope exercised his right to appoint ecclesiastics to any benefice in Christendom, a practice known as 'Papal Provisions'. When used without discretion, as it sometimes was, this meant that the richest benefices in Europe were occupied by foreigners appointed from Rome, who in practice found substitutes to perform the work of the office while they themselves remained in Rome. Absenteeism was one of the more blatant abuses of the time.

Allied to it was 'pluralism', that is to say, the holding of several benefices by the same person. The warrior Pope Julius II possessed one archbishopric, two abbacies and seven bishoprics, mostly in France. A nephew of Pope Sixtus IV drew 60,000 ducats annually from benefices and died in debt. He was also appointed Cardinal by his uncle. A related abuse was that of 'simony', or the promotion of a man to an ecclesiastical office in return for a reward. In this way a Church office could be sold to the highest bidder. This particular abuse was sometimes included as one of the Seven Deadly Sins and from the fourteenth century onwards it was widespread. Even to many prelates within it the reform of such a structure seemed to be an urgent matter. Of authenticated abuses in administration, of the corruption and greed of the Curia at Rome, of the worldliness of bishops, many of whom were sons of noble families and spent large sums of money on their own pleasures, there are many examples. The traffic in benefices went on openly in every part of the Holy See; likewise the sale of indulgences, which became a means of raising revenues. Sexual licence among the priesthood, including the maintenance of concubines, and the opportunities for leading an idle life encouraged people of limited education to join the Holy Orders. Ignorant clergy who seldom or never read their breviaries and could not even recite the paternoster flocked into the monasteries.

Perhaps the worst afflicted country so far as Church abuses were concerned was Scotland. It was farthest away from Rome of all countries under Papal jurisdiction and under extremely remote central control; in fact, it may be said that the Scots bishops ruled themselves, interpreting Rome's decrees as it suited them. The priests owned over a third of the country's wealth and the bishops and abbots lived like princes of a rich land though Scotland was a poor country compared with England. The peasantry were milked by the Church by a process of what may well be described as spiritual blackmail, for, without fee, no priest would perform any of the sacraments such as marriage or baptism or even bury the dead. The private lives of many of the high clergy were disorderly. Cardinal Beaton, Archbishop of St Andrews, had three sons legitimised; David, Abbot of Arbroath, a son and two daughters, Patrick Hepburn, Bishop of Moray, ten children. The rank and file of the clergy not surprisingly followed the example of the more elevated officials of the Church. Opposition to dissemination of the Scriptures was fierce. The Bishop of Dunkeld thanked God that he never knew what the Old and New Testaments were—a sentiment which gave rise to a proverb

> Ye are like the Bishop of Dunkeld, that knew
> neither the New Law nor the Old

and the literature of James V's Scotland, as will be apparent later, is packed with references to popular demand for Bible instruction and to clerical attempts to suppress it.

6 : The Retreating Middle Ages :
Prose and the new Bible

Personal correspondence is one of the most useful sources of
information about the day-to-day lives of citizens of a bygone age
and the first great collections of family letters date from the
fifteenth century. Of these the most readable is the Paston collection, numbering about a thousand separate items, and dating from
1420–1509. The letters were written by members of a Norfolk
family of landed gentry named Paston and treat mostly of domestic
subjects as they touched the family, which was rather a close-knit
one. The various sons, daughters, cousins and adherents to the
Paston cause are made very much alive and their concerns are
infused with a vital immediacy by the numerous hands engaged
over the century in passing domestic information from one member
of the family to another.

The letters treat mostly of intimate subjects as they touched the
family—the progress of the Norwich estates, the succession of
births, deaths and marriages which kept the line going from one
generation to the next, the education of the male children and their
travels in England and abroad. In addition to the personal letters
many documents remain to testify to the administrative interests
of the Pastons—wills, agents' reports, invoices and proclamations,
lists of possessions, particularly books from the Caxton press
which were obviously fashionable acquisitions for a squire of that
time. All these add up to a fairly clear picture of the kind of life
which landowners led in England during a time of war in France
and civil strife in their own country. Every class was at the centre
of an upheaval, for kings and queens obtained power and lost it,
three kings were murdered, political officials intrigued, successfully
and otherwise, and the lower classes complained about their
conditions and several times rebelled openly against authority.
'Law and order' was weakened, ruffianism frequently prevailed

against attempts to control its depradations and few local citizens would take civic responsibility since it might easily mean persecution without any chance of official protection.

A great deal of information about all these events and trends is to be found in the Paston correspondence, accepted by historians as the most accurate record in existence of events in the English fifteenth century. The letters are factual in character, intelligently composed, and observant; their religious faith is strong and their writers are forever determined to weather the national storms. Their fortunes fluctuated, and they were no strangers to reliance upon armed force as a means of securing their possessions when conventional legal methods would not work. Professionally, some of the Pastons were trained for the law, some were minor diplomats, some, when occasion demanded it, were soldiers. The men strengthened their positions and increased their fortunes by making sensible marriages to capable wives, who proved to be good managers of the family estates. The families begotten in these unions were solid and reliable scions, obedient to traditions, conscious of their duties to offspring in respect of education, moral teaching, religious training and social obligations. Healthy minds in healthy bodies seem to have been the ideal aimed at and the Paston men, as revealed in the *Letters*, were excellent examples of the 'squire' class, physically strong, self-confident and self-satisfied, reliable, hard-working, and not over-imaginative or sensitive. They were good balanced fellows, pillars of the English landowning class. Two Paston women in particular, Agnes, wife of William Paston the justice, and Margaret, her daughter-in-law, stand out as especially decisive and efficient administrators and defenders of the estates and the household. Their marriages, business partnerships initially, developed into lasting unions, happy on both sides; one marriage, between Margery Paston and the Paston bailiff or secretary, was at first opposed vigorously by her brother and mother, but finally took place in the year 1470 and was, to all intents and purposes, happy.

The *Paston Letters* are not 'literature'. Their object was not artistic. They were not written for posterity and their survival is an accident. But they do touch literature, not only by providing a more solid social and historical background against which to read, say, Malory's *Morte d'Arthur*, a work having no obvious factual connections with its own time, but also because they are cast in fifteenth-century English prose style, tuned to the subject-matter, capable of communicating insights and nuances, malleable, flashing the writer's personality on and off, not wooden but controlled by a range of vital impulses. Still, they cannot be said to represent the summit of English prose. The primary object of a letter is to communicate clearly and this is how the Pastons regarded it. The notion of epistolary elegance did not seem to occur to any of them and, even if it had, the language at that time was not fully capable of the definition essential for the establishment of a standard which may be called 'literary'. Just as Malory reveals the state of fifteenth-century literary prose so do the *Paston Letters* show what late fifteenth-century colloquial personal communication was like. Neither escaped the faults of indefiniteness and formlessness and, compared with contemporary French prose, both Malory and the Pastons wrote crudely, though Malory, at least, did aim at precision and lucidity. In the fifteenth century English prose was still fashioned out of many dialects; unlike poetry it was still searching for a reliable standard.

In the middle of the sixteenth century, from February 1542 until March 1552, a family called Johnson, wool merchants who went bankrupt in 1553, left a similar collection of letters. These shed bright light on the affairs of family firms in Tudor times and on the kind of business activity which went on in the 1540s and are therefore extremely valuable documents for students of economic history. Comparison of the way of life of the Johnsons with that of the Pastons shows the degree to which the sixteenth-century family had become 'civilised' compared with their predecessors. John Johnson was an excellent example of a well-educated, sophisticated, travelled and sociable young man who came to approach the conventional notion of what a respected merchant ought to be like, sober, steadfast and dedicated to the art of good business, not simply to profit-making. In Henry VIII's reign England was developing a high reputation as a merchant nation and the merchants' social position was solidly established as their financial power grew. Thomas Cromwell was a friend of the Johnsons and their connections in high places—particularly with the rich *parvenus* of Henry's new hierarchy of officialdom—were skilfully developed. Originally, the Johnson correspondence numbered twenty thousand items but of these only a thousand survive. Though no more to be called 'literature' than the Paston material, they reveal something of the emotional contrasts of joy and bitterness, the sense of instability and the Tudor melancholia so obvious in the poetry of their contemporaries Wyatt and Surrey, for the common accompaniments of upper-class life in those days were persecution and personal insecurity pressures from which no-one in an influential position was free. The path to the scaffold, to prison or to exile was a well-trodden one. More prominent men were executed by the Tudors than by any of their predecessors. Not until the French Revolution did so many aristocratic heads fall again. Violent death, on the block, on the gallows, at the stake, in battle, or by personal attack stalked both governors and governed. In Henry VIII's reign, a period of thirty-eight years, over eighteen thousand death sentences were handed down; most of them were carried out. Nearly all the authors discussed in this book at one time or another went in fear of losing their lives or physical liberty.

· · · · · ·

In the reign of Henry VII the most significant figure in the history of English prose development is that of William Caxton, (1421–91) who as an elderly man imported the printer's art into England. As a young apprentice, he had settled in Bruges, where he found himself within the influence of the most sophisticated Court in Europe, that of Burgundy, to which Flanders belonged. About 1450 Johann Gutenberg of Mainz discovered how to print books by means of movable type and the appreciative Burgundians were among the first to benefit from this wonderful invention. Caxton learned typesetting from a printer in Bruges, Colard Mansion, and in 1474 published his first book there. It was a partial translation from French into English of Raôul Lefevre's *Recueil des Histoires de Troye*. In 1475 Caxton brought out another translation from French, this time of a treatise on chess, and in the year following returned to England, there to establish the first English press, close by Westminster Abbey. Under aristocratic patronage he worked there until his death, a period of fifteen years. During this time he published over a hundred volumes, chosen according to standards of upper-middle-class preference. Caxton's library was, as we have remarked, well represented in the collection of the Pastons, listed in their correspondence in the 1480s, and included romances of chivalry and devotional books, some of them possessed less for their content than for what at that time must have been a great novelty. To own a printed book was a mark of the sophisticated man and supported the kind of social reputation which the Pastons wished to have. Caxton started a series of translations from several languages—he printed English versions of Ovid's *Metamorphoses* and Virgil's *Aeneid*, the latter taken not from the original but from a French romance called *Livre des Eneydes*. From Dutch he translated *The History of Reynard the Fox*.

Caxton's publications include Chaucer's *Canterbury Tales* and *Troilus & Criseyde*, the poems of Gower and Lydgate, *Legenda Aurea*, Boethius and Aesop, Cato and the *Sayings of the Philosophers*, Alexander, Plato, Demosthenes and Aristotle, *The Book of Histories of Jason*, *The Life of Charles the Great*, *The Four Sons of Aymon* and a contemporary work of some considerable significance, Malory's *Morte d'Arthur*, printed on 31 July 1485. In his preface Caxton said that he

> enprised to imprint a book of the noble histories of the said King Arthur and of certain of his knights after a copy unto me delivered, which copy Sir Thomas Malory did take out of a certain book of French, and reduced it into English.

Elsewhere he again mentioned Malory as the 'reducer' of the work into English, but added that it was by himself 'into xxi books chapitred, and enprinted & finished'. From 1485 until 1934 Caxton's text was the only one available. (A more authentic text was found in Winchester by W. F. Oakshott in the latter year.) Caxton, therefore, has always been closely associated with Malory and it is important to separate the two. Caxton is a solid historical personality; Malory may never have existed and attempts to attach a biography to him have not made him anything but a shadowy figure. There *was* a Thomas Malory who died in 1470 and who seems to have been something of a rebel, ruffian and rapist, practically a criminal, in fact. That he was the author of the prose chivalric romance called *Morte d'Arthur* (which in correct French should be '*Mort*') seems unlikely.

Caxton's edition was divided into twenty-one books and five hundred chapters. It was reprinted, with some alterations, in 1498 by Wynken de Worde, one of Caxton's immediate successors, in 1557 and twice in 1585. Recent attempts by scholars to distinguish the Malory of ill fame from a 'good' Malory who might conceivably have composed a work that had a civilising effect on its readers (though sometimes it is hard to agree with certain commentators that the unruly conduct of some of the knights in the *Morte d'Arthur* is civilised) have failed. We know little about him, except that he was himself a knight and a prisoner, though the amount of circumstantial evidence available takes up five pages of E. K. Chambers' *English Literature at the Close of the Middle Ages*.

Caxton presented the *Morte* as a single work, but in fact it is not a unity but a group of separate romances, a collection of Arthurian legends, mostly 'reduced' from French sources. No fewer than fifty-six times in the course of the work, Malory, who in the absence of alternative claims and other information we must credit with its composition, informs the reader that the 'French book' is his authority. This source cannot be identified though compilations of this nature were current in fifteenth-century France and drew their material from a thirteenth-century prose romance cycle which included many of the more familiar stories about Arthur, Merlin, Lancelot and the Quest for the Holy Grail. In addition, there existed English versions of the same stories and a body of folk material, legends and oral traditions, upon which a fifteenth-century author could have drawn. In any case, it was not uncommon for medieval writers to claim works in Latin or in French as their direct sources or to ascribe their own imaginative creations to other authors. Such sources are hardly ever identifiable. Chaucer said that a 'Lollius' was his 'author' for *Troilus and*

Criseyde, and the poet of *Wallace* claimed a Latin book by a certain Master John Blair as his source, but Lollius remains a mystery while Blair and his book have never been discovered.

· · · · · ·

Malory not only adapted French and English sources but also abridged and altered them. Moreover, he showed himself capable of making original interpolations for which no authority can be found. Thus his Book XVIII is a remaking of the French *Launcelot* and the English metrical *Morte Arthure*, but bearing the stamp of original composition. Books XX ('How the corps of the Mayde of Astolat aryved before Kyng Arthur, and of the burying and how Syr Lancelot offryed the masse peny') and XXV ('How true love is likened to summer') are both original interpolations by Malory. He was not critical in his choice of sources, and some of the extant versions of the legends which he took as models were by no means the best ones, but the end result is coherent in spite of the absence of fixed plan. No writer can rival him as the story-teller of the Arthurian legends and no author since Malory has added substantially to what we learn of Arthur from him, though many have chosen the tales as subjects for verse and prose narrative, including Dryden, Morris, Tennyson, Swinburne and Charles Williams. Before Malory, no prose work had been attempted on such a large scale and, although to attain to a finely ordered artistic structure was beyond his capacities, the whole work is in style and sentiment remarkably uniform. He aimed to please a middle-class audience and his style of writing is artless:

> And for to pass the time this book shall be pleasant to read
> in but for to give faith and belief that all is true that is contained
> herein, ye be at your liberty

states Malory, thus separating history from fable, the chronicle from art and bare facts from conscious imaginative creation. From the *Morte d'Arthur* it is not hard to draw some obvious parallels between fifteenth-century events, such as the Wars of the Roses and the French campaigns, and the incidents in which Arthur and his knights participate, but there does not seem to be any deliberate attempt on Malory's part to write contemporary history in the guise of Arthurian adventures. The advice in 'The Day of Destiny' is very general:

> Lo ye, all Englishmen, see ye not what a mischief here was? For he that was the most king and noblest knight of the world, and most loved the fellowship of noble knights, and by him they all were upholden, and yet might not these Englishmen hold them content with him. Lo, thus was the old custom and usages of this land and men say that we of this land have not yet lost that custom. Alas! This is a great default of us Englishmen, for there may nothing please no terme

and the kind of society depicted in the Paston correspondence has nothing in common with that chivalric world of Arthur and his knights—in fact, the two are completely at odds. Malory is concerned with writing a chivalric narrative through which factual reality rarely shines. The contrast between *Morte d'Arthur* and the real world of the fifteenth century is that between Lancelot the knight-at-arms and Malory the presumed gaolbird and hired bully. Of all the authors of major works in English 'Malory' is perhaps most conceivably a scoundrel—an English François Villon. Yet the atmosphere of the stories, the idealised conduct of the personages, the code of honour to which they cling throughout the interminable battles and twists and turns of fortune, are all rooted in a mythical bygone 'golden age'.

A useful comparison in respect of atmospheric and tonal qualities, as well as in narrative itself, is with Spenser's *Faerie Queene*, though the world of Spenser, glimpsed through its masking allegory, is far more substantial than Malory's, and represents Elizabethan politics, seen through the eyes of a tough-minded courtier. But in Spenser and Malory one may find the same 'faery' environment, a magical world of no temporal or spatial limitations, the same instructive aims governing both works, though more explicit in Spenser than in Malory, and the same force of national pride giving them impetus. Chivalry is important to both authors. Both influenced the English ideal of character, both make use of archaic language and ideas. Heroic qualities embodied in the best of men are the subject of both. Arthur, backed by a long and complex tradition, is the embodiment of true chivalry, an English version of Charlemagne, cruel, strong but human, for his own people love him. Towards his subjects he feels responsible; to his enemies he is implacable. When his own knights are killed, he mourns. When rewards are due, he gives them. He has diplomatic talents at his disposal, and is a wise ruler in every way; in other words, he approximates to the stereotype of the fighting king or the redoubtable heroic warrior. Most of his knights have no personalities above and beyond the courtly convention and are simply typed characters with names,—Gawain, Lancelot, Galahad, Gareth, Bedivere—though a few stand out and defy strict limitations, like Lancelot, whose love for Guinevere, Arthur's wife, gives a new tragic dimension to the stock courtly relationship. Medieval narrative dealt in types, not individuals of infinite variety, and one knight or villain was much like another, distinguished only by his name. Galahad, the chivalrous hero and soldier of Christendom, the only knight to succeed in the Quest for the Holy Grail, is not a flesh-and-blood personage even by medieval standards, but an idealised, ethereal figure who is interpretable as a Christ-symbol; Lancelot, a type of courtly lover, is brought closer to the audience by his having recognisably human failings, but neither Galahad nor Lancelot are 'characters' of much psychological depth.

Malory's notion of chivalry was that of heroic devotion to a great cause, an old Teutonic tradition embellished by French romantic idealism to give the concept wider scope. His selection of events from the romances is governed by patriotism and he leaves out discreditable incidents which might show up Arthur in a bad light, such as are narrated in the English alliterative *Morte Arthure*. Caxton's claim for his volume, made in the introduction, was:

> All is written for our doctrine, and for to beware that we fall not to vice nor sin, but to exercise and follow virtue.

Roger Ascham said of the *Morte Arthur* (*sic*), *i.e.* Malory's work, that

> the whole pleasure . . . standeth in two special poyntes, in open mans slaughter and bold bawdrye.

> (*The Schoolmaster*, Bk I)

The popularity of Malory and indeed of the whole Arthurian tradition may perhaps be simplistically explained in terms of the expression in literature of a relatively uncomplicated way of life and its deep appeal to men whose responsibilities have become more complex as the centuries roll by. Certainly the Tudors found in *Morte d'Arthur* a style of existence which they thought to be utterly unlike their own, though the fictional violence of Arthur's disciples was not any different in its fictional results because it was prefaced or concluded by an exchange of well-mannered observations, as in this illustration from the combat of Arthur and Accolon in Book IV:

> 'A, sir knyght', seyde kynge Arthur, 'this day haste thou done me grete damage wyth this swerde. Now ar ye com unto youre deth, for I shall nat warraunte you but ye shall be as well rewarded with this swerde or ever we departe as ye have rewarded me, for muche payne have ye made me to endure and much bloode have y loste'.
> And therwith sir Arthure raced on hym with all his myght and pulde him to the erthe, and than raced of his helme and gaff hym suche a buffette on his hede that the bloode com oute at his erys, nose and mowthe.
> 'Now woll I sle thee!' seyde Arthure.
> 'Sle me ye may well,' seyde sir Accolon, 'and hit please you, for ye ar the beste knyght that ever I founde, and I se well that God is with you'.

Arthur does not immediately dispatch this emissary of the wicked Morgan le Fay but in any case Accolon dies within four days from loss of blood, whereupon Arthur has him sent

> ... 'in an horse-bere with six knyghts unto Camelot, and bade bere hym unto my systir, Morgan le Fay, and sey that I send her hym to a present'.

The adulterous relationship of Lancelot and Guinevere was consistent enough according to the conventions of *amour courtois*, which regarded adultery as respectable within this context and love in marriage as rather an unfit subject for romance-writers. By

Ascham's time, however, attitudes had altered, and his *School-master* was a work of the maturer days of the Reformation. What Caxton and what Ascham understood by vice, sin and virtue, were not the same. So far as the later sixteenth-century Puritan was concerned, sin was very largely bound up with sexual relationships. The behaviour of the great lovers of classical and medieval legend such as the Arthurian cycles include would by Ascham have been thought 'vicious'. *The Schoolmaster* was, after all, mainly a discussion of the ideal education for the upper classes, including the proper reading for a young gentleman. Ascham despised the Italian *novelle* and the romance tradition because of their 'Papist' origins and because he thought that they tended to have a bad moral influence on the young. His criticism of the *Morte d'Arthur* type of fiction was founded on moral rather than on aesthetic precepts, and although he professed concern with the techniques of verse writing, Ascham was not a literary critic as such. If one finds pleasure in reading about violence and sex, which seems always to have been the case, one will, in Ascham's opinion, find both in *Morte d'Arthur*. His complaint was that it lacked any power of instruction but was *merely* pleasure-giving, the age-old groan of the Puritan. Tennyson echoed Ascham's sentiments and spoke of 'war and wanton-ness' as being the main features of Malory's work.

This dislike of the romances was characteristic of all the humanists. Erasmus attacked these '*fabulae stultae et aniles*' (stupid and old-womanish tales) because they lured the student away from classical history and poetry. Vives, in a work on the education of women called *De Institutione Femina Christianae* (1523), listed a number of pestiferous books which women ought not to be permitted to read. He gives no English examples but his English translator Richard Hyrde took it upon himself in 1540 to add a few of his own, including some English ones. Vives' *De Officio Mariti* (1528), (Office and Duties of a Husband), translated twenty years later by Thomas Paynell, stated:

There be some kind of letters and writings that pertain only to adorn and increase eloquence withall. Some to delight and

K

please. Some that make a man subtle and crafty. Some to know natural things and to instruct and inform the mind of man withal. The works of poets, the Fables of Milesii, as that of the Golden Ass, and in a manner all Lucian's work, and many other which are written in the vulgar tongue, as of Tristram, Lancelot, Ogier, Amasus and of Arthur the which were written and made by such as were idle and knew nothing. These books do hurt both man and woman, for they make them wily and crafty, they kindle and stir up covetousness, inflame anger, and all beastly and filthy desire. (*op. cit.*, 'De Disciplina Femina')

and Tyndale's *Obedience of a Christian Man* blames the clergy for forbidding laymen to read the Scriptures while at the same time raising no objection to their reading *Robin Hood, Bevis of Hampton* and

a thousand histories and fables of love and wantonness, and of ribaldry, as filthy as heart can think, to corrupt the minds of youth withal, clean contrary to the doctrine of Christ and his apostles

so that Ascham, who first showed in *Toxophilus* that he was violently antipathetic to 'books of fayned chivalry' because of the damage he thought they did to the young and ignorant, was really harping on a well-worn theme.

Nevertheless, the romances continued to be the favoured literature of the reading public for a century after the advent of printing, and Caxton, de Worde, Pynson and Copland kept popular taste well supplied with editions of *Morte d'Arthur, William of Palerne, Huon of Bordeaux, Bevis of Hampton, Sir Eglamour, Guy of Warwick, The Squire of Low Degree, Sir Isumbras, Sir Triamour* and many others. Not only in printed form, but in fifteenth-century manuscripts, still popular before the book trade reached its heights, did these old tales circulate. The love of romances penetrated all classes, aristocratic, bourgeois and peasant, and though the patrons for whom Caxton had prepared his editions had been nobles, the small quarto editions of de Worde and Pynson were aimed at comparatively poor people. There is a record of a sale of *Bevis of Hampton* for 6d, *Sir Eglamour* for 3d and *Sir Isumbras* for 2d, all in the year 1520. In 1498, twenty bound copies of *Bevis*, printed by Pynson, went for 10d each. An outstanding favourite, *Bevis* was still in print in 1650.

More interesting for the literary critic is Caxton's statement that the *Morte d'Arthur* was intended to instruct. One might ask what sort of virtue it was supposed to encourage and what sort of vice to warn against? Again the similarity of Spenser's *Faerie Queene* is apposite. Spenser said that he intended, through the construction of this 'allegory or dark conceit',

> to fashion a gentleman or noble person in virtuous and gentle discipline.

There is much in the *Faerie Queene* which made nineteenth-century critics talk at length about Spenser's love of the beautiful—his 'Platonism'—entering into conflict with his desire to instruct—his 'Puritanism'. A good deal of 'bawdry' and 'wanton-ness', as well as violence, is described in detail in the *Faerie Queene* and the duality of his apparent aim is not hard to discern. But to set the two in opposition and call the result 'criticism' is now a dated and, in a more recent view, wrong treatment of a work of literary art. Caxton and Spenser both intended that their audiences should choose the good and reject the rest or, as Chaucer put it in the *Nun's Priest's Tale*,

> Taketh the fruyt and lat the chaf be stil.

Malory's aim was neither 'moral' in a narrow sense nor 'religious' in a post-Reformation sense. He was concerned with the practice and ideals of chivalry, the whole complex of what was known as 'courtoisie'—gentleness, manhood, generosity, fair-mindedness, loyalty to leader and cause, service and all that it entailed, the proper use of physical prowess and, above all, responsibility to one's class, society and country. Both Malory and Spenser handed down a standard of national behaviour and an ideal English character. The Arthurian legend was associated with nationalism and the individual behaviour of the ruling classes, with their code of responsibility. When responsibility is shirked, the code is violated. Bedivere does not at once obey the order of the dying Arthur to return Excalibur to the Lady of the Lake. Only under threat of death from the stricken leader does he do so, but by this time we have branded Bedivere as an inferior knight, who all but succumbs to temptation. Gawain kills a lady by mistake and is associated with several deaths of a doubtful kind. His brother Gareth keeps away from him on account of his vengeful nature and willingness to commit murder on his enemies. Lancelot's son, the perfect Galahad, rejects his companionship in the field and Gawain refuses to do penance. In an accident, he kills Gareth. Although he dies nobly and is praised by Lancelot as 'a full noble knight as ever was born' without any clear reason being given for this testimonial, Gawain's dominant reputation is that of a ruffian and expert in 'open mans slaughter'. The plottings of Mordred and Aggravayne result in a series of incidents which throw the relations between Arthur and Lancelot into confusion; Lancelot is adulterously in love with Arthur's Queen Guinevere, Mordred stirs up civil war and usurps the throne. The action is not consistent and there are many unexplained incidents and trends. The conduct of the main personages may be judged against Malory's statement that the knight of the Round Table are sworn

> never to do outrage nor murder, and always to flee treason and to give mercy unto him who asks mercy, . . . and always to support ladies, damsels, gentlewomen and widows in their rights and never to use force on them upon pain of death. Also that no man enter battle in a wrongful quarrel for love or for worldly goods. (Caxton's ed., IV, 15, modernised.)

As has been pointed out, this aristocratic ideal is not invariably attained, for the knights are human and subject to temptation or unable to control their natural predisposition to brutality. Malory's standards of chivalric behaviour were practical and his knights are not cavaliers seeking a phantom honour but practical men intent on the pursuit of realistic aims in Arthur's Court. Lancelot's objects are down to earth, to win and keep Guinevere without Arthur finding out, which in the courtly love tradition of discretion in wooing is a straightforward enough aim. Malory strips the legend of most of its impractical embellishments, including supernatural aids and fairy-tale trappings, leaving a few key objects traditionally associated with Arthur. Merlin's prophecies, some never confirmed by Malory, Excalibur the sword and the removal of the wounded Arthur to Avalon by the ladies keep the slender unity before his audience. For the rest, the material is ordered by what appears to be a concern for the aristocratic ideal. Some scholars, like Professor Eugene Vinaver, who edited Malory, have suggested that all this emphasis on high standards of conduct and the chivalric code was reformatory in intent, since the stories were written at a time when such ideals appeared to have fallen into disuse. E. K. Chambers takes a less elevated view of Malory's concern for his own society:

> ... of the England of the fifteenth century, exhausted by generations of dynastic quarrels, of England as we find it depicted in the *Paston Letters*, of the complete breakdown of law and order, of the abuses of maintenance and livery and private warfare, of the corruption of officials, of the excessive taxation, of the ruin of countrysides by the enclosure of agricultural land for pasture—of all this we find no consciousness whatever in Malory's pages. A revival of the spirit of chivalry might have done something to help matters, but a strong hand in the central government would have done more.
> (*English Literature at the Close of the Middle Ages* [1947], p. 97)

The content of Malory is not to be read for much else than its considerable entertainment value and if we seek to discuss *Morte d'Arthur* as a mirror of its age we will not find much relevant material in the tales themselves. More useful to the historian than the dramatic content is the style, which improves in the later books. Its main characteristic lies in its short sentences joined by conjunctions ('and', 'but', 'so', 'then'). Most sentences are 'simple' as opposed to 'complex' and consist of a principal clause and subordinate clauses introduced by 'when', 'while', 'that', 'who', 'which' and used sparingly. The diction is old-fashioned even for its own time and contains, like Spenser's, many archaisms, which help to relieve the monotony, *e.g.*;

Sir Lancelot leapt to him and gave him backward with his

gauntlet a reremayne (*backhand blow*), that he fell to the earth dead. (Book XIX.)

This is considered appropriate treatment for a carter who was unwilling to give the hero a lift in his waggon. The same hero, after the death of his mistress Guinevere, 'dried and dwined away' and Bedivere, sent to throw Excalibur into the lake, said that he 'saw nothing but the waters wap and the waves wan'.

The figures are scanty, for Malory prefers the legacy of Anglo-Saxon to that of French. A warrior in the lists is described as being 'bright as an angel'. Two champions rush together 'like two rams,' 'two bulls' or collide 'as it had been thunder'. The narrative is liberally sprinkled with words like 'hurtling', 'wallop', 'noseling', which suggest violent movement of weapons and fists for, like all narratives of the time, it was designed for oral recitation. The human emotions recorded are uncomplicated—love, hate, pride, anger, pity, fear. Many of the incidents and dialogue read quaintly nowadays:

So whan sir Bewmaynes was a-bedde sir Persaunte had a doughter, a fayre lady of eyghtene yere of ayge—and there he called hir unto hym and charged hir and commaunded hir uppon his blyssyng to go unto the knyghtis bed:

'And lye downe by his syde and make hym no strange chere but good chere, and take hym in your armys and kysse hym and loke that this be done, I charge you, as ye woll have my love and my good wylle.'

So sir Persauntis doughter dud as hir fadir bade hir, and so she yode[1] unto sir Bewmaynes bed and pryvyly she dispoyled hir[2] and leyde hir downe by hym. And then he awooke and sawe her and asked her what she was.

'Sir, she seyde, 'I am sir Persauntis doughter that by the commaundemente of my fadir I am com hydir'.
'Be ye a pusell[3] or a wyff?'
'Sir', she sayde, 'I am a clene maydyn'.

'God deffende me', seyde he, 'than that ever I shoulde defoyle[4]

---

[1] went [2] undressed herself [3] maiden [4] defile

you to do sir Persuante suche a shame! Therefore I pray you
fayre damesell, aryse out of this bedde, other ellys I wol'.

(Book VII)

and again, the animation of the battle between the same Bewmaynes
(really Sir Gareth) and the Red Knight:

And than thus they fought tyll hit was paste none, and never
wolde stynte tyll at the laste they lacked wynde bothe, and
than they stoode waggyng, stagerynge, pantynge, blowynge
and bledyng, that all that behelde them for the moste party[1]
wepte for pyté. So whan they had rested them a whyle they
yode to batayle agayne, trasyng[2], traversynge, foynynge and
rasynge[3] as two borys[4]. And at som tyme they toke their
bere as hit had bene two rammys and horled togydyrs, that
somtyme they felle grovelynge to the erthe; and at som tyme
they were so amated[5] that aythir toke others swerde in the
stede of his own.   (Book VII)

The vocabulary consists mainly of short words, and even when the
main influence on the language was Latin, as was the case during
the fifteenth and sixteenth centuries, English prose writers showed
a preference for such words, avoiding flowery phrases and over-
elaborate terms of description. Malory's special art was mastery
of narrative. Nothing checks the speed of events and he alternates
and interweaves dialogue and narrative. This is far in advance of
contemporary prose writing. It is not heavily Latinised, like
Wyclif's clerical style, Teutonically uncouth, like Pecock's, nor
heavily Frenchified, like that of certain writers of romances, nor is
it so unsubtle as to be unsuitable for anything but direct statement.

It is worthwhile comparing Malory's prose (c. 1470) with that of
Caxton's *Preface* (1485). Caxton's is laced with London dialect; he
himself calls it 'broad and rude'. It is more pedantic and affected
than Malory's, and marks more of a compromise with Latin. Like
all Renaissance prose writers, he is better at short sentences, for his
long ones are unsteady and stretch out endlessly. Nevertheless, if
the whole taken together is apt to flounder, each clause, considered
as a unit, is harmonious. In some respects he is as pedestrian as

[1] part   [2] tracking   [3] thrusting and rushing together   [4] boars   [5] amazed, confused

Ascham, but now and then his flights anticipate the more ornate eloquence of Berners, Lyly, Donne and Browne, whose extravagances were better controlled.

.   .   .   .   .   .

In the history of English prose from Alfred the Great onwards a historical continuity has been traced by R. W. Chambers and others, though not every critic agrees that it exists. Its main feature is honesty of communication and although there were occasional departures from this tradition the ideals of clarity and under-ornamentation prevailed. Teutonic, Romance, Latin, Hebrew and Greek ways of writing and words derived from those languages gradually coalesced to form standard written English. The greatest single influence in fixing the form of the language was the spread of printing and after the fifteenth century the English language ceased to change syntactically. Spelling became fixed, inflections were retained, or dropped, permanently and forms which were obsolete or obsolescent during Elizabethan times, such as *-eth* in the third person singular of the present indicative of verbs (*doeth, thinketh*, etc.) survived in print long after they had disappeared from the spoken tongue. This was especially true of the language of the Bible.

Printing increased the range of vocabulary and of recorded foreign borrowings. Words were borrowed, either through French or straight from Latin (later from Greek), and naturalised by the addition of affixes. A critical and scientific terminology grew up and philosophy, history and the arts acquired vocabularies of their own. By 1600 the tongue that Shakespeare spake was the property of a large number of educated people and Alfred the Great's standard English—the King's English—had at last become a reality. In 1611, the 'Authorised Version' of the Bible, known also as the 'King James Bible', appeared, the work of a committee of forty-seven scholars. Its influence on the life, character and thought of English people goes back thirteen hundred years to A.D. 680, when, so the story runs, a labourer of the monastery of Whitby, called Caedmon, turned part of the Scriptures into verse after he had had a vision. There may have been paraphrases from Latin into Old English even before that. In the eighth century the Venerable Bede, a monk of Jarrow, translated the Scriptures into a language which the common people could understand.

In Chaucer's time, John Wyclif of Lutterworth in Leicestershire, assisted by several others, including Nicholas Hereford at Oxford, who translated most of the Old Testament, produced a vernacular version of the Bible as a defence against the monopoly of the friars in the spreading of the Gospel. His Bible, copies of which were small, light, unadorned and closely written, were aimed at the ordinary man, not the rich man. G. M. Trevelyan described the Wyclif Bible as 'an admirable and scholarly piece of work, a great event in the history of the English language as well as religion'. It illuminated Holy Writ at a time when many of the clergy could not recite the Lord's Prayer, or interpret it, nor the Ten Commandments, nor the Creed. Wyclif died in 1384, two years after the appearance of his Bible, and in 1428 the Pope ordered the Bishop of Lincoln to proceed in person to the place

> where John Wycliffe was buried, cause his body and bones to be exhumed, cast far from ecclesiastical burial and publicly burnt, and his ashes to be so disposed of that no trace of him shall be seen again.

This was the Papal penalty for unlocking the Bible to the common English reader and thus weakening the power of the priests over the people at large, an authority based on the latter's ignorance and illiteracy. Such disinterment and posthumous revenge was considered just treatment until the middle of the sixteenth century.

However, it was not until Caxton's introduction of printing into England that copies of the vernacular Bible were enabled to reach the laity. Caxton's printing of *The Golden Legend* included portions of the Pentateuch, the first five books of the Old Testament, and the Gospels and the results of his attempts to find a compromise between ornament and the pedestrian are not hard to discern. His aim was ease of communication and the avoidance of obscurity, as in this passage from *Exodus*:

> When the third day came, and the morning waxed clear, they heard thunder and lightning, and saw a great cloud cover

the mount; and the cry of the trump was so shrill that the
people were sore afraid . . . All the mount of Sinai smoked,
for so much as our Lord descended on it in fire; and the smoke
descended from the hill as it had been from a furnace. The
mount was terrible and dreadful and the sound of the trump
grew a little more, and continued longer (*op. cit.*, modernised),

which combines Latinisms with a somewhat greater proportion of
Saxon and French words. This clarity has the effect of raising
sharp images in the mind's eye of the audience, suggesting that they
are actually seeing and hearing the action described.

About 1500, a new era began. John Colet, a close friend of
Erasmus and of Sir Thomas More, recently returned from Italy
and steeped in the ancient classics, lectured in Oxford on the
Epistles of St. Paul, perhaps under the influence of Savonarola.
Colet became the chief English humanist of his time and in 1504
was made Dean of St. Paul's, 'the cathedral of that apostle whose
epistles he loved so much', as Henry VII described it. Colet was
the first to introduce the historical method of interpreting Scripture
and his techniques looked forward to those of the seventeenth-
century Anglican apologists. Armed with a battery of classical
learning, inspired by the examples of the humanists Linacre and
Grocyn, who had learned Greek at Oxford, and blessed with a
scholar's desire for terminological precision, Colet helped to
discredit the older allegorical methods of interpreting the Bible,
particularly the New Testament, by seeking the real meaning
which the human writer sought to communicate. His interpretation
of the Pauline Epistles was governed by what he was able to learn
about St. Paul himself, as a man living at a certain period of history.
He tried to understand what the *Genesis* account of the Creation
really meant in terms of contemporary cosmogony and based his
own allegorical reading of *Genesis* on scientific rather than moral
values. Colet founded St. Paul's School and was co-author of a
standard Latin grammar, later called *The Eton Latin Grammar*,
which was used in a modified form until the present century.

Other priests followed his example of preaching on a set subject,
rather like the giving of a course of lectures on a connected theme,

and adopted the practice of using the pulpit as a platform for the dissemination of information, so that opinion about scriptural authority was thenceforth established. Very often the views of pulpit orators were at odds with those of officialdom and, by means of a system of licensing, attempts were repeatedly made to censor or even to muzzle controversial clerics. The Government tried to supervise the pulpit and to stop the flow of polemic, chiefly in London. In an age without newspapers, when printing and publishing were still in their infancy, audiences looked to the pulpit for weekly intelligence and to form public opinion. Strict supervision eventually had a strong effect in country parishes of silencing the pulpits, and only in London itself did preaching of note continue throughout the sixteenth century. John Fisher, Bishop of Rochester, preached sermons in which there is exhibited a considerable degree of literary artfulness. They are packed with comparisons and show the same warm concern with style as Malory did, but more consciously. Like Caxton, he is prone to fall into unwieldiness in long sentences and the influence of Latin is overpervasive. Yet in pieces like the two funeral sermons which he composed on Henry VII and his mother, Fisher shows that he had glimpses of what 'the grand style' in English was to be:

All be it he had as moche of them (transitory qualities) as was possyble in maner for any kynge to have, his polytyque wysdome in governaunce it was syngular, his wytte alway quyeke and redy, his reason pythy and substancyall, his memory freshe and holdynge, his experience notable, his counseylles fortunate and taken by wyse deliberacyon, his speche gracyous in dyverse languages, his persone goodly and amyable, his naturall compleccyon of the purest myxture, his yssue fayre and in good nombre, leages and confyderyes he hadde with all crysten prynces his mighty power was dredde everywhere, not onely within his realme but without also, his people were to hym in as humble subgeccyon as ever they were to kynge, his londe many a day in peas and tranquyllyte, his prosperyte in batayle ayenst his enemyes was mervaylous, his delynge in tyme of perilles and daungers was colde and sobre with grete hardynesse. If ony treason were conspyred ayenst hym it came out wonderfully, his treasour and rychesse incomparable, his buyldynges mooste goodly and after the newest cast all of pleasure. But what is all this now as unto hym, all be but *Fumus* and *Umbra*. A smoke that soone vanyssheth and a shadowe soone passynge awaye.

(*The English Works of John Fisher*, collected by John E. B. Mayor [1876], sermon preached in St. Paul's Cathedral, 10 May 1509, 269–700).

Later sixteenth-century preachers continued in this tradition and inasmuch as their sermons have been published or remain extant for succeeding generations to evaluate, pre-Reformation prelates like Longland, Latimer, Hooper, Bradford, Crowley and Lever stand as models of sixteenth-century eloquence. By the time of Elizabeth's accession people of every class were coming to write, read and understand a common language, whether scholars or churchmen, traders, minor civil servants or farmers. A movement which started early in the fifteenth century gradually made for itself a standard English prose and from Henry V's reign onwards the royal language of communication was English. In 1418 he wrote to the Bishop of Durham:

Worschipful fader in God, right trusty and wel beloved . . . our beloved squier John Hull haath long tyme be in our ambassiat and service in the parties of Spaigne, for the whiche, as he haath compleined to us, he is endaungered gretly and certain goodys of his leyd to wedde (*put up for security*)

which is recognisable English. Henry IV habitually spoke French and Edward III probably knew little or no English.

The fifteenth century saw the disappearance of French as the customary vehicle of social intercourse among the upper classes. What remained was an evolving standard English, founded, understandably, on the speech of the centres of government and of lawgiving. From the middle of the fourteenth century English had been the official language of the courts and in 1384 English laws were stated in the 'mother tongue'. The development of secondary schools, founded by bishops and municipal guilds, benefited the lower middle class, at whom they were chiefly aimed, and the fifteenth century saw the rise of a new 'meritocracy'. No longer was learning and its indispensable key, Latin, kept solely in the hands of the Church; an influential class of grammar-school-educated men, trained in Latin verse and prose and in making translations of Latin authors into English, paved the way for the English Reformation. Indeed, they made it inevitable. The power of the priesthood in Langland's time had depended very largely upon the ignorance and illiteracy of their flocks. By 1500 a new wave of enlightenment had washed over the land. More people could read and there was a constant demand for copies of Chaucer, Langland, Mandeville's *Travels*, prose romances, chronicles about the wars with France, such as Froissart's, pseudo-histories about Arthur and Troy, political satire cast in doggerel rhyme and ballads. Before Caxton came to Westminster, these were circulated in manuscript copies, each laboriously written out by scribes and expensive to possess. Printed books were also costly but, as we have noted, in course of time their prices fell, until by 1560 professional men were easily able to afford the volumes they needed.

. . . . . .

The Bible was not well known. To possess a copy in English without permission from the Church authorities was to be regarded as a potential heretic, and heresy after Wyclif's time was driven underground and associated with poor rebels. Knowledge of the Scriptures was based upon the popular miracle plays, in which dramatised stories of incidents in the Old and New Testaments were presented on feast-days by members of religious and trade guilds. The Creation and Fall of Man, the Temptation of Christ, the Flood, the murder of Abel and Cain, Abraham and Isaac, The Woman Taken in Adultery, the deeds of Herod, Pharaoh and Pilate, the events leading up to and culminating in the Crucifixion, the Resurrection, the Harrowing of Hell, and the Last Judgment were the principal subjects offered by the unknown authors of these plays. They were performed in the principal towns of England and Scotland, in cycles, commencing with the Creation and concluding with the Judgment. These cycles took all day to work through and attracted people from the surrounding country-side by their colourful ceremonial, comic scenes in which Biblical and non-Biblical characters were mingled and their lively dialogue. Although the avowed object of these plays was to teach unlettered people the meaning of the Christian life, and especially of the doctrine of Redemption as evidenced by the sacrifice of Jesus, they were used as a vehicle for social and political comment, complaint about harsh treatment by landlords, crippling taxation, poor food, nagging wives, severe weather which made winter existence a misery and many other unpleasant features of the poor man's lot.

The miracle cycles came into being in the middle of the four-teenth century and were still being played late in the sixteenth century, when Shakespeare was a young man. They were often accused of being sacrilegious and the inclusion of so much secular matter was a constant source of irritation to the bishops. They brought the ordinary English peasant into contact with the Bible by involving him with Biblical incidents, which were treated as though they were contemporary. The Creation was thought of as a historical fact, which had taken place, according to the fourth-century Gospel of Nicodemus, 5,500 years earlier. All Biblical characters were held to be historical flesh-and-blood people who had actually experienced life as the Bible said they had—Adam, Eve, Noah, Abraham and the host of personages who peopled the miracle stage, including the devils from Hell, were all accepted as being real. Some of the more unpleasant characters, like Herod and Pharaoh, were undoubtedly modelled on locally familiar oppressive landlords and public administrators, and their behaviour is strictly in accordance with that of contemporary unjust rulers. Attempts to censor the plays were made at irregular intervals, especially in the later sixteenth century, and the manu-script texts which have come down to us are almost certainly a long way removed from the language of actual performances, although enough of the 'complaint' tradition remains to enable modern scholars to judge that a very great deal of the original material was non-Biblical. It was this 'political' content, often thinly veiled criticism of state policy, which resulted in the suppression of certain plays by Henry VIII's ministers. Plays which served the ends of current policy were, in contrast, encouraged. Miracle cycles were generally innocuous in this respect and were left alone by Henry and his successors until after 1560.

It is sometimes said that the miracle plays were breaking down before Elizabeth's reign because of lack of popular support. This was not the case. Cycles were played enthusiastically in the main cities of the country for many years after Elizabeth came to the throne. The last performance at York, for example, was in 1569, but the accompanying Corpus Christi procession, dating from 1311 in England, was held there until 1584. Although Henry VIII or, more accurately, Wolsey, took the first steps to control them in the mid-1520s and Edward VI maintained a form of censorship on performances, the municipalities which supported the cycles managed to keep them going without much difficulty until about the 1570s. Only then were the miracle cycles stopped, accused by Reformed bishops of being superstititious and idolatrous, tainted by Romish practices and full of sacrilegious matter. But they never ceased to be beloved of the people and would undoubtedly have continued for many years had measures not been taken to end them abruptly. Official texts were destroyed in many cases and only four complete cycles, the Chester, the N-town, the Wakefield and the York survive, in fifteenth-century manuscript versions. A few isolated plays from otherwise lost cycles may be added to these. This cyclic form taken by religious drama was a uniquely English phenomenon. Sharing a common frontier with history, it fell victim to social change and, as a mirror of Northern English agricultural society, the Corpus Christi play provides valuable evidence concerning the kind of entertainment which dwellers in and around English country towns enjoyed in pre-Reformation times.

But the Bible was not to be fettered for long, in spite of authoritarian opposition to its distribution among the people. In 1522 William Tyndale began to translate the New Testament into English; but he had to work out of England in order to escape the hostility of Henry VIII, who stood out at this time for orthodoxy. Printed in Cologne in 1525, the New Testament found its way into England. Tyndale was eventually martyred by strangulation and burning in Belgium in 1536, a year after his completed translation, finished by Miles Coverdale, had been published in England. It was officially recognised by Henry VIII in 1539 and came to be known as the 'Great Bible'.

Tyndale's version is largely preserved in the Authorised Version of 1611. His work made it certain that the King James Bible should be English and not Latin or Latinised, as scholars like Sir Thomas More would have preferred. Tyndale's style is vigorous, dignified and rhythmical, combining Old English (or Teutonic), Romance (or Latinate) influences and the colourful metaphors deriving originally from Hebrew, a highly figurative tongue. Tyndale had picked up his Hebrew indirectly from Pagninus' Latin version of the Hebrew Old Testament, but the effects, even of a second-hand knowledge of that language, carried over into sixteenth-century English, were rich. He said himself that the properties of Greek were more in accord with English than with Latin and that those of Hebrew agreed a thousand times more with English than with Latin.

Like Colet and Erasmus he believed that Scripture was to be interpreted in 'one sense and one only, the sense in the mind of the writer' and claimed fidelity to text; his was a scholar's mind, and his sources were the best available to him. Consider his translation of the first chapter of the Gospel of St. John, which displays a meticulous concern for strong literalness rather than for rhetorical values as dictated by established tradition:

> In the begginynge was that worde, and that worde was with god: and god was thatt worde. The same was in the begynnynge wyth god. All thynges were made by it, and with out it, was made noo thinge, that made was. In it was lyfe, And lyfe was the light of men, And the light shyneth in darcknes, and darcknes comprehended it not.

> There was a man, sent from god, whose name was Ihon. The same cam as a witnes, to beare witnes of the light, that all men through him myght beleve. He was not that light: but to beare witnes of the light. That was a true light, which lighteneth all men that come into the worlde. He was in the worlde, and the worlde by him was made: and the worlde knewe hym not.

He cam into his awne, and his recceaved him not: vnto as meny as received him, gave he power to be the sonnes of god: in that they beleved on his name: which were borne not of bloude nor of the will of the flesshe, nor yet of the will of men: but of god.

The refining influence of Coverdale on Tyndale's style improved the literary quality of the translation, especially that of the Psalms, which still appear in *The Book of Common Prayer*, but the real power is that of Tyndale's English. We know much more nowadays about Hebrew and about Greek manuscripts than did any of these early translators, including the forty-seven scholars who produced the 1611 Bible, but if we call the latter, as Macaulay did, 'a book which, if everything else in our language should perish, would alone suffice to show the whole extent of its beauty and power', we must also acknowledge, as the learned men of 1611 modestly did in their Preface, that

We never thought from the beginning that we should need to make a new translation, nor yet to make of a bad one a good one . . . but to make a good one better, or out of many good ones one principal good one, not justly to be excepted against; that hath been our endeavour, that our mark, (*The Translators to the Reader*)

However, when Coverdale published Tyndale's translation, revised twice by the man himself, he knew that no existing version could win universal support. The so-called 'Great Bible', published in 1539, which went into five editions before December 1541, was a revision of the 1537 'Matthew' Bible, substantially Tyndale's, revised by Coverdale. To give it some official standing, Archbishop Cranmer wrote a preface for the second and subsequent editions which ran:

Here may all manner of persons, men, women, young, old learned, unlearned, rich, poor, priests, laymen, lords, ladies, officers, tenants, and mean men, virgins, wives, widows, lawyers, merchants, artificers, husbandmen, and all manner of persons, of what estate and condition soever they may be; may in THIS BOOK learn all things, what they ought to

L

believe, what they ought to do, and what they should not do, as well concerning Almighty God, as also concerning themselves, and all others.

Nevertheless, the 'Great Bible', like its predecessors and successors during the sixteenth century, was thought of as a possible source of heresy, biased politically or lacking in the soundest scholarship, and within a short time Henry was trying to control its distribution and restrict its readership. Even Cranmer himself was doubtful and in 1542 he questioned the desirability of its retention. On academic grounds, the Catholic Bishop Gardiner asked for changes in translation according to the Vulgate. Henry solved this conflict of interests by proclaiming that the universities of Oxford and Cambridge would organise revisions, but nothing more was heard of this scheme. In 1543 Parliament passed an Act banning 'the crafty, false and untrue translation of Tyndale', prohibiting unlicensed persons from giving public interpretations of the Bible and, most extreme of all, forbidding private Bible study by persons of the lower classes, including, for example, shepherds. A shepherd named Robert Williams bought a copy of Polydore Vergil's *De Inventoribus Rerum* in an abridged English version made by Thomas Langley in 1546 and wrote in it:

At Oxforde the yere 1546 browt down to Seynbury by John Darbye pryse-14d when I kepe Mr Letymers shype I bout thys boke. When the testament was obberagatyd[1] that shepe herdys myght not red hit I prey God amende that blyndnes. Wryt by Robert Wyllyams keppynge shepe uppon Seynbury Hill 1546.

In the same year Henry made another proclamation to the effect that after 31 August 'no man or woman of what estate, condition or degree was . . . to receive, have take or keep, Tyndale's or Coverdale's New Testament' and in London several hundred copies of their Old and New Testaments were burned at St. Paul's Cross. The Great Bible continued to be the version 'appointed to the use of the churches' for the next twenty years. It was twice reprinted in Edward VI's reign, and even though Cranmer and some of his fellow-enthusiasts for Bible translation were con-

[1] abrogated

demned and executed, and Coverdale forced to flee, the book itself was left alone, possibly because Mary Tudor herself had been concerned with it during her father's reign. She had been part author of an English translation of Erasmus's paraphrase of the Gospel of St. John which had been bound with the Great Bible and placed in churches. Bibles were burned, and the works of Luther, Calvin, Bullinger, Melancthon, Latimer, Tyndale, Coverdale and Cranmer banned as heretical or treasonable. A licensing measure adopted in 1551 was reinforced in 1558 and enabled secular authorities to keep control of publishing until well into the seventeenth century.

In 1560 the Geneva version of the Bible appeared. It was the work of a group of Protestants under the leadership of William Whittingham, a relative by marriage of Calvin, who succeeded Knox as minister of the English church at Geneva. In Mary Tudor's reign this group were compelled to flee to Switzerland, where they produced a thorough revision of the Great Bible Old Testament, with reference to the Hebrew text; for the New Testament they used Tyndale's 1535 version as a basis. The Geneva Bible came to be the most successful of the fourteen versions published before 1611, and its dedication to Queen Elizabeth, together with its novel verse-divisions printed in Roman type, marked a forward step in ensuring its popularity. It was immediately adopted in Scotland by the new Reformed Kirk and a Scots edition printed in 1579 (see below, p. 165).

To the Great Bible must be added *The Booke of the Common Prayer and Administracion of the Sacraments*, published in 1549. It was put together anonymously from the Latin missal and provided a model of sonorities in a harmonious English. Coverdale's version of the Psalms which he revised for the Great Bible appears in *The Book of Common Prayer*; it made certain that all church services were henceforth conducted in English, the five years of Mary Tudor's reign excepted.

The value of the Bible as a literary influence was late in showing itself. Biblical phrases and quotations in medieval and early Renaissance literature were taken from the Vulgate; the English Bible, even in its 1611 version, took a long time to affect literary prose and one must wait until the nineteenth century for stylists like Macaulay, Ruskin and Carlyle to reveal their conscious discipleship. Bunyan was touched, not by the English Bible, but by the classical tradition of prose and the Old English melody of alliteration. Milton undoubtedly owed a great deal to the Bible; but syntactically Milton wrote Latinised English, for he was a classical scholar who approached the creation of English epic poetry unconventionally, disregarding normally accepted word order and inventing his own grammar. Only in the mid-eighteenth century, in the works of poets like James Macpherson, the 'translator' of Ossian, may one discern direct and consistent imitation of Biblical, that is, Hebrew, cadences, such as were first apparent in the Geneva version.

However, it must be said that all Bible translators must needs come into direct contact with the original Hebrew and Greek texts, and the 1611 version, together with its sixteenth-century predecessors, is firmly rooted in what is known as the '*textus receptus*' or 'received text', a Greek text prepared by Erasmus which was normally printed in all editions of the New Testament until the nineteenth century. Thus when one speaks about 'the Bible as literature' one is referring to an eclectic product of sixteenth-century linguistic scholarship, in fact, a monument to Renaissance humanism. These sixteenth-century versions were important examples of how humanists were inspired to serve the multitude which many of them affected to despise. The notion that the Bible is to be regarded as literature is one subscribed to and magnified by over-enthusiastic literary parsons, rather than by professional literary critics or historians, and Holy Writ has never really been properly subject to the standards of art to which literature is normally referred. The purpose of making translations of the Bible was never an artistic one but to disseminate knowledge of God's word. As Tyndale put it, addressing a theologian and echoing Erasmus:

> If God spare me life, ere many years I will cause the boy that driveth the plow to know more of the Scriptures than you do.[1]

[1] See *The Cambridge History of English Literature*, ed, A. W. Ward and A. R. Waller (1909), IV, 40f.

Discussions of the Bible in a literary-historical context are therefore unfruitful. Its connections are not with the history of literature in English, but with the growth and development of the English language. In 1950 Professor C. S. Lewis published a pamphlet called *The Literary Impact of the Bible*, in which he pointed out that the moulding influences on the Authorised Version were classical, not 'Biblical', in style. But, in any case, most people in the seventeenth century did not 'read' the Bible. Families owned copies and heard about its contents by having it read aloud to them in churches, schools and at catechism. In their devotions, the majority of people used the Psalter, either in Coverdale's translation or in a metrical version. Only in 1662 were the Epistles and Gospels of the Prayer Book transferred to the Authorised Version, which took a long time to gain acceptance among the Puritans, who thought it was 'prelatical', that is, the work of priests. Until the Restoration, the Geneva and other forms of the Bible continued to be used in preference to the King James translation.

During the forty years or so before Elizabeth acceded to the throne there was a great deal of individual interest in making the Bible accessible to laymen but its effect on the multitude during the sixteenth century was negligible. Biblical phrases started to find their way with increasing frequency into the writings of certain poets, like Skelton or Sir David Lyndsay, who was himself one of the first to try to make poetry out of scriptural incidents from the Old Testament, such as the Flood, and who frequently refers to the Scottish clergy's opposition to a 'popular' New Testament. In Lyndsay's *Ane Satyre of the Three Estates*, Truth lands in the stocks for offering the people a New Testament and is accused of heresy, for although Tyndale's translation of the New Testament circulated in Scotland, the climate of hostile opinion was harsher and extreme reactionaries held the reins of authority for longer than was the case in England. Practically speaking, the only version to which the Scots had access was the Latin Vulgate, which few could read. Most poetical echoes of Biblical sentences were from the Vulgate, not from any contemporary versions. The first Bible edition actually to be printed in Scotland was the Bassandyne edition of 1576–9, which differed only slightly from the Genevan

Scripture, and although the effects of continual domestic study of the book upon the language and national character of the Scots were far-reaching, they were not immediate effects and so far as the first half of the sixteenth century is concerned may be discounted.

· · · · · ·

One humanist recorded in both literary and social or Church history is Alexander Barclay (1476–1552). Most scholars make him a Scot but he may have been English. His literary activity was completed before 1528 though his reputation as an apostate, supporter of the old order and eventual returner to the Anglican fold, sketchily recorded in chronicles and letters, keeps him in the historian's view until the date of his death. His known connections are entirely southern, with the Dominicans at Ely and with St Mary's, Ottery, in Devonshire, according to biographical notices.

In literature he was something of a pioneer, although his critics have not been kind to him. He was the first to write eclogues in English, following Mantuan's example of 1498, and anticipated the works of Spenser and the Elizabethans in this Virgilian poetic form. Spenser, however, does not refer to Barclay and his *Shepherd's Calendar* shows no dependence on the earlier writer.

Barclay's first notable work was his *Ship of Fools*, published in 1509 by Pynson. This was a paraphrase, expanded threefold, of Brant's *Narrenschiff*. It is 14,000 lines in length, cast in the rhyme-royal stanza of *Troilus and Criseyde* and *The Kingis Quair*. Although condemned by most modern critics and not read at all by succeeding generations, *The Ship* contains many references to the life and thought of the times and its application to current events justifies more than a passing reference here. The Fools of Barclay are English, and his characters merry citizens of London, like Dekker's of a century later. The work is more imaginative and colourful than Brant's and, packed with allusions and spiced with wit, it deserves independent consideration as a fascinating example of the poetry of complaint. According to the Prologue, the avowed object of *The Ship* was to

redress the errors and vices of our realm of England as the aforesaid composer and translators have done in their countries.

The contents of this entertaining work, an English version of Brant's characters, reveal the nature of the society in which Barclay moved—a medieval and not a modern society. Its short chapters and constantly changing personages make for great variety of interest, as the following selection of subject-headings suggests:

Of evil counsellors, judges and men of law
Of avarice, of covetousness and prodigality
Of new fashions and disguised garments
Of old fools, that is to say, the longer they live the more they are
    given to folly
Of tale-bearers, false reporters and promoters of strifes
Of him that will not follow nor ensue good and necessary counsel
Of disordered and ungodly manners
Of contempt or despising of holy scripture
Of fools without provision (*i.e.* foresight)
Of disordered and venerious love
Of gluttons and drunkards
Of riches unprofitable
Of him that together will serve two masters
Of too much speaking and babbling
Of them that are always borrowing
Of pluralities
Of adultery
Of him jealous of his wife
Of those who cannot or will not learn but talk much and
    remember little
Of great anger about little things
Of people who do not profit from others' misfortunes
Of backbiters
Of mockers and scorners and false accusers
Of old fools that give example of vice to youth negligent and
    unexpert
Of young fools who take old women for their wives for their
    riches
Of the clattering and babbling of priests and clerks in the queue

Of night watchers and beaters of the streets
Of womens' malice and wrath
Of cooks, butlers and other officers of the household who cheat
their masters

together with vignettes scorning unkindness, conceit, vanities (*e.g.* dancing and dice-playing), fleshly lusts of all kinds and even of 'the foolish description and inquisition of divers countries and regions'—a jeer at the prevailing enthusiasm for exploring unknown territories by men who in Barclay's opinion do not even know themselves, which has an acutely modern ring.

Barclay knew no German and relied on translations, Locher's, Rivière's and probably that of Badius Ascensius. His English is of the unornamented kind which the ordinary man might find attractive and goes straight to the point in reference to the usual objects of the satirist's hatred—ecclesiastical and secular corruptions and the tyranny of nobles—which he lashes enthusiastically.

One addition to his version of Brant, or rather, of Brant's translators, comes in the form of a short encomium on James IV, represented in an acrostic as something more than a conventional hero:

> Inprudence pereles is this most comely kynge
> And as for his strength and magnanymyte
> Concernynge his noble dedes in every thynge
> One founde on grounde lyke to hym can nat be
> By byrth borne to boldness and audacyte
> Under the bolde planet of Mars the champyon
> Surely to subdue his ennemyes echone (stanza 1572)

while the stanza following speaks of the disadvantage of poverty and a bad harvest from which James suffered. Current English policy towards Scotland was directed at preserving the peace and separating the Scots from the French, so that it is quite possible that this passage, following as it does a eulogy on Henry VIII, is simply a 'diplomatic' statement. On the other hand, the eulogy was written when Henry VII was alive and was presumably intended for him rather than for his son, so that Barclay's Scottish sympathies may be no more than a summary of the official foreign policy of the pre-Flodden years.

Rather more has been said by the critics in favour of the *Eclogues*, the first pastoral in English. If *The Ship* is a medieval poem, the *Eclogues* exemplify humanist influence on Barclay. They number five, three translated from the satirical *Miseriae Curialum* of Piccolomini and two from 'Mantuan' (Baptista Spagnola), who printed ten eclogues. The form was originally Greek, associated with Theocritus, who wrote pastoral idylls about Sicily for an urban audience in Alexandria. Virgil adapted the form mainly for satirical purposes and it was this aspect of the pastoral which attracted Petrarch and Boccaccio. Like Mantuan's, Barclay's treatment is critical and satirical, not 'idyllic', and the five poems contain a number of identifiable topical references to personalities and incidents of the day. His Prologue to the work states that it is a compilation reflecting different stages of his own life and it is likely that Barclay started writing his first eclogue early in the century, long before the publication of *The Ship*—though the last eclogue certainly dates from the 1520s. The first three deal with courtly abuses and the dangers of political power; the last two with the behaviour of rich men to poets and with the complaints of the citizenry.

Specifically historical references are scattered throughout the work and include allusions to Henry VII and VIII, Archbishop Morton, Bishop Alcock of Ely, Bishop Foxe of Winchester, Wolsey ('a butcher's mad dog') and the Earl of Surrey's second son, drowned off Brest in 1513. The real attraction of Barclay is, however, the attraction of medieval satire, with its searing denunciations of officialdom and uninhibited accounts of the more brutal side of domestic life: Here Barclay addresses a courtier on the subject of sleeping conditions:

> But if it be fortune thou lye within some towne
> In bed of fethers, or els of easy downe,
> Then make thee ready for flyes and for gnattes,
> For lise, for fleas, punaises,[1] mise and rattes.
> These shall with biting, with stinking, din and sound

[1] bugs

Make thee worse easement than if thou lay on ground.
And never in the court shalt thou have bed alone,
Save when thou wouldest moste gladly lye with one
Thy shetes shalbe unclene, ragged and rent,
Lothly unto sight, but lothlyer to cent[1]
In which some other departed late before
Of the pestilence, or of some other sore,
Such a bedfelowe man shall to thee assigne,
That it was better to slepe among the swine.
So foule and scabbed, of hard pimples so thin,
That a man might grate hard crustes on his skin
And all the night longe shall he his sides grate,
Better lye on grounde than lye with such a mate.
One cougheth so fast, anothers breath doth stinke,
That during the night scant mayest thou get a winke.
Sometime a leper is signed to thy bed,
Or with other sore be grievously bested.
Sometime thy bedfelowe is colder than is yse,
To him then he draweth thy cloathes with a trice,
But if he be hote, by fevers then shall he
Cast all the cloathes and coverlet on thee.
(*op. cit.;* ed. B. White [1934], III, 75–100)

The ensuing description of a score of 'courtiers', or Court servants, spending the night in the one room, passing wind, belching, talking in their slumbers, arguing, vomiting and getting up to relieve themselves, not one of them quietly, with the tethered horses neighing outside, is as repulsive a portrait of the miseries of a servitor's existence as may be found anywhere in English literature. Neither Langland nor Skelton is quite so extensively graphic, and Barclay's intensely personal account of the physically repulsive has about it a touch of Villon.

The fifth eclogue contains several vignettes of English life. One of the most interesting is the description of a game of football, a forbidden pastime in Henry VIII's reign, referred to in scathing terms by Elyot as

[1] smell

nothing but beastly fury and extreme violence; whereof
procedeth hurt and consequently rancour and malice. (*The
Governor*, I, xxvii)

Barclay speaks of this and other sports more kindly:

> Eche time and season hath his delite and joyes,
> Loke in the stretes, behold the little boyes,
> Howe in fruite season for joy they sing and hop,
> In Lent is each one full busy with his top
> And nowe in winter for all the greevous colde
> All rent and ragged a man may them beholde,
> They have great pleasour supposing well to dine,
> When men be busied in killing of fat swine,
> They get the bladder and blowe it great and thin,
> With many beanes or peason put within,
> It ratleth, soundeth, and shineth clere and fayre,
> While it is throwen and caste up in the ayre,
> Eche one contendeth and hath a great delite
> With foote and with hande the bladder for to smite,
> If it fall to grounde they lifte it up agayne,
> This wise to labour they count it for no payne,
> Renning and leaping they drive away the colde,
> The sturdie plowmen lustie, strong and bolde
> Ouercommeth the winter with driving the foote-ball,
> Forgetting labour and many a grevous fall.   (V, 87–106)

and although his verse is often wooden and lacking in fire, he
almost as often hits off a wordly-wise characterisation in a few
pungent lines. Here he talks of servants:

> Some shall be theves, some dronkenner than swine,
> Some shall love brauling or to lying encline,
> Some slowe, some gluttons, some fall to ribaudry,
> Adoutry, murther, with other villany.
> Some be forgetfull, some peart, some insolent,
> Some craftles fooles, some proude and negligent,
> If thou chaunge, some better for to have,
> Thou voydest a lubber and hast agayne a knave,

And if thou have one with knavishness infect,
Then all the other shall folowe the same secte. (III, 705–14)

and here of inferior poets, whom he nails to the wall in a single felicitous line:

Unapt to learne, disdayning to be taught. (IV, 703)

Both *The Ship* and the *Eclogues* are of interest to the paroemi-dologist, or proverb-collector. Chaucer, Langland and the Pastons all used proverbs extensively and Erasmus made a collection of them, drawn from the classics, which he published under the title *Adagia*. Its object was to show how Latin might be elegantly employed, as well as to entertain readers with the adages themselves. John Heywood's *Dialogue conteining the number in effect of all the Proverbes in the Englishe tongue* did not appear until 1546, while the first Scottish MS collection, James Beaton's, was never handed down in its original form. Barclay was thus the first man to have current sayings printed in English, though his proverbs were an integral part of his principal works and were not intended to be isolated. Few passages in *The Ship* are without these worldly-wise utterances. By the time of Elizabeth's accession, they had become a desirable attribute of polished literary style and every educated man was writing them.

Though closer to folk-lore than to literature and often untrace-able as to source, proverbs have much to tell the historian about the mood of contemporary society, since even the oldest ones are generally modified to suit the modern occasion. Such observations as:

Better is a fende in courte than a peny in purse (I, 70),
In every place lyke to lyke will drawe (II, 35)

from *The Ship*, or

Because the blinde man halteth and is lame,
In minde he thinketh that all men do the same (IV, 509–10)

Eche man for himself and the fende for us all (I, 1009)

from the *Eclogues*, express the uncertainties (in this instance) of courtiers concisely and dogmatically. Throughout both these works it is easy to trace signs of the acute discontent felt by urban Englishmen of all classes during the early years of the sixteenth century.

Barclay's other works include a translation of Sallust's *Jugurthine War*, published by Pynson and referred to in Chapter 4, and an *Introductory to Wryte and to Pronounce Frenche*, published by Robert Copland in 1521 at the behest of the Duke of Norfolk. The best-known French grammarian of the period, Palsgrave, practically accused him of plagiarism. Whatever may be the truth of this, Barclay did try to reproduce French speech phonetically and was a minor pioneer in foreign language teaching, though Palsgrave's enormous volume *L'Esclarcissement de la Langue Françoyse*, published by Pynson in 1530, completely superseded other authorities in the matter of laying down grammatical rules for French.

The name of Barclay turns up in documents of the reigns of Henry VIII and Edward VI. He is mentioned in connection with the elaborate preparations for Henry's meeting with Francis I at the Field of the Cloth of Gold in 1520, a demonstration of sham friendship with the French made memorable by the most gorgeous pageantry. Barclay was informed upon in 1528 by one of Wolsey's agents who described him (in the course of a letter which also contained a denunciation of Tyndale) as an apostate tainted by Lutheranism. In 1529 another informer reported that he had called Wolsey a tyrant. However, no action seems to have been taken against him and his heretical stage gave way to one of orthodoxy. After a sojourn abroad, he returned to England and was henceforth known as a devout Franciscan. He must have been one of the friars ejected when the conventual houses were suppressed but his name does not appear on any list of pensioners. He is said to have resisted the order issued by Cromwell in 1538 demanding that friars discard their habits and become secular priests or laymen. John Foxe records a meeting between him and Cromwell in St Paul's Churchyard at which Cromwell is purported to have said:

Will not that cowl of yours be left off yet? And If I hear by one o'clock, that this apparel be not changed, thou shalt be hanged immediately, for example to all others. (*Actes and Monuments*, ed. Townsend [1843–9], V, 396)

This attitude of Barclay's is corroborated from several other sources, more reliable than Foxe, and there is no doubt of his intransigence in the matter of his garb of office, even at the risk of imprisonment or worse. He was well known as a reactionary preacher who refused to accept Henry VIII as Head of the Church. From 1546 until 1552, the year of his death, he held various livings, at Much Baddow in Essex, Wokey, Somerset, and finally at All Hallows, Lombard Street, in the City of London.

Barclay's declared aim, to 'English such foreign authors as might benefit the mind and morals of English people', puts him in the special category of 'translator' but he was much more than just a medium owing his strength and reputation to foreign sources and remarks like C. S. Lewis's 'with Alexander Barclay . . . we touch rock bottom' (*English Literature in the Sixteenth Century*, p. 129) do him less than justice.

The Reformation inevitably lowered the status of the priesthood. Barclay was naturally loth to witness the departure of the old order and its replacement by a movement which must have seemed to him to presage ecclesiastical anarchy. The forces of anti-clericalism, always strong in England and given voice by Langland, Chaucer and Wyclif nearly two centuries earlier, as well as by men of ecclesiastical rank like Fisher and Colet, were associated with the aspiration of the new *bourgeoisie*, who thought of the Pope as 'the great Antichrist of Rome' and the Papacy as 'the great and abominable harlot of Babylon'. Such views were not shared by Henry VIII himself, whose attitude to religion was Catholic but intensely personal, and it was far more dangerous to be an extreme Protestant, like Latimer, Ridley or Crowley, than to be a stubborn old Franciscan who would not discard his habit.

7 : The Changing Language : Standard English and Middle Scots

ONE obvious place where history and literature touch is in the language which they have in common, in this case the English language at a time when it was rapidly developing a written, and even a spoken, standard. Philologists do not believe that any agreed standard existed in Chaucer's time, though his use of dialect for comic purposes, *e.g.* in *The Reeve's Tale*, indicates a Londoner's feeling of superiority over country bumpkins, and the Parson's contempt for those from the north whose speech sounds to his southern ear as though it were a continuous 'rum, ram, ruf', may mean that the first signs of the socially unacceptable in spoken English were beginning to appear. In the Wakefield *Second Shepherd's Play*, written about 1430, Mak the sheep-stealer, in his pose as an official, imitates southern speech, which is ridiculed by the shepherds. From the scanty evidence available it seems that 'official', 'socially acceptable' and 'resented by the underdog', all phrases that might nowadays be attached to an incipient standard, could certainly be applied to Southern English by the middle of the fifteenth century. But that a general consciousness of this existed during the century is not apparent before Caxton published his Preface to *Eneydos* in 1490. This was a translation, as we have stated elsewhere, not from Virgil, but of a French prose 'redaction' or rearrangement of the *Aeneid* called *Livre des Eneydes*, published at Lyons in 1483. In his introduction, Caxton shows that he is unsure of what the appropriate English for such a translation ought to be, and concludes that the educated audience which he has in mind will prefer polished phrases.

> When I had advised me in this said book I delivered and con-cluded to translate it into English and forthwith took a pen and ink and wrote a leaf or two which I oversaw again to correct it.

And when I saw the fair and strange terms therein I doubted that it should not please some gentlemen which late blamed me saying that in my translations I had over curious terms which could not be understand of common people, and desired me to use old and homely terms in my translations, and fain would I satisfy every man and so to do took an old book and read therein and certainly the English was so rude and broad that I could not well understand it. And also my lord Abbot of Westminster did do show to me late certain evidences written in old English for to reduce it into our English now used. And certainly it was written in such wise that it was more like to Dutch than English. I could not reduce nor bring it to be understanden and certainly our language now used varyeth far from that which was used and spoken when I was born . . . in these days every man that is in any reputation in his country will utter his communication and matters in such matters and terms that few men shall understand them. And some honest and great clerks have been with me and desired me to write the most curious terms that I could find. And thus between rude and curious I stand abashed. But in my judgment the coming terms that be daily used are lighter to be understood than the old and ancient English. And for as much as this present book is not for a rude uplandish man to labour therein nor read it, but only for a clerk and noble gentleman that feleth and understandeth in feats of arms in love and in noble chivalry . . . But I pray Master John Skelton late created poet laureate in the university of Oxford to oversee and correct this said book and to address and expound where as shall be found fault to them that shall require it, for him I know for sufficient to expound and english every difficulty that is therein. For he hath late translated the epistles of Tully and the book of Diodorus Siculus and diverse other works out of Latin into English not into rude and old language, but in polished and ornate terms craftily, as he that hath read Virgil, Ovid, Tully and all the other noble poets and orators to me unknown. (*Eneydos*, preface)

John Skelton, an enthusiastic Latinist, used Reuchlin's *Vocabu-*

1 Falkland Palace

2 The Interview Room in Falkland Palace

3 Stirling Castle: the Palace Block and the Great Hall

4 and 5 Hampton Court Palace.
Right: Tudor chimneys.
Below: The Privy Chamber in
the Wolsey Rooms

6 St George's Chapel, Windsor Castle

7 Stalls in Henry VII's Chapel, Westminster Abbey

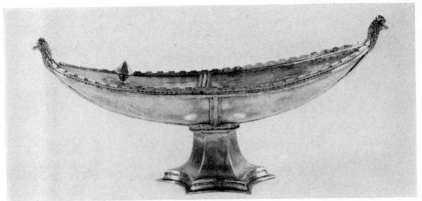

8 The Ramsey Abbey Incense Boat, one of the very few pieces of monastic silver which escaped destruction during the Dissolution of the Monasteries

9 Nonsuch Palace in Surrey, which was built by Henry VIII

10 Sir Thomas More

11 Erasmus by Holbein

Doctor Brants Narrenschiff

j · 4 · 9 · 9 ·

Nüt on vrsach.

Olpe.

Uo: haß ichs narren schiff gedieht
Mit grosser arbeyt vff gerieht
Vnd das mit doren also geladen
Das man sie nit durfft anders baden
Eyn yeder het sich selbs gerißen
Aber es ist dar by nit blißen
Vil mancher hat noch sym geduncken
Noch dem villicht er hatt getruncken
Nuw rymen wellen dar an hencken
Die selben soltten wol gedencken

12 Title page of *Doctor Brants Narrenschiff*, published in Basel, 1499

A fole blynde, forsoth and wytles is that man
Whiche thoughe his wyfe openly defylyd be
Before his owne face, yet suche a chrafte he can
To fayne hym a slepe, nat wyllynge it to se
Or els he layeth his hande before his iye
And thoughe he here and se howe the mater gose
He snortynge slepyth, and wyll it nat disclose.

13 A woodcut from Alexander Barclay's *Ship of Fools*, 'Of avoutry, and specially of them yt are bawdes to their wyves, knowynge and wyll nat knowe, but kepe counseyll, for covetyse, and gaynes or avauntage'

Within our shyp that fole shall haue a hode
Whiche an olde wyfe taketh in maryage
Rather for hir ryches and hir worldly gode
Than for pure loue, or hope to haue lynage
But suche youth as mary them selfe with age
The profyte and pleasour of wedlocke lese certayne
And worthely lyue in brawlynge stryfe and payne.

14 From Barclay's *Ship of Fools*, 'Of yonge folys that take olde
wymen to theyr wyves, for theyr ryches'

15 Title-page of a grammar book by John Stanbridge (1463-1510), printed by Wynkyn de Worde

16 An advertisement handbill by Caxton

If it plese ony man spirituel or temporel to bye ony
pyes of two and thre comemoraciõs of salisburi vse
enpryntid after the forme of this presēt lettre whiche
ben wel and truly correct, late hym come to westmo;
nester in to the almonesrye at the reed pale and he shal
haue them good chepe .·.·

Supplico stet cedula

Th:Eliott Knight.

17 Sir Thomas Elyot, drawing
from a portrait by Holbein

The Prologue.   Fol.i.

Muſing and marueling on the miſerye,
frō day to day in earth ẏ doth increaſe
And of that ſtate the inſtabilite,
Proceding of that reſtles buſines:
Wherof ẏ moſt part doth their mindes
Inordinatly on hungry couetouſnes,   (adies,
Uaineglory, deceit,and other biciouſnes.

But tombling in my bed I might not lye,
Wherfore I went forth in a May morning:
Comfort to get of my melancolye,
Somewhat before freſhe Phebus vpriſing,
Where I might here,the birdes ſwetely ſing:
Into a parke I paſt for my pleaſure,
Decked right well by craft of dame nature,

How I receiued comforte naturall,
For to diſcriue at length it were to longe:
Smelling the holſome herbes medicinall,
              I.i.   Wherof

18 A page from Sir David
Lindsay's *Dialogue between
Experience and a Courtier*
(Purfoote, 1566)

19 James IV of Scotland

20 and 21 Two views of Queen
Margaret. *Right:* as
painted by Van der
Goes on a panel form-
ing part of the Trinity
Altarpiece and *Below:*
with John, Duke of
Albany

22 The printer's device of Walter Chepman

23 Andro Myllar's device

24 Sir Thomas Wyatt, after Holbein

25 A page from the Royal MS of Wyatt's poems

26 Henry Howard, Earl of Surrey

27 Henry VIII as a young man, by Joos van Cleve

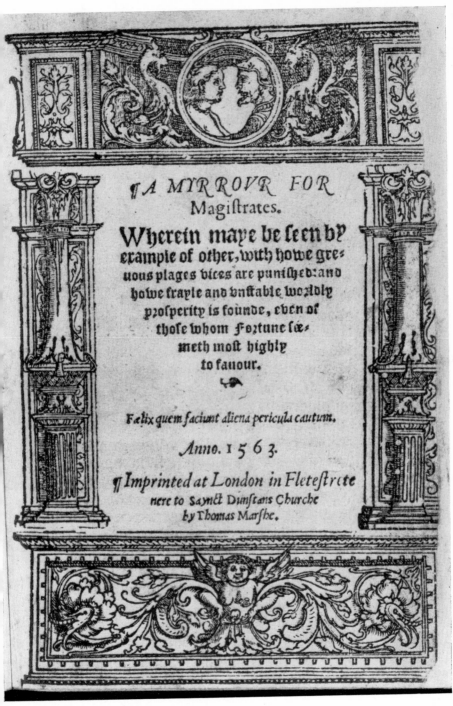

¶A MYRROVR FOR
Magiſtrates.

Wherein maye be ſeen by
example of other, with howe gre‑
uous plages vices are puniſhed: and
howe frayle and vnſtable worldly
proſperity is founde, euen of
thoſe whom Fortune ſee‑
meth moſt highly
to fauour.

Felix quem faciunt aliena pericula cautum.

Anno. 1 5 6 3.

¶Imprinted at London in Fleteſtrete
nere to Saynct Dunſtans Churche
by Thomas Marſhe.

28 Title-page of *A Mirror for Magistrates*, 1563 edition

29 Thomas Cranmer

31 Cardinal Wolsey

30 Cardinal Beaton

larius Breviloquus (1478), long a source-book for humanists, to aid his understanding of Poggio's 1449 translation of Diodorus the Sicilian's Greek into Latin. Poggio completed Books I–V of a work called *Bibliotheca Historica*, a world history from the origin of man to B.C. 59 of which only Books I–V and XI–XX survived intact. Skelton knew no Greek and his English version is based on Poggio. It was composed about 1485, and so stands as one of the earliest attempts to make a Greek work available to those who could read only English, though it is unlikely that anyone capable of reading Skelton's English would have been ignorant of Latin. In fact, Skelton's prose could hardly have been understood by a non-Latinist; for as his twentieth-century editors point out:

> Latin contributions echo through his mind and thrust themselves into his English style, warping and twisting it at times into outlandish and grotesque forms.
> (*The Bibliotheca Historica of Diodorus Siculus translated by John Skelton*, ed. F. M. Salter and H. L. R. Edwards [1957], introd. xxxii.)

Later, they describe Skelton's prose as the most extreme example of the kind of excess fostered by medieval masters of rhetoric such as Geoffrey de Vinsauf (*c.* 1210), who sought to amplify or dilate matter practically as an end in itself. Ornament for its own sake—aureation, weak constructions masked by flowery language, 'doublets', like 'shewe and declare', 'strong and myghty', 'coveyte and desyre', 'avoyde and eschewe', together with long-drawn-out extensions adapted for sound rather than sense, like 'souveraigne dame, governour, prynces and quene of all the hole lond' or 'furious and myghty strong lyon', mark such writing. Tautological habits of style may be discerned in nearly all Renaissance prose-writers, from Berners onwards, but much of Skelton's English is a model of what we are now taught to consider 'bad' writing.

Not all of Skelton's prose falls into this category, however, for here and there in the Diodorus he shows a gift for graphic description which foreshadows the poetry to come. As an example of this, take his account of the Ethiopians' hunting methods:

For drede of wilde bestes they slepe on tree toppes. They buske
M

theym-self upwarde in the grey mornyng, and forth they goo with wepens into the concours of watres, and hide theym-self a litle of in the busshes and the woddes. And in the hote season of somer the wilde oxen, leopardes, and many other of all maner of wilde bestes, for hete and for thirst they have thare recours unto the said watres, of purpose theire thristy drought to represse. Then comme the Ethiopians out of the trees, and when the bestes be pampred full of watre so that they unnethe (*hardly*) can easily wagge away (*escape*), they forcibly assawt theym with long proppes and poles brent at the ends and harded with fire, with bowes and arowes, with stones and stownes, and shew theym-self by bushmentes (*surprise-parties*). (III, 24)

which is comparable to King Alfred's descriptive writing, or again, consider the attractive picture of the capture of a 'monster':

But it was so they approched nere unto hym and sawe his glasyng ien glowyng and flamyng like unto fire, and how he lay likking his lippes with his toung, and the horrible sharpenes and hardenes of his scales, as often as he moved theym how they sheverd and ruskeled to-gedre like as it had bene harneis of plate, and his tuskes that stode out tusked as a tentrehoke, his lothely wide mowth discoloured ugly to behold, they were wondrously agast. (III, 36f.)

His editors sum up Skelton's prose as being characterised by a high degree of Latinity in vocabulary and syntax, as full of tautology, periphrasis and alliteration, decorated with conventional diction and aiming chiefly at ornamental volubility. The two passages quoted above are, therefore, not very typical of his general prose style, which was quite unsuited to the communication of logical thought. His most durable contribution to humanism was made through vocabulary, and he is credited with adding about 700 new words to the English language, which is itself a remarkable achievement.

Skelton's over-embellished prose was very far from being an ideal example of how English ought to be written and Caxton did not attempt to imitate it; in fact this style was soon outdated as written English struggled to rid itself of 'inkhorn' terms and rhetorical flatulence. Nicholas Grimald's translation of Cicero's *De Officiis* (1553) points a sharp contrast with Caxton's and Skelton's notions of what the correct English for translation ought to be like: in his address to the reader, Grimald, also a contributor to *Tottel's Miscellany*, describes his ideal, stipulating that it be

> short and without idle words: that it be plain and without dark sense: that it be probable and without any swerving from the truth: . . . if it be uttered with inkhorn terms, and not with usual words: or if it be phrased with wrasted or far-fetched forms of speech, not fine, but harsh, not easy but hard, not natural but violent it shall seem to be.

It is clear that Grimald has in his mind a solid ideal of English prose, plain and direct, but refined by Ciceronian standards of precision. As he says:

> For although an Englishman has his mother tongue and can talk apace as he learned from his dame, yet is it one thing to tittle-tattle, I wot not how, or to chatter like a jay, and another to bestowe his words wisely, orderly, pleasantly and pithily. Such as have English meetly well, and but a smattering, or small taste in the Latin, which number is great among the scholars of this realm, may hereby fall into such acquaintance and familarity with this excellent Latin man (*Cicero*), that neither shall his device seem hard, nor his art obscure, nor his style strange.

He suggests that his translation ought to be read with Cicero's Latin at hand, so that both the reader's English and his Latin might be improved. After 1558 Grimald's rendering in English was accompanied by the Latin text. It became a standard translation during the reigns of Elizabeth and James I and has the virtues of literalness; save in places where such literalness also implies clumsiness, it is also clear and accurate as a version of the Latin.

· · · · ·

Regarding English as a spoken standard, the first clear statement is found in Elyot's *The Governor* (1531). He is discussing the teaching of young noblemen under the age of seven and states:

> ... it shall be expedient that a nobleman's son, in his infancy, have with him continually only such as may accustom him by little and little to speak pure and elegant Latin. Similarly the nurses and other women about him, if it be possible, to do the same: or, at the least way, that speak no English but that which is clean, polite, perfectly and articulately pronounced, omitting no letter or syllable, as foolish women oftentimes do of a wantonness, whereby diverse noblemen and gentlemen's children, as I do at this day know, have attained corrupt and foul pronunciation.
> (Book I, v)

With other occasional remarks in personal correspondence dating from the second half of Henry VIII's reign, this has been taken as evidence that a received standard of correctness in English speech was emerging by the 1530s, though most references to 'speaking correctly' related to Latin or French rather than to English. In 1552, a friend of Montaigne's named Etienne Pasquier observed in a letter that every nobleman's house in England, Scotland and Germany possessed a French tutor for the children. Elegance in French, a goal pursued by well-born Englishmen anxious to acquire *le douceur*, or charm of Gallic culture, was avidly sought after by the Tudors, since it was one of the hallmarks of a superior education. Compared with French, English was considered to be a crude language, capable of great improvement, and dialect versions of it came more and more to be considered signs of provincialism fit only to be laughed at. But a clear understanding that good birth and good speech went together was slow to evolve and in Henry's reign it was voiced only by grammarians. John Hart, who published his *Orthographie* in 1569, said that his standard was that of the 'learned and literate', speaking 'the best and most perfect English' and went on to accept London and the Court as growing 'the flower of the English tongue'. At the same time, he was not disposed to laugh at provincial dialects, and said that if people from far north and west wish to spell phonetically, then they ought to be able to do so without fear of ridicule.

Thomas Whythorne, the author of the first autobiography in

the English language, discovered in manuscript in 1955 and recently printed, was a Somersetshire man, probably born in or near Chard. Whythorne refers to Hart's *Orthographie*, which was actually written before 1551, and to Sir John Cheke's system as outlined in a letter written to the translator of *The Courtier*. He developed a modified version of Hart's phonetics, reinforced with more conventional spelling and wrote the whole of his autobiography in it. The work contains several references to dialects and occasionally even reverts to Somerset English:

> Heer yee shall vnderstand þat alþouh þe syti of Glosester standeth not in þat kuntrey which iz kommenly kalled þe west kuntrei, or west part of þe realm (az iz kornwall, Devonshier, and Somersett sheer) yet þe kuntrey speech wher þe sitt of Glosester standeth, iz lyk to þe western speech (az appeared by þis forsaid poor womans speech, for shee youzed in her talk, þat maner of pronounsing of her wordz az þei bee sett in her testimoniall). and alþouth shee was born in Gloster, & I in þe furþest part of Somerset sheer sowthward from Gloster, which iz threeskor myl and mor from her natyv plas, yet bekawz shee sownded her wordz after þat kuntrey maner and fasion, I in mirth kald her alwaiz kuntrywoman and took vpon mee to be her kuntreyman. (*The Autobiography of Thomas Whythorne*, ed. James M. Osborn [1961], 169–70)

This entry probably refers to an incident in the 1560s. Whythorne was a university man of letters, a musicologist who published the first collection of English madrigals and the scion of a well established family, born in 1528 into a life of moderate gentility. His phonetics suggest that he preserved his West Country accent, without self-consciousness, and although an exaggerated version of the speech of that area continued to be used to represent yokel talk on the stage, as a play like *Gammer Gurton's Needle* (c. 1550) reveals, it was not a stigma denoting lower-class origins. The dialects of the North of England were apparently less acceptable and by the end of the sixteenth century an order of social preference in spoken English had been established, commencing with the speech of the Court, then of London and the surrounding countries within a distance of sixty miles of the capital (including Oxford and Cambridge), the western counties, Gloucester, Devon and Somerset and, at the bottom of the hierarchy, those who lived beyond the River Trent.

About the same time Henry Machyn, a Londoner of the artisan class, thought to have been an undertaker, was keeping his diary. From 1550–63 he recorded his impressions of events, starting with the many funerals with which he was professionally associated and later developing his account into a more general chronicle. The value of the *Diary* both to the social historian and to the philologist is immense since, as H. C. Wyld, who analysed his grammar, points out:

> it enshrines, not a counterfeit presentiment, such as we might find in comedies, of lower-class speech, but the genuine thing, naturally and consciously set down by a man who is obviously putting his own English on paper. (*A History of Modern Colloquial English* [1956], p. 99)

Wyld adds two extracts from the *Diary*, to show Machyn's style and his unorthodox spelling. Spelling, which since the introduction of printing continued to follow the traditions and habits of scribes, still looked as though it reflected late Middle English vowel pronunciation, whereas in fact it is quite clear, even from the *Paston Letters* and other documents written before Caxton's maturity, that a recognisably modern pronunciation was soundly established in about 1460. Whythorne's phonetics certainly suggest that he spoke in a manner clearly intelligible to a modern listener.

Throughout the sixteenth century English as written and English as spoken gradually drew more and more closely together and from Berners to Ascham the written language of the Court may be seen to contain many apparent 'vulgarisms' used also in colloquial speech. Wyld observes that 'this intimate relation between the highest type of colloquial English and the English of literature cannot be too strongly insisted upon', since the writers of literature were the same men who were making English history,

> that is, who were living and fighting; sailing strange seas, and discovering new worlds; ruffling at Court, or deliberating in the

councils of Church and of the State; conferring and negotiating abroad with princes and prelates, and often, at the last, going 'darkling down the torrent of their fate', and dying joyfully and gaily, like Christian gentlemen, on the battle-field or 'the deck, which was their field of fame', or, by some strange reverse or fortune, by *a no less splendid death upon the scaffold or at the stake. (ibid.*, p. 101; my italics.)

Sir Thomas Wyatt the poet was one of these. In a dispatch to Henry VIII, he described how he took part in the arrest of an Welsh traitor in Paris:

I mysellff went with the provost withowt light, and coming in to his chamber fownd Weldon with hym that was lefft for eache. And I told hym that sins he wold not come to visit me, I was come to sek hym. And shewd hym what payne I had taken that at the dore had hurt my leg with a fall, that in dede I fere me will not be hole this month. His colour chaingid as sone as he herd my voyce. And with that came in the provost and set hand on hym. I reched to have set hand apon lettres that he was wrytyng, but he cawght them afore me and flang them bak ward in to the fire. Yet I ouer threw hym and crached them owt, but the provost gat them; and with that he chargid the provost on th'emperours byhallf, whose servant he sayd he was, that his wrytynges and hym sellf myght be delyuered in to his handes or his maister de Hostelles. And with that owt off his bosome he toke a bagge of cerecloth with wrytynges therein, and delyuered to the provost. (*The Life and Letters of Sir Thomas Wyatt;* ed. K. Muir [1963], p. 117, Wyatt to Henry VIII, 7 January, 1540)

Reference to volume five of *English Historical Documents*, 1485–1558, edited by C. H. Williams (1967), a valuable collection of extracts from written and printed sources, chronicles, sermons, political tracts, royal correspondence, diplomatic and administrative documents, Acts of Parliament, wills, private letters and diaries, will illustrate the truth of Professor Wyld's first statement. The 'standard' of the Court was really a spoken one and a great many usages were permitted in sixteenth-century written English which would nowadays be considered undesirable in spoken English and completely unacceptable in modern written prose. Comparison of an author's literary prose with that of the same man's private correspondence reveals no clear division of standards such as a studied application to attain particular refinement in the former might be expected to produce. Henry VIII, More, Tyndale, Ascham and even Queen Elizabeth herself may all be cited in evidence of this.

Nevertheless, the humanist influence on English was a 'purist' one, associated, as is well known, with Ciceronianism. Erasmus himself was not a Ciceronian and in fact published in 1528 a dialogue called *Ciceronianus* in which he rebuked these imitators. In opposition to Cicero's ornate style Erasmus placed the Attic, or 'plain', style. He described the extremes to which a Ciceronian imitator was wont to go, explaining ironically the meticulous concern with the niceties of composition which even a letter demands:

> I read as many letters of Cicero as possible; I consult all my lists (*i.e.* lexicons of words and phrases); I select some words strikingly Ciceronian, some tropes, and phrases, and rhythms. Finally, when furnished sufficiently with this kind of material, I examine what figures of speech I can use and where I can use them. Then I return to the question of sentences. For it is now a work of art to find meanings for these verbal embellishments. (Quoted in *The Senecan Amble*, by George Williamson [1951], pp. 12–13)

Only at this point does he consider what his subject is to be. This tilt at the habits of the rhetorician nurtured on the grandeur of style suggests that the plain way of writing is to be preferred, as by Erasmus, it was. In a letter of 1527, he said:

> Even if I could attain perfection in portraying the figure of Ciceronian phrase, I should prefer a style of speaking more genuine, more concise, more forceful, less ornate, and more masculine. And yet, though ornamentation has been lightly considered by me, I should not spurn elegance when it comes of its own free will.   (*Ibid.*, p. 19)

The ideal of plain, simple narrative which all students of English find in native literary prose and which lies at the heart of Tyndale's Biblical translation was held by Tudor humanists to be roughly equivalent to the Attic style. Copiousness, flowing periods, coupled synonyms and due observance of the conventions of medieval rhetoric were referred to as Ciceronian. A third style, the Isocratean, stood somewhere in between; it was clear, logical and rhythmic without being diffuse. As a Latinist, Sir Thomas More was a follower of Isocrates; in English, Ascham may be cited as an outstanding example of a writer who preferred measure and balance but was shy of onomatopoeia.

> No, I will never so return thither again, to spend my age there in need and care, where I led my youth in plenty and hope, but will follow rather Isocrates' counsel, to get me thither where I am less known, there to live, though not with less care, at least with less shame.
>
> (*Ibid.*, letter to Bishop Gardiner [1553], pp. 30–1)

Precise compartments for each of these styles are not appropriate where the writing of English prose is concerned, however, and they overlap in many respects. English does not lend itself to analysis in the same way as Latin, so that Ascham, Latimer, Cheke and even Berners in his introduction to Froissart, although comparable as exponents of 'classical' English and as precursors of Euphuism, must not be thought eccentrics or in any way extreme, nor opposed to the 'Attic' style favoured by Erasmus or to the native tradition preferred by Tyndale.

Cheke's letter to Hoby in 1561 took as a principle the statement that 'our tongue should be written clear, pure, unmixed and unmangled with borrowings from other tongues' and admitted borrowing only as a last resort; he was the leading proponent of linguistic purism and refinement in England at the time, and together with Wilson and Ascham, represents an ascetic detachment diametrically opposed to the warm irregularity of Malory. The influence of classical translation, mostly from Latin, during the first half of the century affected spoken English as it did written English. The condemnation of outlandish dialects as inferior to the English of the Court and the universities was inevitable and understandable, but, in addition, censure was passed on exaggerated styles of speech, such as Shakespeare parodies in the character of Osric, the affected courtier of Elsinore, of whom Hamlet made a butt.

.   .   .   .   .   .

The language spoken in the lowlands of Scotland was called 'Inglis' or English by the Scots until about 1500, to distinguish it from 'Erysche' or Gaelic, the tongue of the Highlands. The adjective 'Scottis' is not used by any poet until 1513, when Gawain Douglas employed it in his translation of Virgil's *Aeneid:*

> . . . to mak it braid and plane,
> Kepand na sudron bot our awyn langage,
> And spekis as I lernyt quhen I was page.
> Nor yit sa cleyn all sudron I refus,
> Bot sum word I pronunce as nyghtbouris doys:
> Lyke as in Latyn beyn Grew termys sum,
> So me behufyt quhilum or than be dum
> Sum bastard Latyn, French or Inglys oyss
> Quhar scant was Scottis—I had nane other choys.
>
> *(Aeneid,* I, 110–18)

[to make it (the translation) colloquial and unadorned, keeping no southern (English) save what is in our own tongue and spoken as I learned it when I was a page. Nor indeed do I completely reject all southern terms but certain words do I pronounce as my neighbour does, just as in Latin there are some Greek terms. In this way I am compelled, rather than be silent, to use certain minglings of Latin, French or English, when Scots was wanting—I had no other alternative]

A few years earlier, Dunbar was accused by his poetic adversary Kennedie of rejecting Gaelic:

> Thow lufis nane Irische, elf, I understand,
>   Bot it suld be all trew Scottis mennis lede;[1]

[1] tongue

> It was the gud language of this land,
>   And Scots it causit to multiply and sprede
>
> (*Flyting*, 345–8)

which, if the Spanish ambassador to James IV's Court, Pedro d'Ayala, is to be believed, was one of the eight tongues spoken by the King. Gaelic and Latin had been the official languages of Scotland in the early fourteenth century and *The Book of the Dean of Lismore* (1513–26), the earliest manuscript anthology of Highland origin, includes sixty Gaelic poets, forty of whom are Scottish, twenty Irish. The sixteenth century saw a decline in the bardic tradition following the defeat of John, Lord of the Isles, in 1494, and the retreat of the Highlanders to the north-west, so that it was probably fashionable to decry Gaelic in Dunbar's Edinburgh as a disappearing language which must then have been associated with a decisive political defeat. The Lord of the Isles had claimed sovereignty of the land north of the Forth during Edward IV's reign, and with Edward IV's help, since the English King had arranged by treaty to instal John as his vassal in Scotland and rule the country from London. In 1464 John was forced to ask for mercy from James III but in 1493 he was still plotting against James IV, and his title of 'Lord of the Isles' was taken away. James had homage paid to him by many Highland chiefs in 1498 and, more spectacularly, sailed along the north-west coast of Scotland with a fleet of ships in 1505. Although his achievement as conqueror of the Highlands was more nominal than is often supposed, the forfeit of the title of Lord of the Isles, claimed by a branch of the Macdonald clan since the fourteenth century, undoubtedly represented a grave loss of face for the Highlanders. The remarks of Kennedie about 'Irische' are in this context easier to understand.

The historian John Major tells us that half the people of Scotland spoke 'Irish'. The other half spoke 'Inglis', an offshoot of the Northern dialect of Middle English, which became a language of literature in the late fourteenth century, when Barbour's *Bruce* was composed. Victorian philologists like Skeat, Murray and Gregory Smith called it 'Middle Scots', but more recent lexicographers have subdivided Scots into 'early', 'middle' and 'late middle'. If Barbour is 'early', the poet of *Wallace* is 'middle', Henryson is 'transitional' and Douglas is 'late middle', while Lyndsay, whose work shows forth a literary language at the end of its natural life, maintains a conservative hold on 'late middle' at its fullest extent of historical evolution.

Of prose there is remarkably little, and Scotland has no parallels with Malory, Berners or Elyot. Most histories, like Major's *History of Britain* (1521), were written in Latin, and translations of these are word-for-word versions of their originals, turned into Scots prose. The *Historia Scotorum* of Hector Boece (1527) was translated by John Bellenden in 1536; John Lesley's *History of Scotland*, from 1437–1561, inspired by the author's reading of Fabyan, Polydore Vergil, Froissart and Stow, was dedicated to James VI in 1570 and thus comes too late to be significant. Lindsay of Pitscottie's *Historie and Cronikles of Scotland*, a Protestant version of Bishop Lesley's Catholic work, is also a work of the 1570s. He writes in the Froissart tradition of colourful incident and is in this respect a contrast to Lesley, who was a devotee of the plain style.

Discounting devotional treatises, like John Gau's *The Richt Vay to the Kingdome of Hevine* (1533), a translation twice removed from a German Protestant source and of no literary significance, the student of Scots literature can find only one outstanding example of mature prose. This is the *Complaynt of Scotlande*, which internal evidence dates from 1549. It is based to a large extent on Alain Chartier's *Quadrilogue Invectif* (1422). Chartier, an industrious writer, was the French Ambassador to Scotland in James II's reign, and produced a description of the courtier's tribulations called *Curial*, which Caxton translated in 1484.

Discussions of the spoken tongue of sixteenth-century Scotland have therefore to be based mainly on the works of the 'Middle Scots' poets and on this single prose volume of 1549. No convenient personal letters exhorting young men to speak in a certain manner, rhetorical treatises like those of Elyot and Cheke or instructional manuals in Latin grammar are available by way of evidence. The relationship between colloquial and literary Scots is impossible to ascertain, though the old-fashioned notion that the language of Dunbar and Douglas was an artificial medium, never actually used outside literature, no longer recommends itself to the philologist. 'Aureation', one obvious feature of Middle Scots, which is apparent in *The Complaynt of Scotland* as well as in the works of the poets, is not the ruling characteristic of their vocabulary, nor was it used with equal frequency by all Scottish writers. In any case, it was a well established rhetorical device, used in ceremonial descriptions by English poets from Chaucer to Spenser. The word itself is a coinage of Lydgate's and is used by him in a number of contexts to mean 'eloquent'; its etymological connection with 'gold' is weak and its associations, as J. Norton-Smith observes in his recent edition of the poet's works, are strongly metaphorical. Lydgate himself employs it to express, for example, the 'colour' and the 'sound' of inspired language, and it is in this sense that Dunbar and Douglas chose to develop the style. Dunbar concludes his *Goldyn Targe* with an address to Gower and Lydgate:

> O morall Gower, and Ludgate laureate,
> Your sugurit[1] lippis and tongis[2] aureate,
>   Bene to our eris[3] cause of grete delyte;
> Your angel mouthis most mellifluate
> Oure rude langage has clere illumynate,
>   And fair ourgilt[4] oure speche, that imperfyte
>   Stude, or your goldyn pennis schupe[5] to write;
> This ile before was bare and desolate
>   Off rethorike or lusty fresch endyte[6] (lines 262–70)

and Douglas opens his Prologue to Book I of the *Aeneid* with a paean to Virgil:

> Maist reverend Virgill, of Latyn poetis prynce,
> Gem of engyne[7] and flude[8] of eloquens,
> Thow peirless perle, patroun of poetry,
> Roys,[9] regester,[10] palm, lawrer[11] and glory,
> Chosyn charbukill,[12] chief flour and cedyr tre,

---

[1] sugared   [2] tongues   [3] ears   [4] gilded over
[5] prepared   [6] (talent for) writing   [7] inspiration   [8] flood
[9] rose   [10] fixed criterion   [11] laurel   [12] carbuncle

> Lantarn, laid stern,[1] myrrour and A per se,[2]
> Maister of masteris, sweit sours[3] and spryngard well
> Wyde quhar[4] our[5] all rung is thyne hevynly bell
>   (lines 3–10)

Henryson is more sparing in his employment of 'aureation' and does not usually attempt to sustain his metaphorical configurations for more than a few lines at a time, as in:

> Than fair Phebus, lanterne and lamp of licht
> Of man and beist, baith frute and flourisching,
> Tender nureis[6] and banischer of nicht,
> And of the world causing, be[7] his moving
> And influence, lyfe in all eirdlie[8] thing,
> Without comfort of quhome,[9] of force to nocht
> Must all ga die that in this warld is wrocht.[10]
>
> As king royall he raid[11] upon his chair[12]
> The quhilk[13] Phaeton gydit[14] sum tyme unricht;[15]
> The brichtnes of his face quhen it was bair
> Nane micht behald for peirsyng[16] of his sicht.
> This goldin cart with fyrie bemis[17] bricht
> Four yokkit steidis[18] full different of hew,
> But bait[19] or tyring,[20] throw the spheiris drew.
>   (*The Testament of Cresseid*, 197–210)

Here the device is flashed on and off at irregular intervals, conveying a greater subtlety than in either of the preceding passages.

Aureate prose is used to advantage in *The Complaynt of Scotland*. The centre-piece of the work, 'A Monologue Recreative', is a vision of Dame Scotia and her three sons, representing the estates, introduced by the medieval convention of the tired author going for a walk at Midsummer to recover his energy to continue writing. The scenery strikes him as so beautiful that he stays up all night and greets the dawn, its first streaks appearing in the N.N.E. direction:

[1] lodestar	[2] paragon	[3] source	[4] where
[5] over	[6] nurse	[7] by means of	[8] earthly
[9] whom	[10] created	[11] rode	[12] chariot
[13] which	[14] guided	[15] in the wrong way	[16] blinding
[17] beams	[18] yoked steeds	[19] fodder	[20] wearying

Instantly there eftir I persavit[1] the messengeiris of the rede aurora, quhilkis[2] throucht the mychtis[3] of Titan had persit the crepusculyne[4] lyne matutine[5] of the northt-northt est orizone, quhilk vas occasione that the sternis[6] and planetis, the dominotours[7] of the nycht, absentit them, ande durst nocht be sene in oure hemispere, for dreddour[8] of his auful goldin face. Ande als fayr Dyana, the lantern of the nycht, be cam dym ande pail, quhen Titan hed extinct the lyncht of hyr lamp on the cleir daye, for fra tyme that his lustrant beymis var elevat iiii degres abufe oure oblique oriszone, every planeit of oure hemespeir be cam obscure, ande als al corrupit humiditeis, ande caliginus[9] fumis and infekkit vapours, that hed bene generit in the sycond regione of the ayr quhen Titan vas visiand[10] antepodos thai consumit for sorrou quhen thai sau ane sycht of his goldin scheaip.[11]

The cosmographical passages are prominent enough to suggest that the anonymous author was well steeped in the 'new science' and one may detect a certain similarity in content to Milton's mathematical and astronomical descriptions. Milton himself was a skilled practitioner of aureation, though his vocabulary was much more specifically Latinised than that of the sixteenth-century Scots, who tended to Frenchify their Latinisms. *The Complaynt of Scotlande* is heavily influenced by French and indeed uses French words in preference to Scots words, a characteristic of all the Middle Scots poets in greater or lesser degree. '*Contrair*'. '*esperance*', '*facil*', '*felloun*', '*gloire*', '*gre*', '*maculat*', '*merle*', '*puldir*', '*renye*', appear instead of 'against', 'hope', 'easy', 'cruel', 'glory', 'degree', 'spotted', 'blackbird', 'powder', 'rein' in *The Complaynt* and in the poems of Henryson, Dunbar and Douglas. Spelling is likewise affected, as in '*abusion*', '*felicite*', '*propriete*', '*remeid*', '*souveraine*' and forms like '*the quhilkis*', which includes a definite article as in French '*les pauvres*'—Scots relies a great deal on this for precise reference and phrases such as '*the foirsaidis*' (the aforesaid men) continued to be commonly used

---

[1] perceived   [2] which   [3] powers   [4] shadowy
[5] morning   [6] stars   [7] rulers   [8] terror
[9] dark   [10] visiting   [11] shape

in Scots without the effect of clumsiness which they produced in English prose even in the first half of the fourteenth century. Michael of Northgate's *Ayenbyte of Inwyt* (*c.* 1340) is an example of the latter. (See Kenneth Sisam's *Fourteenth-Century Verse and Prose*, III.)

This strong association with French is historically easy to explain. The political links, the 'auld alliance' of long standing, the many intermarriages between the French and Scots royal houses during the fifteenth and sixteenth centuries and the migration of Scots students to French universities all contributed to deepen the relationship. James V's two marriages were both to princesses of France, and his daughter, Mary, Queen of Scots, was half-French and spoke Scots with a *douce* accent. James VI and his mother surrounded themselves with French poets and poetasters. Ronsard had been a page at James V's Court and both he and du Bellay wrote celebratory verses about Mary's physical beauty.

The Middle Scots writers all drew upon a Latinised vocabulary, not at one remove, as Chaucer knew it, through French transformation, but directly, so that although both Chaucer and the Scots used a range of colloquial French terms, anglicised or 'scottified' as the case might be, the French of the latter was more of a living tongue, spoken in the highest social circles, whereas that of Chaucer and his English disciples was either made up of long-established borrowings from central French or reflected more exclusively academic and technical interests, *e.g.* philosophical or military terminology or the vocabulary of *The Romance of the Rose*, which Chaucer in part translated.

In addition, the Scots had an exclusively literary vocabulary available to them in the romances, which were Anglo-Norman in origin. Works like *Fierabras*, *Aventures of Arthur*, the *Alexander* romances, *Sir Tristrem* and *Gologros and Gawane* (printed by Chepman and Myllar) provided a source of language which bore little resemblance to that of Chaucer and which seemed to contain a larger proportion of colloquial usage. The Scots' comic or burlesque romance stands in sharp contrast to their serious poems, in vocabulary as well as in content and tone.

These differences are best shown by examples: *Christ's Kirk on the Green*, the first of the comic romances, may have been written by James I or by James V, or by some completely unknown author. This makes it difficult to date, since the two Jameses lived a century apart and the earliest manuscripts are of the reign of James VI. The poem, a highly skilled product which conceals its art beneath an apparent naiveté of subject and handling, is much less 'French' than any of the earlier quotations given:

> To dance the damisallis thame dicht,[1]
> And lassis[2] licht of laittis;[3]
> Thair gluvis[4] war of the raffell[5] richt;
> Thair schone[6] war of the straitis:[7]
> Thair kirtillis war off the lincum licht[8]
> Weill prest with mony plaitis.[9]
> That war so nyce[10] quhen men tham nicht[11]
> Thay squeild lyk ony gaitis[12]
> Ful loud
> At Chrystis Kirk on the grene. (stanza 2)

The rhymed alliteration and the 'bob' and 'wheel' device which concludes each of the twenty-three stanzas links this poem with the romances and the ballads, and the whole is clearly recognisable as a burlesque of rustic activity made from a more sophisticated point of view, presumably by an aristocratic or well-educated author. After *Christ's Kirk* came a succession of similar works, of which *Peblis to the Play*, also ascribed to James I, *The Freiris of Berwik*, *The Three Priests of Peebles*, *The Cursing of Sir John Rowell*, *Rauf Colyeir* (Ralph the Collier)—all four anonymous— are the best known. Dunbar and Lyndsay both joined this tradition and wrote poems having similar characteristics, and in his alliterative satirical romance *The Twa Mariit Wemen and the Wedo* Dunbar draws freely on the considerable resources of both the colloquial and the literary vocabularies at his disposal.

Even so, the three women of the last-named work use mainly 'poetical' phrases and their manner is serious, thus emphasising the

---

[1] dressed themselves   [2] maidens   [3] conduct
[4] gloves   [5] doeskin   [6] shoes
[7] Moroccan leather   [8] real lincoln green   [9] plaits
[10] wanton   [11] drew near to them   [12] goats

N

contrast between their apparent dignity and the crudity of their behaviour; unlike the dressed-up rustic damsels at Christ's Kirk who squeal like she-goats when their swains approached them, Dunbar's married trio, elegantly clad, keep their amorous activities secret. They maintain a level of elevated phraseology even when the subject-matter is obscene and one never feels that this was the way in which people really spoke in Scotland at that time. This poetical 'heightening' makes genuine 'colloquial' speech hard to find in Dunbar's works. His serious debates, like that between the Merle (Thrush) and the Nightingale, are formal in tone, and while the *Flyting* with Kennedie shows the immense range of abusive epithets contained in contemporary Scots, one can hardly judge the quality of the spoken language from this torrent of nouns and qualifying adjectives. Dunbar imparts a literary veneer to every word he appropriates. Much the same may be said of Douglas. In the translation of the *Aeneid* proper, he is limited by his original, but in the *Prologues* to the thirteen books he is creating his own poetry:

> Sum latyt latton, but lay, lepys in lawyd lyt,
> Sum penys furth a pan boddum to prent fals plakkis;
> Sum gowkis quhill the glas pyg grow full of gold yit,
> Throu cury of the quynt essens, thocht clay muggis crakis.
>
> (Prologue VIII, 92–5.)

[some men, against the law, are mixing a cheap alloy with silver to be circulated at little worth; others are beating out a mould to cast spurious coins; others, again, stare patiently waiting for the glass bottle to fill with cash through alchemical practices, though the clay jar may crack in the meantime]

This is a very difficult passage, out of which several editors have tried to make sense. The reference to alchemy is ironic, since references to the 'quint-essence', *i.e.* the fifth essence by which base metals may be transmuted into gold, applied in such a context to ways of making money by tricks or fraud. Lyndsay uses the same metaphor in *Ane Satyre of the Three Estates* when he is talking about the idlers who frequent monasteries:

> Fidlers, pypers, and pardoners
> Thir[1] jugglars, jesters and idill cuitchours,[2]
> Thir carriers[3] and thir quintacensours[4]
> Thir babil-beirers[5] and thir bairds[6] (2604–6)

Neither of these examples is 'purely' colloquial, though they both contain words used in common speech; the impression is 'literary', and the choice of nouns is governed by the pressing formality of alliteration. All the comic poems of the Scots *makars*, named and anonymous, have this veneer of discipline and concern for technique and the rollicking stanzas of *Christ's Kirk* should not blind one to the fact that it is a work of extremely skilful construction and a memorial to its author's mastery of rhetorical devices.

For a closer approximation to the common speech of the time, one must really look mainly to Henryson and, in particular, to his versions of Aesop's *Fables*, which he introduced in a Prologue claiming that

> In hamelie[7] language and in termes rude
> Me neidis[8] write, for quhy[9] of Eloquence
> Nor Rethorike, I never Understude. (36–8)

which turns out to be mock modesty but nevertheless indicates that one of the translator's objects was to convey Aesop in words which the ordinary reader would find no difficulty in following. As well as this, he aimed to 'domesticate' Aesop, to turn his characters into Scots peasants while maintaining the animal disguises of classical and medieval fable, and to give these modernised stories a more solid and contemporary background, just as the writers of miracle plays did with the Biblical incidents which they dramatised.

The age was one of satire and complaint, of massive indignation at religious and administrative abuses—a literary trend given a firm grounding by Langland. Protests in verse or embedded in the dialogue of miracle plays, such as those attributed to the 'Wakefield Master' of the 1430s, were levelled against heavy taxes on the poor, harsh landlords, cruel rulers, national enemies like

[1] these
[2] wasters
[3] entertainers
[4] "seekers after the fifth essence"
[5] bauble-carriers (jesters)
[6] bards
[7] colloquial
[8] I have to
[9] anything

the French and Scots, local enemies like dishonest traders and upstarts in petty office, together with the whole sorry mechanism of injustice, legal and personal. The general disaffection came to be concentrated more and more on ecclesiastical corruptions and it has already been pointed out that English poetry was overwhelmingly anti-clerical, thus reflecting public opinion. Scottish literature was of the same kind—in fact, more so, or at least less subtly. Of all European countries, Scotland was below the surface the most unruly, and Henryson's accusations in the *Fables* of deep-rooted corruption were more than justified.

After Henryson came William Dunbar, who was really the first Scottish Court poet. He had much in common with his contemporary Skelton, his poetical inferior, and Dunbar's glances at the petty intrigues of James's Court, which seem to have been considerable, and his complaints about human failings in his world, all highly personal in character, are indispensable to the student of Scottish social history of the century preceding the Reformation. Information on how the people of Scotland lived at these times is scanty and hard to come by and Dunbar and his fellow-poet, or *makar*, Henryson, both help to fill some of the gaps in a lively, personal, intimate and authoritative manner. From them and from Lyndsay, we derive a fairly clear picture of what conditions were like immediately before and after Flodden (1513), so that no student of James IV's reign can ignore contemporary Scots poetry.

Dunbar was the first Scots poet to see his own works printed by a Scottish press. On 15 September, 1507, James IV granted leave to two of his subjects, Walter Chepman and Andro Myllar, burgesses of the City and Burgh of Edinburgh, to import a press and letter

> for imprenting within our realme of the bukis of our lawis, actis of parliament, croniclis, mess bukis and portuus[1] after our awin Scottis use with additiouns and legendis of Scottis sanctis[2] now gaderit to be ekit[3] thairto.

Chepman, a rich merchant, and Myllar, a well-established importer of books who numbered the King among his customers and who had learned his trade in France, issued eleven Scots poems

[1] breviaries   [2] saints   [3] added

in April, 1508, including works by both Henryson and Dunbar. Their devices are most distinctive and appear in all their issues. Chepman's, which resembled that of a Parisian printer called Pigouchet, consisted of a shield, with a monogram of his initials, hanging from a tree and supported by a '*wodewose*', or wild man, and a wild woman, figures of great antiquity often seen in medieval pageants. Beneath this his name appears in full on a ribbon. Myllar's, appropriately enough, took the form of a miller, ascending a ladder to a windmill bearing sacks on his back. From the bottom of the windmill hangs a shield, bearing the printer's merchant mark. In the two upper corners appear two smaller shields, each carrying three *fleurs-de-lis* and at the base of the block Myllar's name is written in full. A book printed for him at Rouen in 1506 is the first known to bear the device. The printer's mark, a sign of authenticity like a hallmark or artist's signature, became more elaborate as the number of practitioners increased. Those of Caxton, de Worde and Pynson are monogrammatic and as such relatively simple.

The Chepman and Myllar editions of the works of Scots poets, which included part of *Wallace* as well as poems by Henryson and Dunbar have, in spite of some puzzling typographical errors, become original sources for editors of (especially) Dunbar since he was still alive in 1508 and could have 'overseen' his own poems—though if he did do this he was not very careful. Corresponding manuscript authorities date from the second half of the sixteenth century. In 1509 Chepman and Myllar printed the famous Aberdeen *Breviary*, a service book which was mainly the work of the enlightened Bishop Elphinstone, founder of King's College, Aberdeen, who probably helped Chepman and Myllar to secure James IV's support for their press. The *Breviary* was the last work to be issued under the distinguished imprint and, unfortunately, these printers were not influential, for no able apprentices took their places as Caxton's successors did. Early Scottish printing had therefore no perceptible effects on the language, which was soon to be subjected to irresistible pressures from the South.

8 : James III and IV of Scotland : Henryson and Dunbar as Commentators on the Times

O F the important Scots poets or *makars*, Henryson deserves the palm. The date of composition of his *Fables* is uncertain, but scholars now regard them as early work, probably of the late 1470s. Even so, in temper they are of a piece with pre-Reformation 'complaint' literature and have something in common with Lyndsay's writings. Henryson's *Fables* depict the Scotland of James III, a land split by factions and feuds, with James and the older nobles on the side of Henry VI and the Lancastrians and the Queen Mother, Mary of Gueldres, regent until her death in 1463, together with John, the Lord of the Isles, the exiled Earl of Douglas and the younger nobles, on the side of Edward IV and the Yorkists. Bishop Kennedy of St. Andrews died in 1465 and from that time until James III's reign ended in 1488 a state of political disunity prevailed in Scotland under conditions which were at times close to anarchy and under a ruler whose historical reputation is a bad one. James is described by most of his biographers as unfitted for his office, shifty, preferring the company of low-class cronies before that of his nobles, treacherous in his fraternal relationships and incapable of giving leadership to a divided land.

In fact, James was a sensitive man, interested in painting, music, and architecture, and the low-born favourites so much derided by hostile commentators included the architect, Robert Cochrane, a scholar, John of Ireland, later author of *The Mirror of Wisdom* composed for James IV, a musician, William Roger, and a swordsman, William Torphichen. The shoemaker and the tailor, Leonard and Hommyl by name, who were known to have enjoyed particularly close association with the King, were presumably arbiters of the royal taste in clothing. As an administrator, James was not talented, nor was he interested in military matters, unlike many of his nobles or even his brothers, who were much better suited to a dominant role than was James himself.

His attempts to secure peace with England by marrying his nobles to daughters of the southern aristocracy began in 1474 when his infant son James was formally betrothed to Princess Cecilia. Mary of Gueldres had been a Burgundian, from a part of France friendly to England. England was caught in the throes of internecine struggle and the balance of power between France and Burgundy was constantly fluctuating. James judged that such a policy would be favourable to future union between England and Scotland and that the time was politically ripe for it. English matrimonial alliances for his brother the Duke of Albany, for his sister Margaret, and later, between the same Margaret and Edward's brother-in-law Rivers were also arranged. The latter was still under consideration even after the English army had invaded Scotland in 1482.

None of these marriages ever took place. The traditional friendliness to France, strongly supported by both nobles and churchmen, and their corresponding dislike and distrust of England, both shared by the ordinary man, made any thought of union far-fetched. Hary's *Wallace* was composed at this time and its opening reveals the feeling of betrayal which the 'inbringing of Englishmen' inspired in a nation which still looked back with pride at the military successes of Robert Bruce in the early fourteenth century:

> Our antecessowris that we suld of reide
> And halde in mynde, thar nobille worthi deid
> We lat ourslide throw werray sleuthfulnes,
> And castis we euir till vthir besynes.
> Till honour ennymyis is our haile entent.
> It has beyne seyne in thir tymys bywent,
> Our auld ennemyis cummyn of Saxonys blud,
> That neuyr yeit to Scotland wald do gud
> Bot euir on fors and contrar haile thar will,
> Quhow gret kyndres thar has beyne kyth thain till.

[That noble worthy deed of our ancestors, of whom we ought to read, and keep in memory, we neglected through plain laziness

and give ourselves over to other affairs. To honour enemies is our entire object. It has been seen in these bygone times, our old enemies, come of Saxons' blood, who have never yet wanted to do any good to Scotland, except when they chose to direct their will to the opposite end, and how great kyndness has been shown to them there (*i.e.* James' aim of alliance)]
(Text from M. P. McDiarmid's S.T.S. ed. [1959–61], I, 1–10.)

and the pride and resolve of the English to subdue Scotland by hook or by crook is the frequently reiterated theme of their enmity which Scotsmen mindful of the deeds of their forebears should never forget. English marriage is a symbol of betrayal in *Wallace* and is used twice as an explanation of downfall and treachery in members of the Scots nobility.

The poet's hero, Sir William Wallace, is modelled to a large extent on tradition, as we have remarked earlier, but some general resemblance may be observed between the fictional Wallace and late sixteenth-century descriptions of the Duke of Albany, such as that given in Pitscottie's *History*. Albany was regarded by the discontented nobles as their spokesman in the campaign against James and his supporters. Later, in the 1480s, Albany would fall from grace and intrigue with Edward IV against James, but at the time of the *Wallace's* composition (1477–9) he enjoyed all the popular support which his brother lacked. *Wallace* has to be studied against this background of political anarchy and what amounted to high treason on the part of Albany and various disaffected elements.

Among the common people, lawlessness was rife, as it was in England, and James III's last Parliament issued ordinances in 1486 designed to accelerate the judicial process and curb the King's prerogative of clemency because of the evils arising

through treason, slaughter, reif,[1] burning, theft and open hership,[2] through default of sharp execution of justice, and over-common granting of grace and remission to trespassers (John Hill Burton, *History of Scotland* [1829–43], III, 191)

[1] rapine   [2] rampage

a statement which should not be taken to mean that utter chaos or anything like it prevailed throughout the land. Contemporary England was far worse in this respect. James III was a trader, with his own ships, and the sumptuary laws of James II, passed in 1458, suggest that easily visible standards of bourgeois comfort existed. Such glimpses of the burgesses and the peasantry as are afforded by poems like *Christ's Kirk on the Green* reveal a well dressed, even overdressed, community and many of the conventional manifestations of successful industry. An Act of Parliament of 1487 recommended that foreign merchants at all Scottish ports be given a courteous reception, so that 'they may be excited to return, to the great utility of the whole kingdom'.

In contrast to this state of comparative affluence enjoyed by the town merchants, the country Scotsman lived at a bare subsistence level, as he had done for centuries, his home of wood, skins and turf shared with his cow, working a strip of land which he held only for five years at a time and which could be confiscated at the behest of his lord. Those who had no lord were treated as outlaws and had to move constantly from one place to another, saved from legal penalty by general amnesties or by the indifference of officialdom.

Henryson's Horatian adaptation of the old fable *The Tale of the Uponlandis[1] Mouse and the Burgess Mouse* describes the contrast in conditions. The town mouse was a guild brother and free burgess, exempt from taxes and free to travel wherever she wished. This description is in accord with what is known of the highest class of free burgesses, the merchants, in James III's reign. The town mouse lives in 'ane worthie wane', a solid dwelling-house, and is well provided with cheese, butter, meat, fish from the sea and the stream, meal and malt. He offers his rustic sister mutton and beef, unleavened cakes and fine bread. In comparison the country mouse's fare is meagre—withered peas and nuts, eaten in 'ane sober wane', an insubstantial erection made from moss and ferns. The town mouse cannot eat such food. Descriptions of Scottish houses, by Piccolomini and d'Ayala, bear out Henryson's evidence as presented in this poem. Piccolomini's picture of the

[1] Country

peasant huts is a miserable one; d'Ayala's of burgh housing is complimentary and he mentions their glazed windows, chimneys and solid hewn-stone construction as well as their solid furniture, which he said was comparable with that used in Italy, Spain and France. This last was written in 1498, over sixty years after Piccolomini's record and after a significant improvement in urban living conditions had taken place. But the countryfolk lived much as they had done in the time of Froissart's *Chronicles*, judging from the latter's account.

Each of Henryson's *Fables* has a *moralitas* attached. The moral of the fable about the two mice is that everyone has his joys and his adversities and ought to make the most of his lot, even though it be small, for abundance and prosperity often lead to a bad end:

Blissed be the sempill lyfe withoutin dreid

says the poet stoically. The town mouse may live in comfort and dine well, but he has to contend with the cat (*i.e.* violence and disorder), who interrupts his meal and chases him all over the place. The country mouse takes herself off and returns to the security of her natural home.

The Cock and the Fox starts, like Chaucer's *Nun's Priest's Tale*, with a short description of a poor widow-woman who owned only a cock and some hens and earned her food by spinning on a distaff. Chaucer's widow had three large sows, three cows, a sheep, plenty of milk and brown bread, broiled bacon and sometimes an egg or two, as Chaucer quaintly puts it. Although described by him as poor and as living in a 'narwe cotage', she clearly enjoys less straitened circumstances than her Scottish sister. *The Tale of the Foxe that Begylit the Wolf in the Shadow of the Mone* starts by recalling the unhappy conditions of the peasants, who worked hard with primitive implements, while *The Tale of the Wolf and the Lamb* reflects the poor man's complaint about the seizure of his strip by landlords eager to evict him, a common practice at the time. The rise of the wool trade with Flanders encouraged land enclosure in Scotland as it did in England and the physical presence of any small tenant farmer could easily be ended at the expiry of the short leases then allowed. In the *moralitas* to this last fable,

Henryson describes three types of wolves, those who pervert the law to their own advantage and harass the poor man for a fee; powerful landlords whose greed is satisfied at the poor man's expense and who will take his 'mailling' or rented farm away from him; landowners by right of birth, who receive 'gressome' or annual rent until it suits them to evict their tenant on one pretext or another or

> With pykit[1] querrillis for to mak him fane
> To flit,[2] or pay his gressome new agane.

In the *Fables*, the result of the change from a feudal agricultural economy to a partially mercantile economy was recorded by a poet with a fine eye for detail and a wealth of human sympathy for poor and unfortunate country dwellers, open to all kinds of rapacity. The *nouveaux riches* in the growing towns he both despises and pities, as in the case of the town mouse, or the 'cadger' (itinerant merchant) whose calculating stinginess places him in a category far below that occupied by the generous town mouse. Another mouse, in *The Lion and the Mouse*, is said to represent the commons, unhappy because of the bad example shown them by their treasonable lords and princes:

> I the beseik[3] and all men for to pray
> That tressoun of[4] this cuntrie be exyld,
> And justice regne, and lordis keip thair fay[5]
> Unto thair soverane king, baith nycht and day.

a concluding sentiment exactly in accord with that of the author of *Wallace*, whose sympathies lay with the peasants alienated from rich, oppressive and capricious barons.

The Scots burgesses were politically weak and hardly affected legislation at all. During the fifteenth century their voice was rarely heard. Difficulties of overland communication and harsh weather conditions kept the inhabitants of one village or 'toun' from associating with those of another except at public gatherings such as the poets of *Christ's Kirk* or *Peblis to the Play* describe. The town burgesses sided with the King but lacked the cohesion

---

[1] forced   [2] remove   [3] beseech you   [4] from   [5] faith

needed to present the barons with a united front and so maintain their own independence. After James III's murder following Sauchieburn public outcry against the regicide forced the estates 'spiritual and temporal' to take steps to preserve the internal peace of the land because of 'the heavy murmur and voice of the people'. No punitive measures were taken against the dead King's supporters—on the contrary, a general amnesty was accorded 'to all the burgesses, merchants and unlanded men' who had fought for James against the adherents of Angus, Drummond, Errol, Glamis, Gray, Hepburn, Home, Huntly and other baronial families.

The spiritual estate, the clergy, did little to alleviate the distresses of the peasantry. For one thing, the high prelates were themselves scions of these selfsame aristocratic families, and the few enlightened men in their ranks, like Archibald Hay and William Elphinstone, were unable to bring about changes. The merchants and the craftsmen, of the class of Henryson's cadger, could look after their own individual interests and were usually able to slip the clutches of the 'unbelled' cat who, for both Langland and Henryson, represented their warring overlords and, for the Earl of Angus, James III himself. According to a popular anecdote, Angus resolved to 'bell the cat' (*i.e.* face the king with an ultimatum demanding the surrender of his favourites) in 1482. However, the peasantry had to wait until the advent of John Knox before they found their own champion.

Henryson devotes some of his stories to criticism of the clergy and the law. *The Fox and the Wolf* is aimed at mendicant friars and their slack methods of receiving confessions. *The Sheep and the Dog* castigates the courts, ecclesiastical and civil alike. The Sheep is sued for a piece of bread by the Dog. The church court is presided over by a Wolf and a Raven serves the summons. The Fox is clerk and notary of the court and the Kite and the Vulture are the advocates. The point of the satire is that the law depends upon so many authorities that debate obscures justice. The *moralitas* explains that the Sheep represents the Commons and the Wolf a sheriff, or judge in the civil courts. All officials are corrupt and the Sheep, robbed by legal process of what was rightfully his, shivers with cold in the middle of winter, and asks God why he is so long asleep.

> Se how I am, be fraud, maistrie and slicht
> Peillit full bair
>
> [Look how I am stripped completely bare by
> fraud, tyranny and deception]

he complains, and goes on to deplore the scarcity of those who will execute proper justice and protect the poor man from oppression. Langland's sentiments in *Piers Plowman* are comparable, though Langland is more impersonal and his illustrations, graphic though they be, lack the poignancy of Henryson's. The unfortunate Sheep who pleads his own case with considerable skill and merit, though full of fear, is, like all Henryson's animals, endowed with delicately etched human qualities and the poet enlists the sympathy of his audience first of all for this particular Sheep left desolate, then for all oppressed men suffering under petty official tyranny.

In a study of Henryson's poems as they reflect the social and economic life and times of the last quarter of the fifteenth century, M. W. Stearns draws many parallels between contemporary historical incidents and references in the works, particularly in the *Fables*. James III's relations with his nobles, his favourites and his treacherous friends are suggested in *The Paddock and the Mouse*. The Paddock (Frog) seeks to drown the Mouse after gaining her confidence but just as he is about to do so and the victim is crying for a priest, a Kite swoops down and grabs the treacherous Paddock, whom he rips to pieces with his bill. Stearns believes that this fable refers directly to the Duke of Albany's intrigues against his brother James III and that certain phrases in the poem relate to actual incidents in the plot-laden career of Albany, but the pattern of seduction with fine words is too general to be closely linked with specific events. It may be, however, that Henryson was thinking of Albany as a type of traitor appropriately cast in a fable.

The Wolf and the Wether relates how a wether, clad in the skin of a dead dog, chases a wolf, who kills the wether when he realises how he has been tricked. Henryson's *moralitas* includes three stanzas condemning those who imitate the high-born in dress and habits though they be no more than servants. He enjoins such people to know their places and not to climb too high lest they fall from the ladder. Such criticism may have been a none too veiled reference to James's favourites but, again, like all fables, it has a universal implication. Henryson used Aesop's ponderous morality as a basis for topical criticism but, tempting as it may be to draw exact parallels, one should guard against treating fables as though they were historical documents. Their outstanding quality is their integrity as sketches of human character and the cunning presentation of small farm and forest animals in their accepted categories according to the authority of medieval bestiaries—the guileful fox, the simple, innocent and steadfast mouse, the predatory kite, the helpless sheep, the vain cock and the voracious wolf—all mingling easily with types of contemporary human beings, representative of the three estates living in their uneasy relationship. Moreover, the supposition by M. P. McDiarmid and others that the *Fables* were composed before 1480 rules out many of Stearns' precise parallels with events known to have occurred after that year.

Henryson himself is practically an anonymous figure. He is described in MSS and printed texts as 'schoolmaster of Dunfermline', a royal burgh and the site of a Benedictine Abbey which probably housed a school. A certain schoolmasterly air lingers in many of his poems and his adaptation of Aesop for purposes of moral instruction suggests his fondness for teaching the young wordly wisdom calmly and benignly by peopling his narratives with attractive little creatures like mice and frogs such as children might keep as pets, sheep and fowl such as they might see in the fields round about, and wolves, symbols of terror and violence (but by 1480 practically extinct in lowland Scotland, so not likely to appear in Dunfermline Toun). Caxton's *History of Reynard the Fox* (1481) and his *Aesop's Fables* (1484) appeared too late to be thought of as sources for Henryson's *Fables*, but Aesop had been studied for centuries as part of the grammar school curriculum. The Scots poet probably depended on French models for his tales, and numerous parallels are traceable. His tone is impersonal but not with the impersonality that implies remoteness and lack of concern. Dunbar, in comparison, seems to think mainly of himself and his own insecurity at Court. Lyndsay, composing his satires at least half a century later under greatly changed conditions, did not have to be so much on guard against causing offence.

·　　·　　·　　·　　·　　·

Henryson's finest poem is *The Testament of Cresseid*. It begs to be considered in conjunction with Chaucer's *Troilus and Criseyde*, since the Scots poet alleged that the source of his literary inspiration was his reading not only of Chaucer's original, but also of an extension of the story of Criseyde's life after she had deserted Troilus for Diomede. It is not known for certain whether or not this second tale of the immortal lovers really existed outside Henryson's imagination but, poetical fiction or not, this 'uther quair', or book, is the device by which he justifies his own urge to set down a further version continuing along similar lines.

The moral tone and philosophical content of *The Testament* is medieval and the literary model is 'Chaucerian' though the temperature is lowered sharply from that of Chaucer's sultry atmosphere to a chilly northern level—at least forty degrees of difference. The vocabulary and treatment is humanistic. John MacQueen's *Robert Henryson* (1967) refers to the poet's additions to the standard vocabulary, which are comparable with Skelton's, to his knowledge of Latin authors and to his acquaintance with Boccaccio's *Genealogia Deorum Gentilium*, from which his information about the assembly of deities was derived. Caxton printed Boethius' *De Consolatione Philosophiae*, containing the story of Orpheus and Eurydice, in 1478 and Chaucer's *Troilus and Criseyde* in 1483, whence it is arguable that these novel printed books stimulated Henryson to compose his own domesticated versions of classical epic. In these respects he shares something of the interests of English humanists but in his subject-matter and his revealed delight in exploring the resources of Latin as an adjunct to English he, and his contemporary Gavin Douglas, are a century ahead of their time.

The poet is writing his *Testament* in late March. The moon is shining into the glazed windows of his room. Outside, the night sky is cloudless after a bitter north wind and a hailstorm have purified the air. Over a fire, with a drink to fortify his flagging spirits and shield him from the cold, he takes up Chaucer's *Troilus and Criseyde*, muses over Troilus's joys and sorrows, then, to keep himself awake, he starts to read another book describing Criseyde's later life and miserable death. It is this story which he takes upon himself to relate. Henryson speaks as though he were a man conscious of his years, no longer capable of experiencing love at first hand. This encourages scholars to date the poem at about 1500.

Henryson's narrative, set in a contemporary Scottish town which bears some resemblance to Dunfermline, borrows four characters from Chaucer—Troilus, Criseyde, or Cresseid as Henryson calls her, Calchas, her renegade father, the priest of Apollo (turned into the priest of Venus in the Scots poem) and Diomede, cast in simple terms as lustful and inconstant, who seduces Cresseid, tires of her after a while and sends her 'ane lybell of repudie' or divorce bill so that she is left in no doubt that his interest in her has gone for ever. 'Repudie' signifies rejection and not 'divorce', as from a legal marriage.

Cresseid, stranded without a friend, becomes a courtesan, a plaything of Fortune. For this reason Henryson does not censure her too harshly for her 'brukkilnes', as other men do, but contents himself with a reference to Fortune's responsibility for her guilt. Cresseid, whose promiscuity lowers her status to that of a common prostitute, eventually returns to her father, keeper of the temple dedicated to Venus and her son Cupid, and reveals her plight to him. He takes her in and shows great sympathy—in this respect Henryson alters the function of Calchas, whom Chaucer describes as avaricious and treacherous. Concealing herself from the people at large, Cresseid makes secret remonstration to Venus and Cupid, whom she blames for her plight and for making false promises to her. She regrets that she ever made sacrifice to such gods.

Falling into a swoon, she has a vision. Cupid rings a silver bell and the seven planets descend from their spheres, each dressed in his or her appropriate garments as determined by astrological tradition—astrology, which included astronomy, was a popular science of the day, and James III, IV and V were all interested in it. Henryson's source for the details of this part of the work is Boccaccio and several scholars, including Stearns, MacQueen and Fox in his recent (1968) edition of *The Testament*, have examined the literary implications of this 'assembly of heathen gods'.

Cupid protests against Cresseid's blaming him and his mother Venus. Judgment is referred by Mercury to the highest and the lowest of the gods, namely, Saturn and Cynthia (The Moon), each of whom returns a verdict on the accused. Saturn, touching her with his frosty wand, announces that her physical beauty, her vibrant personality, her position and her riches are to be taken from her. Her mirth will become melancholy and she will die in penury. Cynthia adds further details of the physical affliction that is to strike her:

> Thy cristall ene minglit with blude I mak,
> Thy voice sa cleir, unplesand hoir and hace,
> Thy lustie lyre ouirspred with spottis blak,
> And lumpis haw appeirand in thy face.
> Quhair thou cumis ilk man sall fle the place.
> This sall thou go begging fra hous to hous
> With cop and clapper lyke ane lazarous.

[Your crystal eyes I make bloodshot; your voice, clear as it is now, will be unpleasing, hoarse and harsh to the ear; your fine skin will be covered with black spots and leaden lumps will begin to appear in your face. No matter where you go, every man shall flee from your path. In such a way will you have to go begging from one house to the next, with cup and clapper, as a leper should.] (337–43)

At this point Cresseid awakens, to find that the horrible dream has turned into a far more horrible reality. Her face has indeed lost its beauty and she is stricken with remorse. When her father discovers what has happened he wrings his hands and joins her in her new-found sorrow. Eventually she asks him to conduct her to the leper hospital at the edge of the town, so that

o

no-one may learn of her affliction. This he does, and every day sends some part of his alms to the 'spitaill hous'. No-one recognises her, not even those who had known her in happier days, since the loathsome disease has changed her appearance so much.

The next seven stanzas are given over to her 'Complaint', in which she compares her past beauty and comfort, elegant living and handsome companions to her present state of ugliness and distress—a familiar rhetorical device for emphasising such change. Her weeping attracts the attention of another female leper, who tells her that tears will avail her nothing and that she should make of necessity a virtue and settle down to live as lepers do. This Cresseid does, moving from place to place, compelled to beg in order to eat and protect herself from the cold. This stress on coldness is characteristic of Scots poets, and the author of *Wallace*, Dunbar and Douglas all dwell upon it as well as on other manifestations of a bleak northern winter.

Now Troilus, a conventional gentleman-knight, enters the scene, fresh from a raid, galloping past with his gallant company on the way back to Troy. The lepers cry for alms and rattle their clappers. Cresseid looks up and sees Troilus. He returns her gaze and, as he does so, it comes into his mind that he has seen her before somewhere. She fails to recognise him, presumably because her sight has been affected by the disease, though Henryson is too subtle to explain this incident logically. Yet Troilus is reminded of

> The sweit visage and amorous blenking[1]
> Of fair Cresseid, sumtyme[2] his awin darling.
> (503–4)

and thinks he sees his beloved just as a strong memory may be recalled by certain stimuli:

> The idole of ane thing in cace may be
> Sa deip imprentit in the fantasy
> That it deludis the wittis outwardly,
> And sa appeiris in forme and lyke estait,
> Within the mind as it was figurait.

[1] glances [2] once

[the image (of Cresseid as he had known her) of a thing may in certain circumstances be so deeply etched in the imagination (the faculty of storing images) that it deceives rational thought, and so the image appears in the bodily likeness just as it had been formed in the memory.]   (507–11)

Admirers of Henryson from William Godwin to George Saintsbury have picked out this incident of the brief reunion of the ill-starred couple as being one of the most felicitous conceptions in any love-literature. According to Aristotelian psychology and related theories of the imagination well known during the Middle Ages, the behaviour of lovers is linked to the degree of intensity with which the image of the beloved is imprinted in the memory by the imagination. Italian, French and English poets, including Jean de Meun, Dante, Boccaccio, Chaucer and Gower among others, depended on this conception of the 'image'. One later example is found in *The Kingis Quair*, possibly by James I of Scotland, in which the image referred to is aural, not visual, namely, the bell ringing to summon the poet to matins, which urges him to tell his story. Since *The Quair* may not be by James at all, but instead a Chaucerian work by a contemporary of Henryson writing in the late fifteenth century, the appropriate stanza is worthy of quotation here:

> Thoght I tho to myself, 'Quhat may this be?'
>   This is myn awin ymagynacioun;
> It is no lyf that spekis unto me;
>   It is a bell, or that impressioun
>   Off my thoght causith this illusioun,
> That dooth me think so nycely in this wis:'
> And so befell as I schall you devis.
> (Text from W. Mackay Mackenzie's ed. [1939], stanza 12.)

Another factor contributing to this complicated effect is the pervasive presence of leprosy, which has half blinded Cresseid. Many commentators on the poem have examined the meaning and significance of this disease in medieval times and some have shown themselves overmuch inclined to dwell on its nature both medically and historically. Henryson's description of the external symptoms of leprosy was the first record of the incidence of Greek elephantiasis (Hansen's bacillus) in northern Europe, an observation recorded by Simpson in 1841, but the Biblical and medieval use of the term had application to a great many afflictions which were not in any way related to Hansen's bacillus, such as bubonic plague, smallpox, syphilis rashes, and lesions, psoriasis, scabies, boils, sores and species of horse-and plant-mange. The name 'Lazarus' became a synonym for the disease or for its carrier and 'leprosy' might signify a beggar's state of misery, poverty and social sequestration.

As his parody of contemporary prescriptions, *Sum Practysis of Medecyne*, suggests, Henryson was keenly interested in medical matters and *The Testament* shows how expert he is at describing the external symptoms of a disease, but that Cresseid's disease is what is now recognised as leprosy is open to question. Some scholars state that the most likely interpretation is that a venereal disease, an advanced stage of syphilis, is responsible for Cresseid's semi-blindness and lost beauty, and this would certainly fit in with the poet's previous account of her promiscuity; as he says, rumour has it that she was forced to become the common property of the Greek Court:

Sa gigotlike,[1] takand thy foull plesance.

he scolds her, though his sympathy for her plight overbears his disgust at her conduct.

Henryson's emphasis on a repulsive disease is to some extent characteristic of late medieval sermon-makers who loved to threaten their flocks with sensational physical punishments, describe the torments of hell in enthusiastic terms and dwell on the loathsome corruptions of the grave. But he is too sophisticated a poet to be explained as though he were merely following a clumsy convention, especially since a historical parallel may be drawn which fits *The Testament*.

About 1500 a violent outbreak of syphilis, lately introduced

---

[1] wantonly

into the country from the Continent, was recorded in Edinburgh. Since it was what is known, ironically in this case, as a 'virgin' disease, *i.e.* one against which the body had not yet developed natural defences, it was often fatal. Quarantine regulations were announced, designed to prevent the spreading of 'grandgore' or 'glengore', as syphilis was called, and Dunbar's scabrous poem *To the Quene* is devoted to an account of how 'the pockis' had laid men low and should be guarded against by surgery and abstinence:

> I saw coclinkis me besyd
> The young men to thair howses gyd
>   Had bettir ligget in the stockis;
> Sum fra the bordell wald nocht byd,
>   Quhill that thai gatt the Spanyie Pockis

[I saw prostitutes close by, leading young men to their houses who would have been better lying in the stocks for some of them would not stay away from the brothels until they had picked up the Spanish pox]   (26–30.)

'Ane Grandgore Act' had been passed in September, 1497. It called for all light women to desist from their vices and the sin of venery and to earn their livings by hard work or be branded on the cheek. The Act even sought to deport and isolate infected persons on the island of Inchkeith in the Firth of Forth. This entry on the statute book may not have been unconnected with the arrival in Scotland of Perkin Warbeck and his motley army in November, 1495—many of these soldiers of fortune had seen service in Naples and it is from Naples in this period of French garrison occupation that some medical historians trace the first European contact with the disease. From what one may learn from contemporary accounts, it appears that in its secondary stage it killed thousands during the first quarter of the sixteenth century in Scotland, and descriptions of its effects, especially on the face, which was frequently eaten away, leave little to the imagination. It is quite within the bounds of possibility that, before death supervened, the features could have been eroded and a woman of beauty made utterly repulsive by gummy tumours. The plight of Cresseid is from this point of view convincing and the harshness of her voice, mentioned twice by Henryson, is consistent with erosion of the palate and uvula, results noted by contemporary physicians.

Yet Troilus is generated by a spark of love for this ugly remnant of womanhood which sends his body into a trembling fit. He sweats, becomes physically weak and alters colour but still neither he nor Cresseid actually recognises the other. The physiological effects are those suggested by courtly love traditions, but this near-recognition, presented by Henryson with such exquisite finesse, is without parallel in contemporary literature. It shows the vitality of the Aristotelian tradition in Scotland at this time, the verbal economy with which the poet has created this striking effect and a degree of intellectual and emotional refinement which far surpasses that of his fellow poets. For an insight comparable to Henryson's one must turn back to the bedchamber dialogue in Fit III of *Sir Gawain and the Green Knight* or forward to the domestic tragedy of *Othello*.

The rest of *The Testament* is anti-climax, for its highest point has already been reached. Troilus throws Cresseid a purse of money and trinkets and rides away, 'pensive in hart', keeping his place in the saddle with great difficulty. From first to last he has not spoken a single word. The lepers crowd around and comment on the unusually large gift with which Cresseid has been rewarded. Soon one of them mentions the name of the donor and Cresseid falls to the ground in a thrill of pain and bewails her sorry lot, blaming herself in an agony of remorse and warning other lovers to cherish true love. She sits down and inscribes her testament, committing her body to the worms and toads (commonly believed to devour corpses), her personal possessions to the lepers who will bury her and her ring, which her lover had once given her, to Troilus, so that he will know the sad manner of her passing. Then she dies. Troilus receives the ring (Chaucer's brooch and belt are in possession of Diomede) and laments. He is supposed to have erected a marble tombstone in her memory, and had an inscription in letters of gold placed on it, the legend

> Lo, fair ladyis, Cresseid, of Troyis toun
> Sumtyme countit the flour of womanheid,
> Under this stane, lait lipper,[1] lyis deid.
>
> (607–9)

and the poem ends with an exhortation to all women, for whom the author says his 'ballet schort' has been composed, to

> Ming[2] not your lufe with fals deceptioun

and to keep the unhappy death of Cresseid in mind. He leaves a vision of suffering womanhood as well as an impression of Cresseid as a fickle light-of-love who was made to suffer far more than she herself had unthinkingly made Troilus to suffer. Such is his delicacy of touch, however, that Henryson succeeds in imparting a warmth of human interest to what in the hands of a lesser writer might have been merely a symbol of misogyny. *The Testament of Cresseid* is a 'man's poem' and does not invite the audience to say of Henryson what Gavin Douglas said a few years later of Chaucer, namely, that he was 'all womanis frend' (*Aeneid*, Prologue to Book I, 449). Nevertheless, the Scottish poem is not, like Chaucer's, open to 'psychological' interpretation as a work in which courtly conventions get in the way of its author's supposed desire to present character studies of the lovers as though they were real people. Henryson is a stern moralist, but capable of writing compassionately about a woman of whom he disapproves in the hope that other women will be guided by his remonstrance. His 'man's poem' seems to have been composed with a female audience in mind and this, if nothing else, marks Henryson as an optimist.

· · · · · ·

The historical background to Dunbar's poems is the reign of James IV, who was born in 1473 and died at the Battle of Flodden in 1513. His father, James III, had been a lively clever man, whose better qualities were unfortunately cancelled out by tendencies that unfitted him to rule a country like Scotland at the time he was compelled to do so. In the end, he was murdered after fleeing

---

[1] leper   [2] mingle, spoil

from the battlefield of Sauchieburn in 1488, supposedly by a man who claimed to be a priest. James IV, fifteen at the time of his accession, inherited a kingdom that might have been in a state of leaderless anarchy, but which the victors at Sauchieburn, the rebel nobles, sensibly turned into a sound administration, with the rightful king as nominal ruler, under apprenticeship to be the effective monarch.

Relations with England were troubled but officially James IV and Henry VII maintained their outward show of friendship, overcast by the suspicion on Henry's part that the rebel party which had overthrown James III because of his partiality to England would not be long in attacking the English garrison at Berwick. Occasional breaches of the 1488 treaty of non-hostility occurred, especially at sea, but on the whole the two nations maintained it. James IV, however, unlike his father, had visions of military grandeur. As we know, he received Perkin Warbeck and his followers in 1495 and married him to a relative, Lady Katharine Gordon, arranging a tournament to mark the occasion. The Spanish were anxious to promote peace between England and Scotland, so that England might not be distracted from membership of the Holy League which the French invasion of Italy in 1494 had forced into existence. Free of Scottish interference, Henry VII would henceforth be unhampered in his anti-French campaign. The marriage between Catharine of Aragon and Henry VII's elder son, Arthur, the heir apparent, was part of the Spanish policy of attracting England to their cause. Similarly, James IV was encouraged by promises of matrimony with an unspecified Spanish princess or *infanta* and agreed to keep the peace with the English King and abandon the 'Duke of York', as Warbeck styled himself.

However, James discovered from a Spanish ambassador sent to him by Ferdinand of Spain, Pedro d'Ayala, whose letters about Scotland have already been referred to as an important source of information about conditions in the country, that no further reliance could be placed on Spanish promises. He thereupon launched a campaign against England in support of the 'Duke of York'. D'Ayala, whose sympathies were with James and whose accounts of the King and the country were extremely flattering, accompanied the invasion. The main interest of the Scots army was in looting and rapine and not at all in Warbeck, who soon returned to Scotland. Polydore Vergil describes how d'Ayala ('a man not learned but very clever and exceedingly discreet') wrote to Henry in an effort to make peace and actually became an impartial mediator between him and James. Henry was as impressed by the Spaniard as James had been and promoted him to several ecclesiastical benefices in England. After much discussion, peace was established on condition that James should expel Warbeck from Scotland, which he did in the summer of 1497. James' campaign had cost him a great deal of money and prestige and had gained him little or nothing except the renewed suspicion of England, as d'Ayala and other counsellors repeatedly told him.

Breaches of the truce at Norham in 1498 provoked James to send belligerent communications to Henry and to d'Ayala, asking the latter to intervene, but Henry, described cynically by Polydore Vergil as 'a lover of peace whenever it could be secured without damage to himself', wrote conciliatory letters to James. A suggestion made by Henry in 1497 that he should marry the English king's daughter Princess Margaret Tudor, and at first ignored by James, was revived by the Scottish king himself. Such a matrimonial alliance would, it was thought, be a sound basis for friendship between the two countries. Richard Fox, Bishop of Durham, was commissioned to arrange the marriage, to take place when the child, only nine at the time, reached marriageable age. James agreed, but asked, with proverbial Scots canniness, for the dowry to be paid immediately. Henry, with equal caution, paid half. A papal dispensation was obtained in July, 1500, to permit the marriage, since the bride and bridegroom had a common great-grandfather, John Beaufort, Marquis of Dorset, and thus brought the projected union within prohibited degrees of consanguinity.

R. L. Mackie in *King James IV of Scotland* (1958), chapter 4, provides a detailed account of the events leading up to and the elaborate preparations for this wedding, celebrated by Dunbar in *The Thistle and the Rose*. Pageants, music, dancing and a sumptuous ceremony marked the occasion. Both Dunbar and Gavin Douglas, the poet of *Eneados*, at that time Provost of the Collegiate Church of St Giles, were present when the Queen-to-be arrived from Dalkeith. An anonymous poet, perhaps Dunbar, wrote what is, in fact, the oldest Scottish Court song known:

> Younge tendre plant of pulcritud,
> Descendyd of imperyalle blode;
> Freshe fragrant floure of fayre hede shene
> Welcum of Scotland to be Quene!

(*Poems of William Dunbar*, ed. W. Mackay Mackenzie [1933].)

and in Holyrood Abbey on 8 August, 1503, a new alliance was made between the traditional enemies. James became Henry VII's son-in-law and, since Prince Arthur had died in 1502, the match placed him third in line for the English throne. Arthur's widow Catherine of Aragon married her brother-in-law Henry. Henry succeeded his father in April, 1509, and Anglo-Scottish relations continued to be friendly. England and France made a treaty in March, 1510, and it looked for a time as though the 'auld alliance' was to become an anachronism.

Yet James still maintained immature romantic visions of himself as the leader of a crusade against the Turk, tried to ally himself with the Venetian Republic, built a fleet of ships and postured as a warrior king, although he was naively ignorant of European affairs, the implications of the Holy League and the price the 'auld alliance' would cost him if he dared to revive it out of a swashbuckling desire to flaunt his own 'honour'. Louis XII, threatened by a ring of foes which included England, wanted James to invade England and so pin down Henry's armies destined for the war against France. James and Louis made a treaty in 1512, the most important clause of which was that neither would enter into truce with England without the consent of the other.

Largely in order to fulfil his promises, James prepared to attack England in the summer of 1513 and, after a final exchange of acrimonious despatches, a state of open war, promoted mainly by James, existed between the two countries. The Earl of Surrey's army met James' at Flodden and stopped the invasion. The date was Friday, 9 September. The English estimate of Scots dead was, according to Polydore Vergil, ten thousand, twice as many as the

English side lost. Other contemporary estimates put the English dead at fifteen hundred, the Scots at over ten thousand. Among them was James himself, 'wounded in two places . . . showing great dignity even now that the life had gone out of him', to quote Polydore's account. The poet Dunbar is popularly supposed to have been one of the ten thousand dead 'flowers of the forest'. Scottish military prestige never properly recovered from this blow, which for historians has long symbolised the end of an era. Flodden witnessed a waste of life, for, even if James had won, he could not have consolidated his victory, and the opinion of professional historians today is that Henry's ultimate vengeance, a full-scale invasion of Scotland, would have come a year later with terrible effects on property as well as on lives within Scotland herself. Either way, Flodden was a calamity, though the fact of the swift carnage makes the defeat more poignant.

James' yearning for military glory had led him and his people to disaster. The country lacked leadership after Flodden, for many of the mortal casualities were nobles and high prelates. James's widow Margaret enjoyed intrigue and the young James V became a pawn in a power game. For the next forty years Scotland was split on the question of whether the 'auld alliance' with France should be maintained, on the degree of reformation to be aimed at and on foreign relations generally, but the immediate effects of Flodden have usually been exaggerated and romanticised. In fact, policies continued exactly as before, with war against England planned. The complications of Scottish government under a Regency, the administration of Albany, the evolution of rival political groups, the growth of the influence of Angus and the Douglases, the alignment of James V with Catholicism and his inevitable clash with Henry VIII in 1542 are all historical events, not literary ones, so need not detain us. They provided poor stimulus to poetry-making but the uneasiness of the times inspired a small number of satirists, of whom Lyndsay is the best known, to pen complaints concerning political and clerical abuses.

Scotland found herself in a strange position at the end of James V's reign. James V was ready to go to war for the 'auld religion' and had forfeited the confidence of many of his subjects. Henry wished to persuade the Scots to follow his own anti-Papal policies, which were intensified by the English king's own excommunication in 1539. In the 1530s James's unpopularity rapidly increased and his selfish and acquisitive methods succeeded in uniting those who wished for a tightening of ecclesiastical discipline with those who saw advantages in breaking with Rome altogether. The Battle of Solway Moss, fought on 24 November, 1542, was won by the English. Within the Scots ranks there was mutiny and voluntary surrender on the part of leading nobles, who had no enthusiasm for the cause of their King. James himself died a few weeks later. Mary, Queen of Scots, who reigned from 1542–67, inherited a kingdom fought over by English pro-Reformers and French pro-Catholics and their respective Scottish adherents. In 1544 and 1545 the English invaded the Border countries and pillaged the countryside. The French sent financial aid and armed expeditions to Scotland to help their allies to eject the English, whose invasion had hardened into a prolonged occupation. French interests in Scotland, whose Queen was French, led to what amounted to a French occupation, in which high administrative offices were given to Frenchmen, and several thousand professional soldiers from France garrisoned Scottish strongpoints. Scotland found herself becoming a tool of the French in her campaign against England, now allied by the marriage of Mary Tudor to Philip II of Spain, with France's enemies the Spanish. In 1558 the French were seeking to recapture Calais, England's only remaining foothold on French soil, and, with Scottish assistance, to gain control of Berwick, England's only remaining foothold on Scots soil. Such a policy held little joy for the Scots, particularly since a proposal was made that, for the first time in their history, taxation should be levied in order to support a paid army of mercenaries.

It is hardly surprising, therefore, that in such an age of political and religious upheaval, of lost Scottish causes, of unstable government by regencies, factions, vested interests of one kind and another, and by legitimate rulers scarcely fitted by temperament and character to deal with the situations facing them, the arts were neglected. There was no Scottish Court after James IV's wherein a cultural Renaissance, similar to those in England,

France and elsewhere, might have flowered. The main Scottish Renaissance died with James at Flodden. Douglas' translation of Vergil's *Aeneid*, which preceded Surrey's partial rendering by many years, was really symbolic of the end as well as the peak of a literary tradition. Political trends from that time forth led inevitably to Union of the Crowns (1603), a slow but certain weakening of nationalist expression, and the adaptation of written Scots to serve the purposes of satire and political propaganda rather than of literary creation in classically inspired styles.

However, the Renaissance as it occurred in Scotland did continue after the 1520s, though in a less spectacular manner than might otherwise have been the case. The humanist historians, like Major, Boece, Bellenden and Buchanan, and the three Scottish universities, particularly Aberdeen (of which Boece was first Principal), were internationally known and Scots students no longer felt the same urge to go to France for advanced studies. Skill in Latin was admired in Scotland as much if not more than anywhere else in Europe and the standard was high. Even before Knox, the number of young Scots receiving instruction in Latin was relatively great. James IV's Parliament of 13 July, 1496, had passed the first Scottish 'Education Act', enjoining all barons and substantial freeholders to send their eldest sons to the grammar school from the age of eight or nine, to remain until

> thai be competentlie foundit and have perfite latyne, and thereftir to remane thre yeris at the scule of art and Jure, sua that thai may have knawledge and understanding of the lawis. Throw the quhilkis Justice may reigne universalie throw all the realme (quoted in R. L. Mackie, *King James IV of Scotland*, p. 82.)

and although Scotland may have been a much later imbiber at the Italian *fons et origo* of the new learning than other countries of that Europe of which she then considered herself an integral part, the Renaissance influence was effective in Scotland. It emerged less in the form of intellectual dependence on ancient models than in that of freedom of conscience in politics and religion. Gavin Douglas' reverence for the classics is tempered by an independent approach to the problems of translating them which no English translator of the sixteenth century possessed. Lyndsay's poems glow with humanity rather than with humanism and the literature of dissent occupies a more significant place in Scottish cultural history than in English at this time.

Courtly poetry in Scotland was centred on Alexander Scott, probably the same Alexander Scott who studied music in Paris in 1540 and eight years later was an organist in Scotland. One of the poems in the Egerton MS:

> Lo what it is to love!
> Lerne ye that list to prove
> At me I say, no ways that may
> The growndyd greiff remove,
> My liff alwaie that doeth decaie,
> Lo what it is to love!

included in the Wyatt canon, is ascribed by a contemporary (George Bannatyne, who compiled the Bannatyne MS) to Scott, and there may have been some exchange of poems between the two shortly before Wyatt's death. Scott and some of the other love poets included within his circle, (but who are really anonymous inasmuch as little or nothing is known about their personal lives), made up an enclosed group, whose 'courtliness' seems to have been an expression of longing for a kind of life which was not possible for them.

After James IV's death, the atmosphere of cultural sophistication which he and his father before him tried to generate was dissipated in the uncertainties of the regency that followed. Whatever his faults, James IV was known and liked by his people, whom he met by travelling around the country and joining in their entertainments. Pageants, summer revels, competitive sports like wrestling and shooting with the bow, tennis, horsemanship, hunting, hawking, bowling and breeding dogs were among the many activities patronised by the King. In speaking foreign languages he was said (by d'Ayala, who probably exaggerated) to be proficient in Gaelic, Latin, French, Spanish, Flemish and Italian and to be a great reader of sacred and profane books. He had his own musicians and enjoyed dancing and card-playing. A colourful and attractive figure, capable of extracting great personal devotion from his subjects, he bears a superficial resemblance to Henry VIII, whose versatility as a Renaissance man dedicated to the cultivation of both mind and body is well known.

. . . . . .

William Dunbar, the poet of James IV's Court, is a personal poet, who sees an unreliable world from his own point of view, that of the solitary underdog, seeking in vain for a fair deal for himself and commenting wryly when others are accorded the recognition which he himself thinks ought to be his own. He was very much a man of this Court, which seems to have been a hotbed of intrigues and ambition motivated by greed, if one is to accept the picture given of it by Dunbar himself. It must be remembered, however, that Dunbar was for most of his adult life an unsuccessful seeker after patronage, possibly in the form of a benefice, (although it is not certain that the poet was in Holy Orders,) certainly in the form of a pension, which he eventually secured. His view of the Court may therefore have been exaggerated, and although his opinions on the life and times were consistent, the interest they generate is not that of an historical document; like Lyndsay after him, but with different motives, Dunbar has something to say about the malice, selfishness, spuriousness and bitter-sweet character of human existence in a community of self-seeking men and women which is not tied to the time or place of composition.

Very little reliable information has come down to us about Dunbar himself. He lived from about 1460 and disappeared from public record after the Battle of Flodden in 1513. His active life as a poet was presumably spent at James IV's Court, which moved around with the King from one residence to another. Several poems are addressed to the King directly, and some others are apparently intended for His Majesty's edification; most of them are supplications for favours, or complaints of a quasi-autobiographical nature, though what seems to be a personal statement may be no more than a conventional observation in the 'complaint' tradition. More than any other poet of the period, however, Dunbar succeeds in conveying the impression that he is speaking for and about himself:

> Nane can remeid[1] my maledie
> Sa weill as ye, sir, veralie;
> With ane benefice ye may preiff,[2]
> And gif I mend not haistalie,
> Exces of thocht lat[3] me mischeif.
>
> I wes in youthe, on nureice kne,[4]
> Cald dandillie,[5] bischop, dandillie,
> And quhone[6] that age now dois me greif,[7]
> A sempill vicar I can not be:
> Excess of thocht dois me mischeif.
>
> *(To the King)*

and in *The Petition of the Gray Horse, Auld Dunbar*, he concludes a sustained comparison of himself to an elderly steed, who has given long service and now deserves a pension, with the King's simulated reply:

> Efter our wrettingis,[8] thesaurer
> Tak in this gray hors, Auld Dumbar,
> Quhilk[9] in my aucht[10] with service trew
> In lyart[11] changeit is in hew.
> Gar hows him[12] now aganis this Yuill[13]
> And busk[14] him lyk ane bischopis muill[15]
> For with my hand I have indost[16]
> To pay quhatevir his trappouris[17] cost
>
> *(Petition)*

lines which are to be explained by the fact that the poet had not received an annual gift of clothing to which he was entitled.

But such biographical information that may be drawn from the poem is extremely scanty. He occasionally wrote about real personages, such as the Italian favourite of James IV, Father John Damien, who in 1504, was made Abbot of Tongland, in Kirk-

---

[1] cure   [2] prove (it)   [3] does   [4] nurse's knee   [5] darling
[6] when   [7] saddens me   [8] In accordance with our written instructions
[9] which   [10] possession   [11] grey   [12] have him stabled   [13] Yule
[14] dress   [15] mule   [16] endorsed   [17] trappings

cudbright. Damien is mentioned in Lindsay of Pitscottie's *Chronicle of Scotland*. Pitscottie says:

> This Abbot tuik in hand to flie with wingis, and to be in France befoir the saidis ambassadours: and to that effect he causet mak ane pair of wingis of fedderis, quhilks beand fessinit apoun him, he flew of the castell wall of Striveling, bot schortlie he fell to the ground and brak his thee bane; bot the wyt thairof he ascryvit to that thair was sum hen fedderis in the wingis, quhilk yarnit and covet the mydding and not the skyis.

> [This Abbot took in hand to fly by means of wings and to be in France before the said ambassadors; and to this end he had a pair of wings made out of feathers, by means of which, when they had been attached to him, he flew from the wall of Stirling Castle, but soon fell to the ground and broke his thigh bone. But he put the blame for that on the fact that some of the feathers were from hens, which were attracted to the midden and not to the skies.]

Dunbar's *The Fenyeit[1] Freir of Tungland* attacks this late medieval Daedalus and in graphic terms describes his ill-fortuned flight; in ridiculing it the poet is laughing at the folly of all high flyers who come to grief, as this one did, in a mire, pecked at by the fowls of the air and of the barnyard who resent the intruder decked in his fine feathers.

> He schewre[2] his feddreme[3] that was schene[4]
> And slippit owt of it full clene,
> And in a mire, up to the ene[5],
>   Amang the glar[6] did glyd[7].
> The fowlis all at the fedrem dang[8],
> As at a monster thame amang,
> Quhill[9] all the pennis[10] of it owsprang
>   In till the air full wyde.
>   (105–12)

[1] pretended	[2] tore off	[3] feathers	[4] bright	[5] eyes	[6] mud
[7] wallow	[8] beat	[9] until	[10] feathers

P

Although he calls 'The Feinyeit Freir' a murderer, a charlatan and bad priest, Dunbar is using a real personage as a symbol of the trickery which secured benefices at a time when an honest hard-working man like himself could not do so. In *Complaint to the King* he makes a list of the rascals who gain promotion when men of birth and education, again like himself, are passed over. A rogue gets a cowl and assumes charge of a convent, though he is steeped in viciousness. Such preferment pleases the devil. Eventually the rascal climbs above his betters, assuming the countenance of a prelate, and sits above them at table when he at one time used to muck out the stable:

> Ane pykthank in a prelottis clais,
> With his wavill feit and wirrok tais,
> With hoppir hippis and henches narrow,
> And bausy handis to beir a barrow;
> With lut schulderis and luttard bak,
> Quhilk natur maid to beir a pak;
> With gredy mynd and glaschane gane,
> Mell-hedit lyk ane mortar-stane,
> Fenyeing the feris off ane lord.
>
> [A sycophant in clerical garb,
> With feet turned outwards and corny toes,
> Hips like a millhopper and narrow haunches,
> Coarse hands fit to push a barrow;
> His shoulders bent and back bowed down
> Which nature fashioned to carry a pack;
> With a greedy look and grimacing face,
> Mallet-headed like a pestle,
> Aping the manners of a gentleman]
>
> (53–61)

Dunbar's opinion of the clergy in general is low, but his scorn falls on individuals, not on institutional abuses. He does not single out the priesthood more than any other class. In *How Dumbar was Desyred to be ane Freir* he claims that he himself once went about preaching in various parts of England and France, deceiving the people at large, but this is probably just another satirical attitude not based on fact. In *Epitaphe for Donald Owre* he lampoons Donald Odhar of the Isles who in 1503–5 led an insurrection against the King and went to prison. (Released forty-two years later, he was undaunted and stirred up another rebellion, this time against James VI.) The *Epitaphe* does not signify the subject's death, nor, by the same token, does the content necessarily reflect Dunbar's real opinion of the men. It is more likely that he was expressing what he knew to be the King's view of 'the fell strong traitor'. The invective is crude, its appeal is to the patriotic emotions:

> And he evir odious as ane owle,
> The falt[1] sa filthy is and fowle;
> Horrible to natour,
> Is ane tratour,
> As feind in fratour[2]
> Undir a cowle
> (7–12)

and the comparison first with an owl, symbolising lechery, then with a monk, is conventional according to contemporary satirical fashions.

Dunbar also wrote several poems of celebration, marking specific events. The best known of these are *The Thistle and the Rose* and *The Goldyn Targe*. The first was composed after James IV's marriage to Princess Margaret Tudor, then aged fifteen, on 8 August, 1503. Written in the allegorical style of Chaucer, it tells how the poet dreams that Aurora (Dawn) and May (Spring) roused him and commanded him to write a piece in May's honour. He rises and observes the rich panoply of nature, described by him in aureate language:

> The purpour[3] sone, with tendir bemys reid
> In orient bricht as angell did appeir
> Throw goldin skyis putting up his heid
> Quhois[4] gilt tressis schone so wondir cleir
> (50–53)

---

[1] crime   [2] refectory   [3] reddish   [4] whose

and welcomes the day that is to make every man happy:

> Haill May, haill Flora, haill Aurora schene[1]
> Haill princes Natur, haill Venus luvis[2] quene
>
> (62–3)

while the birds sing in unison, choirlike.

Dame Nature orders every bird, beast, flower and herb to do her homage, as befits the season, and the Lion, the beast of the highest rank, inclines before her.

> This awfull beist full terrible wes of cheir
> Persing of luke, and stout of countenance;
> Rycht strong of corpis, of fassoun fair but feir;
> Lusty of schaip, lycht of deliverance,
> Reid of his cullour, as is the ruby glance,
> On feild of gold he stude full mychtely,
> With flour delycis sirculit lustely.
>
> (92–8)

[This fearful beast was most terrible to look upon with piercing gaze and bold of countenance; exceptionally powerful in body, of his kind unequalled in handsomeness; sleek to look upon, agile in movement. His colour was red, like the scintillating ruby, on a golden field he stood mighty of mien, Encircled delicately with the lily flower.]

Crowned King of Beasts by Dame Nature, the Lion is enjoined to exercise justice with mercy and conscience and to protect the small creatures from the powerful ones; to treat all alike and control those who would oppress others—all this was conventional advice to a king. The assembled beasts cry 'Vive le Roy!' and humble themselves before him.

The Eagle, crowned King of the Birds, is committed to keep order in his domain. Then the Thistle, warlike and aggressive, is crowned with rubies and told to make sure that the Lily, symbol of nobility, is honoured accordingly and not challenged by nettles or weeds and that, in particular, the French Rose is always esteemed above all other flowers

[1] bright   [2] love's

Conciddering that no flour is so perfyt,
So full of vertew, plesans and delyt,
So full of blisfull angelik bewty,
Imperiall birth, honour and dignite.

(144–7)

Then the Rose is crowned, amidst universal rejoicing and a paean of praise sung by the congregation of birds, greeting the Rose and blessing the hour when she was chosen to be their 'principall'. Their singing rises to such a crescendo that the poet is hurled into sudden wakefulness and the scene vanishes, leaving him in a half-frightened state. He concludes by informing the audience that he had been writing on 9 May, which presumably refers to the May before the wedding, though it might well have been that of 1504. The wedding itself is well documented, from the preliminary reception to the five days of post-ceremonial revelry. No expense was spared to impress the guests from England, who included the Archbishop of York and the Earl and Countess of Surrey. The Earl of Surrey was later to lead the English army which destroyed James at Flodden, but on this occasion he and his retinue enjoyed Scots hospitality, which they boorishly affected to despise. The petulant fifteen-year-old Margaret wrote a letter to her father complaining that she had been neglected during the revels. In later years, the delicate Rose was to turn into a very spiky Thistle, who proved herself a worthy sister of Henry VIII. As her subsequent career demonstrates, she was a calculating woman, far shrewder than her headstrong, restless husband. Widowed at twenty-four, she married the Earl of Angus and divorced him to marry Henry Stewart, Earl of Methven. By James she had six children, of whom only one survived infancy. He was to become James V of Scotland.

The allegory of *The Thistle and the Rose* is more easily followed with reference to heraldic symbolism. The red Lion on the gold background refers to the armorial bearings of Scotland, the Lily signifies France, to which the Rose is said to be superior, and the line 'the fresche Rois of cullour reid and quhyt' calls attention to the Houses of Lancaster and York which, after the Wars of the

Roses, came together in the Tudor dynasty. The context of this line, however, urges the King to be discreet and not to hold any other flower in such esteem as the Rose. This may be read as a comment on James's past and present infidelities—he had five 'natural' children by four different mothers—and he is known to have been in the company of a mistress even as his bride-to-be was making her way from England to the castle at Dalkeith, where she met James for the first time.

Another of Dunbar's allegories, also in aureate language, is *The Goldyn Targe*. Against a richly woven tapestry depicting lush nature walk medieval abstractions, Nature, Venus, Aurora and Flora (as in *The Thistle and the Rose*), June, Apollo, Proserpina, Diana, Cleo, Thetes, Pallas, Minerva, Fortune and Lucina (the Moon). Corresponding to these is a collection of male gods, Mars, Saturn, Mercury, Priapus, Phanus, Neptune, Aeolus, Bacchus and Pluto, all singing and dancing. The poet, who has been surveying this scene from a thicket, is detected by Venus and arrested by her archers.

The rest of the poem depicts a battle between the Flesh, represented by Dame Beauty carrying a bow and accompanied by a retinue of supporters, and Reason, dressed in full armour, bearing a golden 'targe' or round shield, leading Youth, Innocence, Abaising (Depression), Dread and Obedience. Then comes Sweet Womanhede with artillery and a company of Virtues, bearing darts. Battle commences between the two factions for possession of the poet and a number of other abstractions, including High Degree, Estate, Dignity, Comparison, Honour and Noble Array, representing the courtly virtues, join in. But the golden targe cannot be pierced by the darts of Venus until Presence throws dust in his eyes and he is routed. The poet now falls into the hands of Dame Beauty and the lusts of the flesh. Aeolus blows his trumpet and the lush landscape changes all at once into a wilderness as both sides take to ship and sail away, firing their guns and leaving behind the smoke and noise of battle. The poet-dreamer awakes, affrighted by the nightmare ending to his vision, and is happy to discover himself back in the world of spring growth. He ends with a conventional salutation to the poets from whom he claims to have taken inspiration, Chaucer, Gower and Lydgate, his avowed masters in poetic language, though in fact Dunbar surpasses all his predecessors in dazzling verbal skill.

The background to this poem is obscure. The clash between the opposing factions is described in terms of early sixteenth-century military tactics. English armies had depended on bowmen since Crécy and Agincourt. James II of Scotland used cannon decisively against rebels in the 1450s and again to break down the walls of Roxburgh Castle in 1460. He was himself killed when one of these cannons burst. Records show that 'an instrument called a gun' was bought for Edinburgh Castle as early as 1384. Flodden was to be won largely by English accuracy with the longbow and by their superior handling of artillery.

However, the device of the battle had immediate literary origins in *The Romance of the Rose* and it is unrewarding to seek contemporary history in *The Goldyn Targe*. The symbolism of French allegory is nowadays sometimes interpreted, according to recently fashionable Freudian theories of psychology, as a means of explaining the individual subconscious, so that the dream vision comes to signify a sexual conflict between the animal and rational sides of man's nature, expressed in the morality play language of the late Middle Ages. This kind of allegory has a lengthy history and it has been traced back to the fourth-century monk Prudentius, but Dunbar's poem, like *The Romance of the Rose*, is 'pagan', or classical, in its allusions and the mythological figures probably have their source in Boccaccio's *Deorum Genealogia*, as Henryson's gods and goddesses did. Moreover, real-life tableaux made up of these figures had been shown in the streets of English and Scottish towns for hundreds of years, so that Dunbar's mixture of medieval and classical subjects had its vital counterpart in local pageantry. In a poem addressed *To Aberdein*, Dunbar refers to the city's enthusiastic welcome to Queen Margaret, when

> The streittis war all hung with tapestrie;
> Great was the pres[1] of peopill dwelt about,
> And plesand padgeanes playit prattilie.[2]

> (49–51)

[1] throng   [2] elegantly

and it is not impossible that *The Goldyn Targe* is really a description of one of these performances, a kind of entertainment of which James was very fond.

Dunbar is known particularly for his versatility and the way in which he could adapt his skill as a poet to almost any subject or style. His *Flyting*, or cursing poem, with Walter Kennedie as antagonist, a comic version of the priestly castigation of individual sinners from the pulpit, his personal and elegiac poems, verses praising or condemning known personages of the time in extravagant but conventional terms, such as *The Ballade of Lord Bernard Stewart, Lord of Aubigny*, a renowned Scots commander, who died in Edinburgh in 1508 after serving Charles VIII and Louis XII of France, and on whom Dunbar also wrote an elegy, together with the many poems on Court and town all shed light on the life and times of James IV's Scotland. Thanks to him and to the very full Lord Treasurer's accounts, first-hand information is not lacking. *The Tretis of the Twa Mariit Wemen and the Wedo*, Dunbar's longest poem, referred to previously, is of outstanding quality. In the tradition of Chaucer's *Wife of Bath's Prologue and Tale*, which itself has earlier counterparts in medieval European and classical literature going back to Ovid, Dunbar relates how he overheard three gold-digging women discussing their husbands in derogatory terms, making it clear that they consider the marriage bond useful only so far as it benefited them materially, and also that they have developed many ways of extracting full tribute from their spouses, whom they regularly deceive by committing adultery with more attractive partners. The three women are elegant, expensively attired and outwardly respectable, but their coarse language and confessions of sexual promiscuity are more appropriate to 'cow clinks', or prostitutes. Dunbar concludes by asking which of the three would the reader choose for his wife, if he had to get married?

The setting, that of *The Romance of the Rose*, is the vernal scene of spring, when love is supposedly in the air, and the style is that of the confession convention used by fair maidens in the romances and borrowed from ecclesiastical practice. The mock-seriousness of the whole, the pungent and frequently scurrillous descriptive matter, and the cleverness with which Dunbar has combined a number of literary traditions in order to satirise the Court ladies of his circle, not to mention their unattractive husbands, justifies modern critical praise of *The Twa Mariit Wemen and the Wedo*. The unsentimental materialism of the trio of harpies brought to life by Dunbar is a comment on the position of 'women of quality' in the fifteenth and sixteenth centuries who sometimes found themselves the sole executrices of their deceased partners' estates; the widow tells her companions:

> I buskit[1] up my barnis[2] like baronis sonnis
> And maid bot fulis[3] of the fry of his his first wif
> I banyst fra my boundis his brethir[4] ilkane:[5]
>
> (402–4)

and that

> Bot quhen I severit had that syre of substance in erd
> And gottin his biggingis to my barne, and hie burrow landis . . .
> I had for flattering of that fule fenyeit so lang,
> Mi evidentis of heritagis or thair wer all selit.
>
> (337–44)

[But when I had separated that gentleman from his worldly goods, And got his property for my children and his houses in the burgh . . . I had through flattering the fool deceived him for such a long time that I had (written) confirmation of the bequests even before they were all signed and sealed]

after which she makes the poor man's life a misery until he is dead and buried, leaving her free to lead a gay life. How far the poet has real models in mind is impossible to determine. The women are solid believable composites of literary originals, like the Wife of Bath and others in the Ovidian tradition, and of Scottish Court ladies.

Dunbar's women are either remote and symbolic, untouchables to be admired from a safe distance, or refined harlots. His own marital status cannot be known but his poetic *persona* is that of a crabbed old bachelor-idealist, a severe critic of feminine lapses

---

[1] dressed   [2] children   [3] only fools   [4] brothers   [5] each one

from his own unrealistic standard, like the preachers in the St Jerome tradition who displayed obsession with the two medieval extremes—the cults of Marian virginity on the one hand and the fallen Eve on the other. One does not really feel that Dunbar knows much about womankind, in contrast to Henryson, whose perception is acute even when he is judging the weaknesses of the sex.

9 : The Poet of the Scottish Reformation : Lyndsay

THE decadence of the pre-Reformation Church in Scotland—'the auld religion'—is well documented by poets, historians and commentators, some of whom were themselves in Holy Orders. Literature and history come together in their views of the period, which was treated realistically, without sentiment, and not idealised or distorted as was usually the case when English poets depicted the Tudors at work. Skelton and Barclay were not typical and, as we have already observed, the latter may have hailed from Scotland.

Sir David Lyndsay, diplomat and holder of the high public office of Lord Lyon King-at-Arms, was a fierce satirist best known for a topical play called *Ane Satyre of the Three Estates*. It was written about 1530 and is the clearest reflection of the need for reform in Scotland to be seen in contemporary writing. In fact, it is the only complete example of Scots drama of the medieval and Renaissance period which survives; though others existed, no copies of texts remain, either of secular plays or of the miracle and morality plays known to have been performed in that country. That there was a dearth of early Scots drama is true insofar as none of it remains for the literary historian to study, but it is not true to say that there was no Scots drama. Apart from *Ane Satyre*, however, only fragments have come down to us.

Lyndsay is the poet of the Scots Reformation,—though not of Protestantism in the doctrinaire sense, for he was a staunch Catholic, despairing of the state of things in the monasteries and seeking to effect change in the maladministration of the realm. His criticism bears many points of resemblance to that of Henryson, but Lyndsay is much less inhibited and his shafts are more accurately aimed at specific targets. Contemporaneous with Lyndsay, other Scottish poets, similarly fired by indignation, wrote about the plagues of their age. Among their pieces are included the anonymous or near-anonymous *Cursing of Sir Johne Rowlis Upon the Stelaris*[1] *of his Fowlis* and *The Gude and Godlie Ballatis*, probably written in part by Bishop Wedderburn of St Andrews, Alexander Scott's *New Yeir Gift to the Queen Mary*, Sir Richard Maitland's *Satire on the Age*, George Buchanan's Latin *Somnium*, *Palinodia* and *Franciscanus*, attacking the Franciscan friars, the Earl of Glencairn's *Epistle from the Holye Armite of Allarit* and others.

In prose the histories touched upon elsewhere appeared, Major's *History of Britain*, Buchanan's Latin *History*, Robert Lindsay of Pitscottie's *Chronicle of Scotland* (to 1565), John Knox's *History of the Reformation*, printed in 1586, and Bishop John Lesley's *History of Scotland* (the vernacular version extending to 1561), which survive as the chief contemporary or near-contemporary guides to the period. Documents of the Church itself, particularly those of the Provincial Council of 1539, 1552 and 1559, reveal the same picture. The 1559 Council admitted that the fiercest accusations of its enemies were true and agreed that reform was overdue. But by this time it was too late, for what had started out as a reform of the Catholic institutions by Catholics had become a root-and-branch rejection of all that Rome stood for. However, although Scotland reformed more radically than other countries, the process by which she did so was far less violent than was the case in France or Germany. A few martyrs were burned but although laws were enacted in 1545–6 for the rooting-out of heresy they were never put into effect. Feeling against the clergy was by that time too hostile. George Wishart, a follower of Knox, perished at the stake in March, 1546, by order of Cardinal Beaton, but in May the Cardinal himself was murdered in his bed, screaming for mercy. In Scotland, there were to be no general bloodbaths.

·   ·   ·   ·   ·   ·

The Cardinal could not have claimed that he received no warning of the fate that befell him. In 1539 his cousin, Archibald Hay, wrote a discourse on him on the occasion of his election to the rank of Cardinal. It was called *Panegyricus*. A panegyric is usually a

[1] thieves

laudatory eulogy, singing the praises of its subject as though he were spotless. *Panegyricus* does indeed contain about 14,000 words of praise, largely undeserved. The other 46,000 words present a gloomy picture of the state of Beaton's Church during the closing years of James V's reign. The work is a main source of information concerning a clerical body which had lost the qualities proper to its professions through many years of backsliding and gross ignorance. Hay's avowed object in writing it was to acquaint his cousin with the facts, so that he might use his ecclesiastical authority to extirpate the main abuses and, by his own personal example, lead the Church back to righteousness.

Needless to say, the Cardinal took little if any action to reform either the priests or himself, though he did call a Provincial Council at Edinburgh in January, 1546, when it was too late to effect serious changes in the conduct of clergy. A nineteenth-century historian, Patrick Fraser Tytler, described Beaton as

> a prelate stained by open profligacy, and remarkable for nothing but his abilities as a statesman and politician, . . . fitted to produce the worst effects upon the great body of the inferior clergy (*History of Scotland* [1829–43], V, 412.)

and although due allowance must be made for the fact that the standards of the nineteenth century and those of the fifteenth were different, so that what both Tytler and ourselves might regard as abuse of public office was much less clearly defined in Beaton's day than in our own, it is clear that the Cardinal deserved most of the opprobrium heaped upon his head by later historians. Lyndsay wrote a mock confession by Beaton called *The Tragedie of the Cardinall* which indicates that his contemporaries held him in low esteem

> Bot Edinburgh, sen syne, Leith, and Kyngorne
> The day and hour may ban that I was borne

[But Edinburgh, and after it, Leith and Kinghorn, may curse the day and hour that gave me birth]   (*op. cit.*, 202–3)

says the Cardinal, explaining how his political counsels brought nothing but dire misfortune to Scotland. In the end, he warns 'all proude Prelatis' to take heed of his example.

Panegyricus, therefore, was but a straw in the wind, though it laid almost every sham and immorality imaginable at the door of the Scots clergy, who were respected neither by their flock nor by one another. Good priests were hard to find; most suffered from greed, ambition, pride, unreliability, insincerity; were insolent, perfidious, untruthful, dishonest, lustful, hypocritical and above all ignorant and lacking in knowledge of the Scriptures. Hay proposed the foundation of a college, equipped with a library and printing press, to instruct the clergy in Latin, Greek, Hebrew, Arabic, Chaldee, dialectic, moral and natural philosophy, canon and civil law, medicine, arithmetic, geometry, astronomy and music, and obviously felt that he himself was supremely well-fitted for the post of first Principal.

He blames monks for their worldliness, veniality and neglect of duties, for, as he says, many priests spend most of their time in hunting, hawking, dicing, eating, keeping dogs, apes and jesters with their surplus money, and in other pleasures which the writer admits he would blush to name. Lured into Holy Orders, not by any spiritual call but by the attractions of a comfortable and profitable life, clerics receive the benefits of nepotism and simony, so that the good man is discouraged by the knowledge that rascals with influence to back them easily obtain rich livings whereas a man of tried life and scholarly attainment is passed over. Church funds are misapplied, either by lavish spending or by hoarding in a treasure house, and the poor and needy go without succour. Priests serve at the altar suffering from the after-effects of yesterday's drunken debauch.

Ignorance on the part of priests is a very muddy spring, from which flow the majority of the Church's disasters. Bishops blame the examiners of candidates for the priesthood, but the bishop is often responsible for the examiner, the archdeacon. The examiner is often a greater blockhead than the one examined, and admits candidates without selection, lest he lose part of his income, considering it inadequate to admit to ecclesiastical office candidates not as learned as possible but as great in number as possible (Quoted in W. Murison, *Sir David Lyndsay* [1938], 198–9)

and elsewhere

Were the very wise writer of Ecclesiastes now alive, he would ascribe it to the height of vanity that brute beasts should be admitted to ecclesiastical benefices, sometimes even invited to accept them. (*Ibid.*, 199)

When the 1549 Provincial Council met, belatedly, to try to restore order it concluded that the urge for reformation was caused mainly by a crass ignorance of book learning ('*bonarum litterarum et artium crassa inscitia*'), and Hay contrasts the current state of affairs with earlier days when the Bible was read and taught, saying that our ancestors

searched the Scriptures to ascertain the law of the Lord and impart it to others; we are sunk in the vilest pleasures of the flesh

and thus lose the benefits which our predecessors gained from perusing Holy Writ.

Hay wrote *Panegyricus* in Latin, in about 1540. He prophesied a violent and bloodstained future for the Church and pronounced a warning to the effect that unless the twin abuses of avarice and ambition that had brought the Scottish clergy to this miserable condition were brought to an end, the priests would be cast out and others put in their places. He says that if he were to tell of the terrible crimes committed by so-called ecclesiastics and of the wickedness in their hearts, no-one would credit that such savage monsters went about in human guise, but, since he does not wish to incur hatred and attract unwelcome reprisals on himself, he will not provide details of the many pretended miracles, cunning words and deeds and abuses of both sexes, seductions by priests to whom the name of 'father' is especially well-suited, and even incestuous relationships from which such scoundrels are not deterred. Hay's language is temperate and his reputation among contemporaries was high. A learned man of liberal opinions whose decisions were always regulated by plain common sense and not by an excess of emotion or irrational prejudice, he seems to have been a rare bird among the predatory crows with whom he had to work.

Other commentaries and documents dealing with the pre-Reformation Church in Scotland which survive from the period 1520–60 confirm that Hay's *Panegyricus* was not exaggerated in its account of the faults of prelates. The record of *Papal Negotiations with Mary Queen of Scots* makes it clear that Roman Church representatives from the Vatican were equally alarmed at what they saw was going on in Scotland. For the voice of Reformation speaking through literature, one must look to Sir David Lyndsay.

·   ·   ·   ·   ·   ·

Lyndsay's *Three Estates* preceded *Panegyricus* by several years. It is an important play, the only extant example of early Scots drama, for although miracle and morality plays were performed in Scotland as they were in England, and records exist of politically inspired interludes played before James V, no complete texts remain, only fragments. Not only is Lyndsay's play unique, it is also the most brilliant composition to have been written either in England or Scotland up to that time; its closest rival, Skelton's *Magnyfycence*, is inferior dramatically, though Skelton is far more of a poet than Lyndsay and experimented metrically to an extent not considered by the Scot, whose aims were earthily satirical and reformatory. He has been compared both to Aristophanes and to Shaw, a parallel suggesting a timelessness lacking in Skelton's heavyweight production. The matter of the *Three Estates* is in many respects modern, though its setting and techniques are medieval and would have been considered old-fashioned in Tudor England.

Lyndsay, born in Fife in 1486, became a courtier in his twenties. He secured the post of gentleman usher to the infant James V but lost it for four years while power resided in the hands of the Queen Regent's husband, the Earl of Angus. Lyndsay's tutorship of James was at best sporadic, for the young man was never able to speak French, and could not even read English until he was fifteen; but Lyndsay was always able to remain close to the struggle for power between rival noble factions and the King. His experience in the midst of intrigue furnished a background and an inspiration for his satirical compositions.

The subjects of his satire were political and religious and, besides his dramatic work, he wrote a number of poems criticising public morality. *The Dreme*, *The Complaint* and *The Papyngo* (Parrot) are the best of these, all written about 1530. However, the content of the poems is more forcefully represented in the play, first performed before James V and his French Queen, Marie of Lorraine, in January, 1540. By this time Lyndsay had advanced in the service of the Court and attained the title of Lord Lyon King-at-Arms, an office (chief herald) of which he had performed the duties for some years, in 1542. He had gained considerable experience as an ambassador in Flanders, France, Denmark and England, while Spain and England sought to break the 'auld alliance' between Scotland and France. Lyndsay seems to have fluctuated between the practically and the sentimentally grounded policies of preferring peace with England and maintaining the ancient link with France; in his last poem, *The Monarche*, he bewails the necessity for war and prophesies that no lasting peace will be possible until England and Scotland are united under one king, a coalition then half a century in the future.

When he was in England, Lyndsay was noticed by Henry VIII as a man of discretion, and he was the personal friend and shrewd adviser of James V for many years. His poems contain many admonitions to the King, whom he advises to be just, to keep the laws, to know good from bad counsel, to guard against ignorant prelates, hasty engagements in warfare and oppressing the poor. There is nothing new in any of this, but the personal note in Lyndsay is louder than in any stock expression of royal accountability which most historians of the period were wont to utter. His sympathy for the Commons was, like James', a consistent part of his character and he was no theoretical reformist. The distinguishing feature of his criticism is his unremitting hatred of corrupt clergy, and his method in the *Three Estates* is to show how social upheaval results from foolishness. All the abuses referred to in *Panegyricus* are touched upon in advance in Lyndsay's play or

Q

in the poems; writing with a popular audience in mind, like the authors of *The Gude and Godlie Ballatis*, he knows how to sneer with the voice of the common man and to appeal to a ribald sense of the ridiculous by creating a stream of concrete images, often scurrilous or suggestive. Thus the Bishop explains how he fulfils the duties of his office:

> I gat good payment of my temporal lands,
> My buttock-mail, my cotes and my offrands.
> Howbeit I dare nocht plainly espouse a wife
> Yet concubenes I have had four or five,
> And to my sons I have given rich rewairds,
> And all my dochters marriet upon lairds
> *(op. cit.;* ed. M. P. McDiarmid [1967].)

'Buttock-mail' referred to the ecclesiastical fines which he imposed upon fornicators, and 'cotes' to his 'cut' of a dead man's estate, payable in return for confirming his testament.

The Pardoner, a favourite target of English medieval complaint, appears as a conventional symbol of corruption into whose mouth many topical allusions are put. Pardoners were finally banned by the Council of Trent in 1545, so that this is one of the last literary appearances of the familiar figure. Lyndsay's Pardoner, not a smooth villain like Chaucer's, but an obviously 'bad' type, declaims:

> I am Sir Robert Rome-Raker,
> A perfite public pardoner
>   Admittit by the Paip,
> Sirs, I sall shaw you, for my wage,
> My pardons and my privilege,
>   Whilk ye sall see and graip.[1]
> I give to the Deil with good intent
> This waeful wickit New Testament,
>   With them that it translatit!
> Since laymen knew the verity,
> Pardoners gets na charity
>   Without that they debate it.

[1] handle

Deil, fell the brain that has it wrocht
Sa fall them that the Book hame brocht!
   Als I pray to the Rood,
That Martin Luther, that false loon,
Black Bullenger and Melancthoun,
   Had been smoored[1] in their cude[2]
By him that bure the croun of thorn
I wald Sant Paul had never been born,
   And als I wald his books
Were never read into the Kirk,
But amang freirs into the mirk,
   Or riven[3] amang the rooks!
My patent pardons you may see,
Come from the Cam[4] of Tartary
   Weill sealt with oyster shells.
Thocht ye have na contritioun
Ye sall have full remissioun
   With help of books and bells.

Later in the play there is a scene in which the Pardoner tries his skill on a poor man, who eventually attacks him and throws his relics into a stream.

The three Estates, common in contemporary French plays, are the Lords Spiritual, the Lords Temporal and the Commonalty, or more precisely, the burgesses, who in Scotland had hitherto enjoyed little influence. The pattern of the play is that of the moral interlude, though it can hardly be described as an 'interlude' since in its original version it took nine hours to perform. A full account of the 1554 text (the earlier one is not extant) would take up a great deal of space and a short summary would do the play scant justice, for it is a play to be seen, heard and studied for its allusions to contemporary clerical customs. It is informed by a highly developed sense of the ridiculous as in Brant's *Narrenschiff* and the French tradition of the '*sottie*' or play about fools, and is separated from nearly all English plays of the time by its sheer dynamic exuberance.

[1] smothered   [2] crib   [3] ripped apart   [4] Khan

The action is divided into two parts, of which the second is of greater interest. Part I is set in the Parliament of the Estates and deals with governmental reform. Rex Humanitas, the ruler, who resembles Magnyfycence and James V, meets with Correction, Verity and Good Counsel after a wild youth, but not before he is assailed by misrule in various shapes and forms. From the embrace of Lady Sensuality, into whose clutches irresponsible courtiers have lured him, he falls into the power of Flattery, Deceit and Falsehood, each portrayed as fools or jesters. This trio, led by Flattery, keep Good Counsel and Chastity at a distance and persuade Spirituality to accuse Verity, or True Religion, of heresy. Divine Correction routs them and they seek protection from the Spirituality, the Merchants and the Craftsmen respectively. Rex Humanitas is saved. Good Counsel exhoits him to do justice and to take the lessons of history to heart:

> The principal point, sir, of a king's office,
> Is for to do to every man justice
> And for to mix his justice with mercy,
> But rigour, favour or partiality,
> Wha guides them weill, they win immortal fame;
> Wha the contrair, they get perpetual shame.
> The Chronicles to knaw, I you exhort;
> There sall ye find baith good and evil report;
> For every prince after his quality,
> Thocht he be deid his deeds sall never die!

sentiments which were thoroughly in accord with the prevailing view of the didactic value of history as stated by Polydore Vergil, John Major and other commentators, and more particularly by the writers of handbooks on the training of rulers.

After an independent comic episode about a poor man and a pardoner, which could be played as a separate interlude, Part II commences. It is tigerish in its anti-clericalism. The Estates, led by Flattery and other Vices, enter walking backwards, to signify a long-standing complacency. Rex Humanitas comes in to preside over a Court of Inquiry into complaints. The latter are summed up in a Piers Plowman-like figure called John the Commonweal, previously introduced by Lyndsay in *The Dreme*. John is represented as an honest labourer, raggedly attired, the true common man and as such a member of a class not included in any of the Estates—the ruled as distinct from the rulers. John is the national underdog. He starts by explaining to Rex Humanitas why he is so poorly dressed and accuses the misguided Estates, directed by

> Thou feignyit Flattery, the fiend fart in thy face!
> When ye was guider of the court we gat little grace!

Divine Correction punishes these Vices. Flattery, Deceit and Falsehood are placed in the stocks by the serjeants-at-law, who join in a ribald chorus:

> Put in your legs into the stocks,
> For ye had never a meeter hose!
> Thir stewats[1] stinks as they were brocks![2]
> Now are ye siccar,[3] I suppose!

Sensuality and her followers are routed and Good Counsel urges reform, advising changes in taxation, for the poor people are impoverished and driven from their smallholdings. Scotland can never succeed in keeping England at bay when she is oppressed from within her own borders by thieves, and John rehearses a list of rascals, including able-bodied beggars, minstrels, pardoners, entertainers, slackers, dicers and card-players, confidence tricksters, jesters, leadswingers, great fat friars of all the monastic orders and indeed every man who wears a cowl and lives well without working. John compares them to well-fed hogs. Then he launches into a diatribe on the oppressions brought about by the assize courts which prosecute petty thieves, while winking at important or rich criminals who overcome legal barriers by bribery.

John hesitates at first to accuse the priesthood—an unsubtle irony so far as Lyndsay's audience was concerned—but, encouraged by Divine Correction, he provides a lacerating account of ecclesiastical corruptions. This is the main object of the playwright's satire.

---

[1] these rascals   [2] badgers   [3] held fast

The Poor Man supports his argument against harsh death duties, bishops who live like princes, changing their women

> . . . like ramis rudely in their rage[1]
> Unpizzlet[2] rins amang the silly ewes

and the transfer of large sums of money sent to Rome for bribes, stripping the country of her wealth. The Merchants agree on the truth of this—and records confirm that the Scots Parliament had tried without success to stop this outgoing of money for the best part of a century. Pluralism, or traffic in benefices, is also deplored.

Good Counsel hands the Bishop the Bible but the latter throws it away, saying, like the Bishop of Dunkeld (*q.v.*):

> I read never the New Testament nor Auld
> Nor ever thinks to do sir, by the Rood!
> I hear Freirs say that reading does na good

The playwright takes his own where he finds it and adapts it to his satiric purpose. What he has to say about the export of capital to Rome, bribery and pluralism, nunneries run like bordellos and other abuses is confirmed by historians and historical records dating from the period 1530–60. John Bellenden's translation of Hector Boece's Latin *History of Scotland*, made in 1531, contains the following addition:

Till seventy years ago no kind of benefice, except only bishop-rics, went to Rome; and since then we see what infinite amount of gold and silver is taken out of the realm by their continual promotion. The realm must, through this never-ceasing promotion of prelates be brought to such incurable poverty that it shall be an easy prey to our enemies. It cannot sustain such a great charge in time of war as was done formerly by our fore-fathers. But because neither spiritual nor temporal estate of this realm has any love for the commonweal thereof, but each man is set only for his own singular way, I will deplore no more the calamities daily befalling through their imprudence.

(*op. cit.*)

---

[1] sexual excitement   [2] rampant

In 1556, the Papal representative for Scotland in Rome, Cardinal Sermoneta, informed Pope Paul IV that nearly half of the country's revenues was paid over to the Church. One year later the Pope commissioned a deputy to visit Scotland and make certain that some of this money was used to effect essential repairs in church buildings. In 1559 Henry II of France asked Paul to bring about reforms in Scotland and stressed the urgency of the matter. But no tangible results were ever attained.

Sermoneta also referred to the brothel-like character of the Scottish nunneries, particularly those of the Cistercian order (an order which formerly enjoyed a reputation for extreme asceticism), and to the illegitimate children conceived and born in cloisters. He stated that when these children become adults, they were married off with the help of large dowries taken from Church revenues. The Queen Regent later made a similar statement in a letter to the Pope in 1557. The Pope transmitted her information to Cardinal Trivulzio, entrusted with Scottish reform, saying

> ... nuns and other dedicated women go out of bounds, and wander through houses of laymen, admit suspects into their convents, and make bold to indulge in pleasures and carnal lusts ... men and women, ecclesiastics of various ranks, seculars and regulars, commit crimes, iniquities and scandalous enormities, offending God, shaming Christianity, causing loss of souls, bringing scandal to God's faithful. (*Papal Negotiations with Mary Queen of Scots;* ed. J. Hungerford p. 4: quoted in W. Murison, *Sir David Lyndsay* [1938], 161.)

The Lady Prioress, shown by Lyndsay to be wearing a gay dress under her habit, emerges as a cruder version of Chaucer's pilgrim with the 'crowned A' and is accused of being a 'cow-clink' or prostitute. The Poor Man complains about legal delays, Verity and Chastity against their respective subjection and banishment and the Lords Temporal against the large dowries paid to the daughters of high clerics who marry scions of the nobility (with which the nobles find it hard to complete). All the known and obvious abuses and shams find expression in the play. They seem to have been well founded in fact.

The concluding part of the play's action is retributive. The churchmen, Bishop, Abbot and Parson, are deposed, blaming one another and protesting their treatment. Divine Correction dresses John the Commonweal in a rich robe and instals him in Parliament. Fifteen Acts of Reform are announced, passed by the three Estates. These abolish the blatant abuses and enjoin, among other things, that spiritual matters be judged in spiritual courts, temporal in temporal courts, that only qualified persons be licensed as priests, that benefices should not be purchasable, that vicar's death dues be abolished, that no more money should go to Rome except for archbishoprics and, particularly interesting in the light of current (1970) controversy, that priests should be permitted to marry.

The closing scenes show the hangings of Deceit, Theft and Falsehood on a gallows, each making a final speech revealing their dishonest wiles before being drawn up. Falsehood's soul is symbolised by a crow, which the stage directions say shall be 'castin up' as the villain goes to the 'widdie' or gallows. The crow was a sign of predatoriness and deceit. Flattery is banished, not hanged, since, although folly in the Estates has been shown up, it is still rampant. Flattery preaches a sermon on a farcical text—'the number of fools is infinite'—, saying that kings, nobles, conquerors and all men are liable to fall victim to the charms of Lady Sensuality, to flatter themselves and to contribute their portion to earthly foolishness. Although later poets, like Ramsay and Scott, credit Lyndsay with having been a major force in the Scottish Reformation and an essential preliminary to Knox's entry upon the scene, it is more accurate to say that the author of the *Three Estates*, no doctrinal Protestant, was a savage critic of general corruptions in the land, of which those in the 'auld Kirk' were at that time by far the most flagrant.

Dramatically, the play is full of life and, although it deals with corroborated fact, it is not heavily censorious like *Magnyfycence* or *King John*, its nearest English relatives. Gleeful, vital, colourfully contrasting, mocking, clowning and, like the French *'sottie'*, teetering on the very brink of absurdity, *Ane Satyre of the Three Estates* is a cure-all, rude and crude and shot through with bold bawdry. Its scenes are informed by cheerful ribaldry, not a depressing text corrective of specific faults, a fact which goes far to explain why it was so popular. Its factual side, historically faithful as it may be, would not be sufficient to keep the play alive, yet it continued to be read in modernised versions until the nineteenth century, and, as Scott tells his audience in *Redgauntlet*:

> So down the carles sat ower a stoup of brandy, and Hutcheon, who was something of a clerk, would have read a chapter of the Bible; but Dougal would hear naething but a blaud (*ballad*) of Davie Lindsay, whilk was the waur preparation.
>
> (*op. cit.*, 'Wandering Willie's Tale')

A contemporary observer, Robert Heron, claims that almost within his own remembrance 'Davie Lindsay was esteemed little less necessary in every family than the Bible'. Until 1800, editions of Lyndsay were more common than those of either Henryson or Dunbar.

A flesh-and-blood humanity shines out from the changing scenes of the *Three Estates*, peopled as they are by Scots figures at least as convincing as any of Chaucer's pilgrims or Langland's shifting crowds in the Fair Field of Folk. Modern audiences fortunate enough to have witnessed Tyrone Guthrie's production at the Edinburgh Festival (from which modernised text the quotations used here are taken) soon found that this relic of pre-Reformation Scotland possessed durable qualities of entertainment which a ponderous didactic treatment would have reduced. By perceiving the abuses of his Church as absurdities and treating state corruption as an object of ridicule Lyndsay transcended his local background and imparted 'universality', that is to say, timeless and human interest judged according to the cultural standards of Western Europe, to what at first reading might seem to be valuable solely as a document of contemporary conditions.

10 : The Poets of Henry VIII's Court : Wyatt and Surrey

$\mathbf{W}$YATT's musical competence has never been proved to be more than superficial. Although his poems contain references to music and specifically to the lute, critics have pointed out that while Skelton's knowledge of musical terminology as shown in his verses is precise and extensive, Wyatt's is vague and limited. With Surrey, Wyatt is recognised as a 'chieftain' of a new company of 'courtly makers', after a statement made by Puttenham in his *Arte of English Poesie*, published in 1589. Puttenham attributed their worth to the fact that they had brought Italian poetic metres and styles to England. Wyatt and Surrey are usually discussed together, as though there were not much difference between them; Wyatt is credited with introducing the sonnet into English, while Surrey is enshrined as the first to employ blank verse.

Studies of Wyatt by modern scholars and critics are numerous—among these one may mention Muir, Southall, Mason and Tillyard—and it is not the intention here to enter into a profound discussion of Wyatt's love lyrics or to evaluate his place in the English poetical line. Stevens' chapter on 'The Courtly Makers, from Chaucer to Wyatt' sets his lyrics in the larger context of the stylised courtly-love tradition. Our concern here will be simply to observe him as a man of the Court and to draw a portrait of him.

He was a man of Kent, born of a noble house in 1503 and educated probably at Cambridge. As a young courtier, he took part in various formal activities, and progressed from page to more responsible offices such as that of Gentleman of the Privy Chamber and Clerk of the King's Jewels. He was probably taught to play the lute or at least to strike out an accompaniment, and to sing, but there is no record of this. In the mid-1520s he was sent as a member of several embassies to France and Italy. In 1529 he translated Plutarch's *Quyete of Mynde* and from 1528–30 was

Marshal at Calais. The rest of his life was spent on embassies to Spain, Paris and Flanders. He suffered as the victim of Court intrigues which resulted in his imprisonment on various charges in 1534, 1536 and 1541. He was tried for sedition and acquitted in 1541 but lived only one more year, dying at the age of 39.

Wyatt provides historians with an animated English example of the Italian ideal of the courtier, who combined arms and letters, chivalry and learning, prowess in war with social grace, a welding of medieval knight to Renaissance humanist. Castiglione's *Courtier* of 1528 was, as we know, a text-book for young nobles in Italy and France but in England the model was considerably domesticated and 'courtliness' made more rugged and masculine than was the case over the Channel. Wyatt was not an Italianate Englishman, but an Englishman who adapted Italian forms without in any way surrendering his own vigorous personality. He was a learned and more versatile Paston, 'a kind and faithful public servant in a hard-hearted and faithless Court', as Trevelyan calls him, well travelled in Europe, but not regretting his absence from it, as he states in his *First Satire to Poyntz*

> I ame not now in Fraunce to judge the wyne,
> With saffry[1] sauce the delicates to fele;
> Nor yet in Spaigne where oon must him inclyne
> Rather than to be, owtewerdly to seme.
> I meddill not with wittes that be so fyne,
> No Flaunders chiere letteth[2] not my sight to deme[3]
> Of black and white, nor taketh my wit awaye
> With bestylnes,[4] they beeste do so esteme;
> Nor I ame not where Christe is geven in pray
> For mony, poison and traison at Rome,
> A commune practise used nyght and daie:
> But here I ame in Kent and Christendome
> Emong the muses where I rede and ryme; . . .

When he fell out of favour, Wyatt retired to his country seat and lived as a literary squire, hunting and composing verses. He is the wise country mouse who regards the Court with suspicion—'my

[1] saffron (orange)   [2] prevents   [3] judge   [4] bestiality

dear old enemy, my fraward master'—, who compares his painful life to 'these unmeasurable mountains' and is forever falling in love, as C. S. Lewis says, 'with women he dislikes'. Lewis classes him and Surrey as poets of the 'Drab Age', frequently on a level with Barclay (no compliment coming from Professor Lewis), or, alternatively, making verses at the other extreme of excessive precision. 'Both phases', says Lewis again, 'are what we should expect in a man who was escaping from the late medieval swamp; first, his floundering, and then, after conversion, a painful regularity' (*English Literature in the Sixteenth Century*, p. 225).

This religious metaphor may beg the question but it is not to be denied that Wyatt's verse has been overrated by some critics who see him as the first true Renaissance poet, and underrated by others who think that he has an uncertain ear and comes at the end of a transitional period. He has been dissected by the European school, who estimate him as a product of three main influences, that handed down by English literary Chaucerians, those resulting from personal contacts with French poets like Marot and St Gelais, gained while a member of Sir Thomas Cheney's embassy in 1526, and that of Italian models, first of all Petrarch, then near-contemporaries like the *quattrocento* poet Serafino and his school of Petrarchans from whom Wyatt appropriated some bad habits. Later, after Anne Boleyn's execution in 1536, he started to write satires after Luigi Alamanni, whom he translated in his *Satire to Poyntz*, already cited, then after Horace, whose mood of naive Epicureanism he rendered freely. Wyatt's discontent with Court life may be a pose, adopted according to a well-rooted convention, but his own life had indeed been one of disillusionment and even personal danger.

In 1540 he wrote the *Penitential Psalms*, translating from Pietro Aretino's model, but later developing his own original flow and replacing Aretino's doctrinal passages with his own free version of the *Psalms*. These *Psalms* represent his most mature work. He studied and developed three Italian metrical forms, *sonnetto*, *ottava rima* and *terza rima; terza rima* had to wait until the nineteenth century for English poets to use it, but *ottava rima* was taken up by Spenser, Daniel, Drayton, Crashaw and Gay, among others.

The dominant influence upon him from 1527–41 is undoubtedly Italian; French qualities are not marked, though they are detectable, but Chaucer's example, as observed by Wyatt in Pynson's edition of *The Canterbury Tales* (1526), determined his understanding of rhyme, spelling and, especially, versification. From this text he evolved his own notion of the decasyllabic line;

> A face that shuld content me wondrous well
> Should not be fayre but lovelye to behold
> With gladsome chere all greffe for to dispel;
> With sober lokes so wold I that it shuld
> Speke without wordes, such wordes as non can tell.
> The tress also shuld be of crispid gold
> With witt and thus myght chaunce I myght be tyed
> An knytt agayne the knott that shuld not slyde.
>
> ('A face that shuld content me')

This is a late epigram written in prison, referring either to Anne Boleyn, or to an ideal paramour of which Anne was the living approximation. As a courtly lover, Wyatt would have in his mind a Platonic vision of Eros, an unachievable goal of which earthly pulchritude was but a mean reflection. Wyatt's love-lyrics fight shy of direct description and can rarely be linked directly with any specific woman, though there are some exceptions, *e.g.*:

> What wourde is that that chaungeth not,
> Though it be tourned and made in twain?

which refers to an 'Anne', possibly Boleyn, and the lines

> Sure sins I did refrain
> Brunet that set my country in a rore
> The unfayned cher of Phyllis hath the place
> That Brunet had

point to Boleyn and to no other as the 'brunette' from whom he had by then recoiled in favour of the shadowy 'Phyllis'.

Wyatt's relations with Anne Boleyn, unfortunately for himself, seem to have been physically intimate, and when the King expressed a desire to make her his Queen, Wyatt was placed in a fright-

eningly insecure position. Later, Henry was to have several of
Anne's lovers executed and, eventually, Anne herself, but Wyatt,
though imprisoned, escaped the block. One of his poems, headed
by a Latin inscription protesting innocence and saying that his
enemies encircled him, refers to the beheadings of five of his friends
on 17 May 1536, one of which Wyatt almost certainly watched from
his cell. The refrain is Senecan.

> The bell towre showed me suche syght
>   That in my hed stekys day and nyght;
>   Ther dyd I lerne out of a grate,
>   For all vavore,¹ glory or myght,
>   That yet *circa Regna tonat,*
>
> By proffe, I say, ther dyd I lerne:
>   Wyt helpythe not deffence to yerne,
>   Of innocence to pled or prate;
>   Ber low therffor, geve god the sterne,
>   For sure *circa Regna tonat.*

A contemporary poem, not certainly Wyatt's though credited to
him, is an elegy on the executed men, and refers to them by name.
Anne's brother Rocheford, Norris, Smeaton, Weston and Brereton
were all alleged adulterers with the Queen, an offence dealt with as
high treason, and according to the King's own crude statement,
committed by 'more than a hundred'. None of the accused either
affirmed or denied his guilt, but Anne herself admitted that
Norris, Weston and Smeaton, a Court musician, had made over-
tures of love to her. The poem concludes:

> And thus farwell eche one in harte wyse!
> The Axe ys home, your hedys be in the stret;
> The trykklynge tearys dothe fall so from my yes²
> I skarse may wryt, my paper ys so wet.
> But what can hepe³ when dethe hath playd his part,
> Thoughe naturs cours wyll thus lament and mone?
> Leve sobs therfor, and every crestyn⁴ hart
> Pray for the sowlis of thos be dead and gone.

¹ favour   ² eyes   ³ hope   ⁴ Christian

If Wyatt wrote this he must have been oppressed by the dread prospect of his own imminent execution, for Anne herself met the headsman on 19 May. Wyatt, however, was released the following month, when, presumably, he wrote the poem on his innocence, bewailing that

> These blodye dayes haue brokyn my hart
> My lust, my youth dyd then departe
> And blynd desyer of astate;
> Who hastis to clyme sekes to reuerte
> Of truthe, *circa Regna tonat.*

By three independent sixteenth-century commentators Wyatt is said to have told either Henry VIII or his Council before the King married Anne that she had been his (Wyatt's) mistress and was therefore unsuited to be Queen of England. Such frankness, together with the fact that he seems to have become alienated from her by 1532 and was therefore certainly not in the same category as the five accused of adultery with her in her person as Queen, is thought to have saved Wyatt from the scaffold. His poem

> Some tyme I fled the fyre that me brent,
>   By see, by land, by water and by wynd;
> And now I folow the coles that be quent[1]
>   From Dovor to Calais against my mynde.
> Lo! how desire is boeth sprong and spent!
>   And he may se that whilome[2] was so blynde;
> And all his labor now he laugh to scorne,
> Mashed in the breers[3] that erst was all to[4] torne.

refers to Wyatt's journey to Calais in October, 1532, as one of a retinue of courtiers accompanying Henry and Anne to a meeting with the King of France. A month previously she had been created Marchioness of Pembroke and established as Henry's mistress. On 1 June, 1533, she was crowned Queen, and Wyatt is known to have attended the coronation as deputy for his father.

Apart from that mentioned above, there is little direct autobiography in Wyatt's poems. His love lyrics, mostly written in the

[1] quenched   [2] once   [3] briars   [4] utterly

early 1520s, were stereotyped in subject matter, and the figure of the unhappy lover is not necessarily that of Wyatt, but a conventional male courtly symbol, trapped, rejected and tortured by his unfaithful fair. Occasionally, he strikes a more personal note, as in 'They fle from me that sometyme did me seke', and in such instances even his use of the convention is his own and not simply a putting-together of familiar clichés.

> Sens that my language without eloquence
> Ys playne unpainted and not unknowen,
> Dyspache myn answere with redy utteraunce

runs one verse known to be Wyatt's and included in the Blage MS of Trinity College, Dublin. Sir George Blage, (1512–51) was a member of parliament who narrowly missed burning at the stake for heresy in 1546. He accompanied Wyatt to Spain (1537–9) and Surrey to France (1543) and collected poems by Wyatt, Surrey, and a number of unidentified authors. Some of the unidentified poems may be Wyatt's, for they are undoubtedly in his style.

> Dryven to Desyre, a drad[1] also to Dare,
> Bitwene two stoles my tayle goith to the ground

and

> Spytt off the spytt[2] whiche they in vayne
> Do styk[3] to force my fantasye

have the 'jerk and sting' of a Donne conceit.

·   ·   ·   ·   ·   ·

Over thirty of Wyatt's letters to Henry VIII, Cromwell and others, including his own son, have survived. They afford some insight into his professional life as an ambassador and one or two of his poems may be linked with his movements in other countries between 1537 and 1539.

> Tagus, fare well! that westward with thy stremes
> Torns up the grayns of gold alredy tryd:
> With spurr and sayle for I go seke the Tems
> Gaynward the sonne that shewth her welthi pryd;

[1] afraid   [2] spite   [3] hesitate

seems to have been composed in about June, 1539, as Wyatt was on his way home from Toledo.

The correspondence includes descriptions of incidents in which Wyatt was involved, such as the apprehension of a renegade Welshman called Robert Brancetour in Paris, quoted elsewhere as an example of colloquial Court prose. In the same letter (to Henry VIII) there is a graphic account of a lengthy dialogue between Wyatt and the Emperor of France concerning this same Brancetour. Here is a snatch of it:

'It may be', quod th'emperour, 'that thei have done. I woll wryte to the Cardinal of Toledo, that is inquisitor maior, that I may be informid, but this is but on partie'.

'Nay, sir', quod I, 'this is *ex officio* that thei troble our nation, ffor thei have that that tho a man lyve never so upryghtly by thire examinations thei shall trap hym, where there is no publication of wittnesis'.

'I can not tell yow', quod he, 'but gyve me, gyve me that by wrytyng wheroff ye fynd ye grevid and I shall wryte by the next in to Spain to informe me'.

'Sir', quod I, 'Monsieur de Grandvele hath alredy the very copie of that part of the lettre that was sent me'.

'Well', quod he, 'I shall se it'.

'But there is yet more, sir,' quod I, 'prechers be set forth that diffame the kyng and the nation and provok your subiectes agaynst the kinges'.

'As in that', quod he, 'prechers woll speke agaynst my selff when there is cause. That can not be lett'.

'Why, Sir', quod I, 'your selff have ere this commandid other ways. When I was in Toledo in like cass'.

'I woll tell yow, Monsieur l'embassadeur', quod he, 'kynges be not kinges of tonges, and if men gyve cause to be spoken off, thei woll be spoken off: there is no remedy.

(*The Life and Letters of Sir Thomas Wyatt*, 7 January 1540; ed. K. Muir, [1963] p. 126)

R

Wyatt's despatches reveal that he had a diplomat's tact and clarity of communication, vivid and precise in detail but not cluttered with trivia. He was no pliable, bowing courtier, but a tough-minded emissary of his King who shared many of Henry's qualities including that of physical agility. His place in literary history is that of a pioneer, but since he was not printed during his own lifetime his influence was mainly personal. When a few of his poems were published fifteen years after his death they were subordinated to those of his disciple Surrey, whose greater polish attracted the Elizabethans more than Wyatt's rough-hewn gallantries, intricacies and strained conceits, inherited by him from the Italianate tradition. Examples of these are the tortured allusions to love as a galley steered by cruelty through angry seas, sails ripped by tempestuous sighs; a spring bursting its banks; a gun exploding due to overcharging, or a mountain weeping from its many fountains—all of which encouraged Warton and successive critics to make ironic remarks about Wyatt, while finding little fault in Surrey, a poet who in their view cast out the metaphysical excesses of Petrarchanism.

.   .   .   .   .   .

An inseparable literary companion of Wyatt is Henry Howard, Earl of Surrey, elder son of Thomas Howard, who became the Third Duke of Norfolk in 1524. Surrey was born in 1517 and spent his life as a courtier and soldier in the service of Henry VIII. Henry's illegitimate son, the Duke of Richmond, was a close friend of Surrey. The two men went to France in 1532 and travelled with the Court of Francis I. He was present at the trial of Anne Boleyn and served as a soldier under his father's command at the time of the so-called 'Pilgrimage of Grace'. The fact that an army, sent to crush a rebellion with which southern Catholics were bound to feel some sympathy, was under the command of a great Catholic family placed the Howards under suspicion. Surrey was involved in a brawl on account of an accusation of treason in 1539 and went to prison for a short time. However, he was soon reinstated and employed in organising defences. In 1541 he was made a Knight of the Garter. He is recorded as having been present at his cousin Catherine Howard's execution in 1542 and in the same year endured another spell in prison for duelling. With his father, he went to Scotland in 1543 and in 1543 served with the Emperor Charles V at the siege of Landreçy. An incident of riotous behaviour in London had put him back in prison earlier in that year. In 1545 he served as Marshal of the Field at the siege of Montreuil, where he was wounded and took part in several campaigns, showing himself to be reckless in the field of battle—in fact, he was reprimanded for taking needless risks. Recalled to England in March 1546, he was arrested in December, tried on treason indictments and beheaded on 19 January, 1547.

From this factual account it may be deduced that Surrey was headstrong, quick-tempered, dashing, quarrelsome, given to plain speaking, quick to take offence and to settle disputes by recourse to violence. Compared with Wyatt, he was a fiery individual but he held the elder man in great admiration and poetically he was the latter's disciple. He marks an obvious metrical advance on Wyatt, and his cadences appealed more to Victorian critics nurtured on the sensuous and passionate line of the Romantics than did the rougher-hewn Wyatt; but more recently it has been understood more clearly that, of the two, Wyatt was the real pioneer and that Surrey to a great extent drew upon the older man's example.

Surrey's output was more slender and less original than Wyatt's. He left about forty-five poems, four translations from classical authors, Horace, Martial and Virgil, and nine Biblical paraphrases. Emrys Jones' edition (1964) includes most of these. The Blage MS contains one poem and one fragment signed 'H' which were probably by Surrey. Like Wyatt, he imitated Italian models, especially Petrarch, from whom he sometimes translated directly. Warton said in his *History of English Poetry* (1781) that Surrey was 'the first English classical poet' (sec. xxxviii), by which he meant that here for the first time a native poet had responded to the spirit of the new learning. Surrey wrote verses with an eye on Latin diction just as English prose writers had been trying to do for twenty years. It is easy to see why the Elizabethans preferred him to Wyatt, as C. S. Lewis informs us, because he provided them with a ready-made model, polished, metrically precise and in choice of phrase elegantly turned. There is nothing definitely 'Chaucerian' about Surrey and his English qualities are less marked than Wyatt's. The poem which begins

> When sommer toke in hand the winter to assail
> With force of might and vertue gret his stormy blasts
> to quail,
> And when he clothed faire the earth about with grene,
> And every tree new garmented, that pleasure was to sene,
> Mine hart gan new revive, and changed blood dyd stur
> Me to withdraw my winter woe, that kept within the
> dore . . .

is as close to Chaucer as Surrey ever comes. Emrys Jones suggests (*op. cit.* p. 116–7) that it resembles the opening of *Troilus and Criseyde*. In another poem, commencing

> In winters just returne, when Boreas gan his raigne
> And every tree unclothed fast, as Nature taught them
> plaine

several echoes of Chaucer may be heard. The autobiographical

> So crewell prison howe could betyde, alas,
> As prowde Wyndsour, where I in lust and joye
> With a kinges soon my childishe yeres did passe,
> In greater feast than Priams sonnes of Troye,

which refers to Surrey's confinement to Windsor for committing assault on another courtier, Sir Edward Seymour, who had accused him of sympathising with the 'Pilgrimage of Grace' rebels, is a reminder of the medieval *'ubi sunt?'* form. Surrey is looking back with regret at past happinesses and glories, no longer in existence. A related emotion is captured in his epitaph on Wyatt, one of his finest poems:

> A hand that taught what might be sayd in ryme
> That reft Chaucer the glory of his wit;
> A mark that which, unparfited for time,[1]
> Some may approche, but never none shall hit.

[1] incomplete owing to lack of time

A toung that served in forein realmes his king
Whose courteous talke to vertue did enflame
Ech noble hart; a worthy guide to bring
Our English youth by travail unto fame. (11. 13–20)

Another poem, apparently of reminiscent indignation, begins:

London, hast thow accused me
Of breche of laws, the roote of strife?

and refers to his imprisonment in the Fleet prison for, as the
Privy Council records state,

eating off flesshe, as of a lewde and unsemely manner of
walking in the night abowght thr stretes and breaking with
stone bowes off certayne wyndowes (1 April, 1543)

Surrey had apparently roused respectable citizens from their early
morning slumbers by shooting at their windows with his bow and
throwing stones. Surprisingly enough, the second half of this
poem is thought by one critic (*i.e.* H. A. Mason, *Humanism
and Poetry in the Early Tudor Period* [1959], 243–5), to be Surrey's
manifesto of Protestant sentiments, a piece of new-critical perception which makes the scion of the country's oldest Catholic family
a convert to iconoclasm. In fact, Surrey is writing about London
and his intention is ruggedly satirical; the 'martyr's blood' which
calls for justice is his own. 'Membre of false Babylon' is the poet's
name for the centre of government whose officials committed him
to prison for breaking windows:

Thy wyndowes had done me no spight

cries Surrey, before launching into an exaggerated diatribe on the
respectable burghers of the City

. . . prowd people that drede no fall,
Clothed with falshed and upright
Bred in the closures of thy wall

Surrey's translations from Books II and IV of Virgil's *Aeneid* owe a great deal to Gavin Douglas' full-dress rendering of 1513. Their chief interest for the literary historian is that they were the first examples of 'blank verse' in English. Alamanni had experimented with unrhyming verse and so had several of his contemporaries, but it was almost certainly from Alamanni, whom Surrey may have met in Paris, that the English poet learned how the technique of adapting the Latin hexameter to suit a modern vernacular might be mastered. However, such a change as this was already in the air and to say that Surrey imitated the Italians is as misleading as to say that he imitated Chaucer's rhyme-royal. Blank verse was as close an approximation to natural speech as poetry could achieve without falling into *vers libre* or near-prose; in Surrey it was allied with a vocabulary consisting of 'aureate' or 'inkhorn' terms, not controlled by the tyranny of the Germanic alliterative tradition, but grounded in ordinary speech:

> Beholding this, what thought might Dido have?
> What sighes gave she? when from her towers hye
> The large coasts she saw haunted with Troyans workes,
> And in her sight the seas with din confounded.
> O witlesse love, what thing is that to do
> A mortal minde thou canst not force thereto!
>
> (Book IV, 536–41)

Compare Douglas' rendering of the same lines:

> Quhat[1] thocht thou now, Dydo, seand thir[2] thingis?
> Quhou[3] mony sobbys gave thou and womentyngis[4]
> Quhen[5] thou, out of thi castell from the hycht,
> The large costis[6] beheld thus at a sycht
> Ourspred with Trojanys, in fervent bissynes
> Can spedely for thar vayage addres,[7]
> And of thar clamour befor thine eyn dyd se
> Dyn and resounding al the large see?
> O wytles lufe! quhat may be thocht or do[8]
> At[9] thou constrenys nocht mortell myndis tharto?
>
> (IV, ch. viii, 1–20)

[1] what   [2] seeing these   [3] how   [4] lamentings   [5] when
[6] coasts   [7] prepare   [8] done   [9] that

Douglas wrote in rhyming couplets and his translation greatly expanded his original. Emrys Jones makes a detailed comparison of Surrey, Virgil, and Douglas, showing the degree of Surrey's indebtedness to Virgil (*ed. cit.*, pp. 134–47); Surrey is much closer to his model and aimed to achieve an English version of the Latin. He borrowed phrases and words from Douglas and indeed used the Scots *Eneados* as a second source but his translation is more emphatic, more precise, and more compressed than Douglas's which is an independent work in its own right, almost a substitute for the original and thereby coming close, as we have observed earlier, to Goethe's ideal of translation. Surrey's is a version of Virgil, Douglas's is a new poem, involving not only the mechanics of turning Latin into Middle Scots, but also the augmenting of the sense by means of copious additions drawn from the commentary of Badius Ascensius on the *Aeneid*.

The classical translations were probably early work, the sonnets following them; but this is not certain. The Vulgate paraphrases from *Ecclesiastes* and the *Psalms* were made late in 1546, mostly during Surrey's final incarceration in the Tower. The short lyrics opening

> When recheles youthe in an unquiet brest

and

> The soudden stormes that heave me to and froo

were intended as prologues to his versions of Psalms 88 and 73, the sentiments of which Surrey has adapted to his own condition. His sources were the Hebrew scholar Joannes Campensis's paraphrases published in 1532. Campensis, a Dutchman, was a pupil of Reuchlin and both Wyatt and Surrey knew and used his work. Faced with the sharp prospect of the axe, Surrey found his mood reflected in Psalm 88, which he recreated in intense metaphor, more graphic than its original:

> My soule is fraughted full with greif of follies past;
> My restles bodye doth consume and death approcheth fast;
>   Lyke them whose fatall threde thy hand hath cut in twayne,
> Of whome there is no further brewte which in their graves
>   remain.

Oh Lorde, thow hast cast me hedling to please my fooe,
Into a pitt all botomles, whear as I playne my wooe.
The burden of thy wrath it doth me sore oppresse,
And sundrye stormes thow hast me sent of terrour and distresse.
The faithfull frends ar fled and bannyshed from my sight,
And such as I have held full dere have sett my frendshipp light.

(5–14)

Wyatt and Surrey did not see their poems in print. Outside their immediate circle, their works were not known until 1557, when a Devonshire-born printer called Richard Tottel (1530–93) brought out a volume known to critics as Tottel's *Miscellany* but originally published under the title *Songes and Sonettes written by the ryght honorable Lorde Henry Haward late Earl of Surrey, and other*. The 'other' included Wyatt, Nicholas Grimald and a group of contemporaries, of whom Sir John Cheke, John Heywood the dramatist, Thomas Norton, co-author of *Gorboduc*, and Thomas Vaux are the best known. Only Surrey, Wyatt and Grimald are named, however, and that only in the first edition. Surrey contributed forty poems, Grimald is credited with another forty (reduced to ten in the second edition), Wyatt, by far the largest contributor, with ninety-seven. Two editions appeared in the space of two months in the summer of 1557. A third and a fourth followed in 1559, and by 1587 nine editions of the book had been published. By this time it had grown to include 310 poems. H. E. Rollins, who edited Tottel's *Miscellany* (1929) described its importance:

> Tottel's *Miscellany* is one of the most important single volumes in the history of English literature. If its contents as a whole hardly seem to deserve high praise today, still its influence demands that it be treated with genuine respect. As the first printed anthology, it is of the greatest historical importance: the beginning of modern English verse may be said to date from its publication in 1557.　　　(*ed. cit.*, II, introd. 4)

In the same year Tottel printed Surrey's *Aeneid*, which he stated on the title page to have been done in 'a strange metre', *i.e.* blank verse. Its most immediate influence was on Thomas Sackville, who used it in *Gorboduc* in imitation of Seneca's iambics, and on the *Induction* and *The Complaint of Henry Duke of Buckingham* written for *A Mirror For Magistrates*. Commentators have pointed out evident traces of Surrey's influence. Sackville was the author of one of the first verses praising Surrey, discovered in the 1930s in a hitherto unknown manuscript of *The Complaint*:

> Not Surrea he that hiest sittes in chair
> Of glistering fame for ay to live and raighn
> Not his proud ryme that thunders in the aier
> Nor al the plaintes wherin he wrote his pain
> When he lay fetterd in the fyry chain
> Of cruell love . . . (unfinished)
> (quoted by Emrys Jones, *ed. cit.*, xxiv, n. 2)

Perhaps Surrey and Sackville would make more logical literary relations than Surrey and Wyatt, with whom, after Tottel, he has always been associated. Rollins (*ed. cit.*, II, introd. 110) observed that 'the earliest Elizabethan poets, like Thomas Sackville, took the *Miscellany* as an infallible guide and text-book', and provided a substantial account of the many imitations and borrowings from Tottel which established the style and popularity of later anthologies besides affording philologists and dictionary-makers an exhaustive source of archaisms.

The lines

> What natures worke is this, in one wightes corps to hyde
> So gaye gyftes and so badd, ill mixte without ameane
> The happie head of wit, the tongue well sett to speake
> The skilfull pen in hand to paynt the wittes device . . .
> What saye we then by thee whose wittie workes we see
> Excell in kynde of vearse as worthie Chawcers mate

come from a poem in the Arundel Harington MS, an anthology compiled by John Harington, poet and friend of Surrey's (ed. Ruth Hughey, [1960], I, no. 282), and are credited to Sir John Cheke. The subject is almost certainly Surrey, who, with Wyatt, was the only poet of the first half of the sixteenth century who, in his own time, might have been compared with Chaucer.

11 : Poetry and Drama as a Mirror of History

IN a work called *The Art of Rhetoric* (1553–60), composed about the same time as *Gorboduc*, Sir Thomas Wilson explained how characters should be drawn, making particular reference to those personalities whom the authors of historical drama seek to recreate. Basing his prescriptions on Cicero and Quintilian, Wilson tried to improve on the stock portrait composed by medieval writers, which was grounded in an ordered catalogue of moral and physical features:

> In describing of persons, there ought always a comeliness to be used, so that nothing be spoken which may be thought is not in them. As if one should describe Henry VI. He might call him gentle, mild of nature, led by persuasion, and ready to forgive, careless for wealth, suspecting none, merciful to all, fearful in adversity, and without forecast to espy his misfortune. Again, for Richard III, I might bring him in cruel of heart, ambitious by nature, envious of mind, a deep dissembler, a close man for weighty matters, hardy to revenge and fearful to lose his high estate, trusty to none, liberal for a purpose, casting still the worst, and hoping ever for the best. By this figure also, we imagine a talk for some one to speak, and according to his person we frame the oration. As if one should bring in noble Henry VIII of famous memory, to enveigh against rebels, thus he might order his oration. *What if Henry VIII were alive, and sawe suche rebellion in the realme, would he not say thus and thus?* Yes, methinks I hear him speak even now. And so set forth such words as he would have him to say.   (*op. cit.*)

The authors of the dreary composite work *A Mirror For Magistrates*, printed in a succession of parts from 1559–87, seem to have read Wilson's injunction and acted upon it. The *Mirror*, originally the brainchild of Thomas Sackville, was a collection of recitatives about the misfortunes of noble personages in English history. It was patriotically conceived in the style of Boccaccio's *De Casibus Illustrium Virorum* and written in verse. The information on which tales depended was appropriated from contemporary *Chronicles*, as the title page of the 1555 section states, and the character of the narratives is historical rather than literary. The fact that all of them are gloomy gives the compilation a monotonously depressing dignity. Its nearest relation is Lydgate's *Fall of Princes* (1430), itself adapted from Boccaccio's work.

The 'falls' treated in the 1559 *Mirror* were nineteen in number. The most important historically included Richard II, James I, Henry VI, Edward IV, Owen Glendower and Jack Cade, together with a number of aspiring noblemen who lost their heads, were exiled or imprisoned or arrived at some miserable end. The 1563 additions include Sackville's *Induction* (really a separate preface to a projected series of which only one, on Henry, Duke of Buckingham, was actually written by the poet and included in the *Mirror*). This group contained the story of Jane Shore, Edward IV's concubine, who was disgraced by Richard II and forced to do public penance. The 1578 and 1587 editions dealt with more recent personages and incidents. James IV, Wolsey and the Battle of Flodden are three of the subjects. All told, the *Mirror's* reflections number thirty-three.

Although it is poetically uninspiring, the *Mirror* remains an important pioneer work since it dramatised history and linked political blunders with verse tragedy for the popular theatre. *Gorboduc*, by Sackville and his fellow-Oxonian Norton, translated the methods of the *Mirror* into an actable stage play and is usually described as a forerunner of Shakespeare's tragedies. It was written in blank verse, first used in English by Surrey. Of all known metres it provided the closest approximation to direct speech. The purpose of *Gorboduc* was political—to illustrate for Queen Elizabeth, a newly acceded monarch, the possible problems that might arise if she did not soon choose her successor. The hope that Elizabeth would marry, bear a male heir and thus make the succession indisputable was never to be realised. *Gorboduc*, in some respects a prefiguration of *King Lear*, underlines the prevailing belief that political bungling is avoidable and that the great fear of the Tudors, civil disobedience, is to be blamed on the bad judgment of individuals and not, as men thought in the late Middle Ages, on Fortune's caprices. Political responsibility was wholly man's own.

Sir Philip Sidney, writing before 1583, set the poet above the historian. In his *Apology For Poetry*, he stated:

> . . . the best of the historian is subject to the poet, for whatsoever action or faction, whatsoever council, policy or war stratagem the historian is bound to recite, that may the poet (if he list) with his imitation make his own, beautifying it both for further teaching and more delighting, as it pleaseth him, having all, from *Dante* his heaven to his hell, under the authority of his pen.

A Mirror For Magistrates suggests by its very title what it aims to do, that is, to provide a reflective surface in which 'magistrates', or rulers, may observe past human conduct, thus learning lessons to be put into effect in the course of their own administration. The dedication to the work, first printed in 1555, four years before the first edition, and written by its general editor William Baldwin, makes this clear:

> For here as in a looking-glass, you shall see (if any vice be in you) how the like hath been punished in other heretofore, whereby admonished, I trust it will be a good occasion to move you to the sooner amendment. The very titles of the tragedies emphasise the relation of sin to punishment, by way of offering a deterrent to sin.

The analogy of the mirror is Platonic in origin and was much used during the Middle Ages to describe works in which man was afforded a view of his own virtues and vices by way of stimulation to his supposedly almost blunted conscience—*The Ship of Fools* and similar compositions are examples. By the year *A Mirror For Magistrates* was first made available to the public, Tudor political doctrine had crystallised into the theoretical reliance upon one ruler usually known as the 'Divine Right of Kings'. Sovereignty had been embodied in the person of Henry VIII and English royal power exalted in opposition to Papal authority. The king became the Law and occupied the Pope's place as vice-regent to God. Rebellion against the king was considered the same as rebellion against God. Tyrants were sent by divine decision to punish the people, for since kings could not alienate a God-given right, the character of the king, good or bad as it may be, had to be endured and the law obeyed. Baldwin's *Dedication* explains this in fairly simple terms:

> For it is Gods own office, yea his chief office, which they bear and abuse. For, as Justice is the chief virtue, so is the administration thereof, the chiefest office; and therefore hath God established it with the chiefest name, honouring and calling Kings, and all officers under them by his own name, Gods. Ye be all Gods, as many as have in your charge any ministration of justice. What a foul shame were it for any now to take upon them the name and office of God, and in their doings to show themselves devils. God can not of justice, but plague such shameless presumption and hypocrisy, and that with shameful death, diseases or infamy. How he hath plagued evil rulers from time to time, in other nations, you may see gathered in Boccaccio's book entitled the *Fall of Princes*, translated into English by Lydgate. How he has dealt with some of our countrymen your ancestors for sundry vices not yet left, this book called *A Mirror For Magistrates* can show.
>
> (*op. cit.*, spelling modernised by the author, from L. B. Campbell's ed. [1960].)

. . . . . .

The sixteenth century witnessed a slow process of recovery from the anarchy of the fifteenth, the latter described in an official document referring to the reign of Henry VI as urgently in need of reform:

> not plenty, peace, justice, good governance, policy and virtuous conversation, but unrest, inward war and trouble, unrighteousness, shedding and effusion of innocent blood, abusion of the laws, partiality, riot, extortion, murder, rape and vicious living have been the guides and leaders of the noble

realm of England. (*Rotuli Parlementorum*; ed. H. G. Richards and G. Sayles [1935], V, 464)

This was the England of Malory. The Yorkist doctrine of the hereditary right to rule offered Henry VII an opportunity to restore order effectively. After his victory over Richard III at Bosworth in 1485 and his immediate claim to the throne, Henry might reasonably have been considered yet another adventurer, even a usurper, since his accession was by no means undisputed. His English royal descent had come through his mother, Margaret Beaufort, grand-daughter of John Beaufort, who was in his turn the illegitimate offspring of John of Gaunt, Edward III's son. The Beauforts had been declared legitimate under an Act passed in Richard II's reign but the latter's successor, Henry IV, had tried to cancel their right of succession by inserting an appropriate clause in their 'letters patent' or royal authority supporting their aristocratic rights. Elizabeth, Edward IV's daughter, and the young Duke of Clarence, son of Edward's brother, were both surviving members of the Yorkist house, but John of Gaunt's descendants had included the Lancastrian kings of the fifteenth century. Henry Tudor's claim, through the Beauforts, was really a Lancastrian claim, historically a strong one though legally open to question.

Henry was a shrewd man and did not press his rights by descent. Instead, he took the crown and immediately set about establishing a sound administration, dedicated to maintaining the law. Within a couple of months of his victory at Bosworth he had claimed hereditary right by statute for the lawful heirs of his body and no others, and passed other statutes concerning the return of Crown lands, levying of taxes and collection of revenue. In a ceremony presided over by himself, he exacted an oath from the Lords and Commons to the effect that they would not aid criminals, maintain private armies, create rebellions or unlawful assemblies or in any way obstruct the course of civic justice. Five months after Bosworth, Henry married Elizabeth of York (as he had promised to do over two years earlier while he was still an exile in Brittany gathering his forces for a campaign against the usurper Richard). Their second son was to become Henry VIII, their elder daughter Margaret, the wife of James IV of Scotland. In the reign of Henry VIII, relations with Scotland were to play a significant part in determining his policies.

Henry VII, in theory at least, was making his son's colourful reign possible by laying down the basis for strong government so that any lack of logic in his claim to be the rightful successor might be compensated for by *faits accomplis* and the beginnings of a constructive policy. At the end of *Richard III*, Shakespeare makes Richmond, the future Henry VII, declaim:

> Proclaim a pardon to the soldiers fled
> That in submission will return to us;
> And then, as we have ta'en the sacrament,
> We will unite the white rose and the red:
> Smile, heaven, upon this fair conjunction,
> That long hath frown'd upon their enmity!
> What traitor hears me, and says not amen?
> England hath long been mad, and scarr'd herself;
> The brother blindly shed the brother's blood,
> The father rashly slaughter'd his own son,
> The son, compell'd, been butcher to the sire;
> All this divided York and Lancaster,
> Divided in their dire division.
> O! now, let Richmond and Elizabeth,
> The true succeeders of each royal house,
> By God's fair ordinance conjoin together;
> And let their heirs—God, if thy will be so,—
> Enrich the time to come with smooth-fac'd peace,
> With smiling plenty, and fair prosperous days!
> Abate the edge of traitors, gracious Lord,
> That would reduce these bloody days again,
> And weep poor England weep in streams of blood!
> Let them not live to taste this land's increase,
> That would with treason wound this fair land's peace!
> Now civil wounds are stopp'd, peace lives again:
> That she may long live here, God say amen!
>
> (V, iv, 29–54)

This chronicle account of the motives governing Henry's calculated actions was not inaccurate, though the practical application of his remedies was not to be so easily carried through. Much of his time was spent in putting down rebellions, passing and enforcing laws to prevent such insurrections, dealing with rival claimants, like Lambert Simnel, and in keeping the Scots at peace by promoting a policy of friendship which James III tried constructively to reciprocate in the face of his own nobles' hostility. Later in Henry's reign appeared the imposter Perkin Warbeck, who claimed to be Richard of York, the younger of the princes murdered in the Tower by Richard III. First in Ireland, long a seat of disaffection, then in France and the Netherlands, then in Ireland again and finally in Scotland and Cornwall, this self-styled 'Duke of York' tried with varying success to promote his own cause. Accompanied by 1,400 adventurers from half a dozen countries, Warbeck was very well received by James IV, who treated him at his own valuation as future King of England and on his account made a half-hearted attempt to invade England in the summer of 1497. However, by this year it could be said that no serious internal threat of armed rebellion against Henry existed, and the capture and eventual execution of Warbeck improved his relations with James, who became his son-in-law in September, 1503.

This was the marriage celebrated by Dunbar in *The Thistle and the Rose*, though, unfortunately, it did not have the improving effect on Anglo-Scottish relations that Henry hoped it would. It was preceded by a treaty of perpetual peace, ratified in January, 1502, the first 'peace' between the two countries since the treaty of Northampton in 1328. It clashed with the 'auld alliance' between Scotland and France, renewed once again in 1491–2, and put James in line for succession to the English throne. Henry VIII renewed it in 1509 and, from that time onwards, the fortunes of the two kingdoms could not be separated, although their relations were very far from being peaceful. James IV, pledged to both France and England, long-standing enemies, and James V, pledged to support Catholicism, fast becoming a lost cause, kept the quarrel alive.

Political historians agree that the years to 1503 were the best of Henry VII's reign. He had by then set England on a more prosperous course than had seemed likely at the opening of his administration and the internal strife that had bedevilled the times of his predecessors seemed to be a thing of the past. Most Englishmen believed in the rule of law and in its divine origin. Natural law was held to be an expression of divine law and the civil law, by which the king governed, was rooted in natural law. Henry VII conformed to the popular notion of how a ruler acting according to established methods of justice should behave, and so etched a distinct pattern for his successors. The country needed an efficient government which ordinary people as well as warring nobles would support and the victor of Bosworth provided it, thus continually strengthening his own position.

The increasing exaltation of royal authority in opposition to that of the Pope marked the greater part of the reign of Henry VIII, who inherited an orderly and economically sound administration from his father in 1509. The elder Henry had been a conserver of money, a careful attender to matters of taxation and an accumulator of capital who believed in fines as punishments for legal transgressions. Moreover, he supervised the national accounts himself. His son, richly endowed by his father's wise handling of the national revenues, turned out to be extravagant, profligate, anxious to cut a dash in the world, as other European princes had recently done, and careless of interests other than his own. He entered into costly military adventures against the old enemy France, against Scotland and against the Emperor Maximilian with France as an ally. By 1525 he had made severe inroads into the royal treasury, and in spite of attempts to raise money by imposing extra taxation on his subjects, Henry was inevitably short of ready cash for his schemes. His relations with successive parliaments over accounts and the raising of revenue were bad.

However, Henry VIII was a true 'prince', highly gifted both physically and mentally, and generously endowed with the 'virtuous' qualities of the leader which were the mainspring of a Renaissance state. Henry possessed this *virtù*, the heroic mould had cast him, and he was well fitted to fill the role of England's champion against foreign interference. J. D. Mackie described him as 'a king "whose conscience would not suffer him to do wrong"; it always told him that he was right'. Because of this arrogant streak, which ran through all the Tudors, his policies were pragmatic, designed to serve his own personal interests and those of no-one else; he surrounded himself with competent and hard-working men, whom he used and discarded when it suited him to do so. His marriages were all conceived in this same spirit of desire for possession, the gaining of an heir and, with like cold-bloodedness, were dissolved by decree or by the headsman's axe.

The immense influence of Cardinal Wolsey over the country's fortunes was a central feature of government until 1529. Wolsey, a butcher's son whose lowly origin was the butt of poets and satirists from Skelton to Shakespeare, advanced rapidly until he was made Papal Viceroy (Legate *a latere*) in 1518. This put him in a position of supremacy over the Church in England. His amassing of a huge fortune, made up of Chancery fees, stipends from all kinds of sources, profits from pluralism, sundry pensions and gratuities, was eventually symbolised by his four residences, of which the best known was Hampton Court Palace on the Thames. If Henry was an autocrat in secular affairs, Wolsey fulfilled a like function in ecclesiastical matters and indeed secular also, for he was the efficient instrument through which the power of the King was exercised—the Lord Chancellor of the Realm.

Wolsey was a very capable man and many of his reformatory intentions were good, but his own personal ambition and avarice, well known to readers of history and usually characterised on the stage by an obese personage concentrating in himself the Deadly Sins of Pride, Envy, Luxury, Greed in all its conceivable variants and especially Anger—for the Cardinal was a man of irascible temper—have made a balanced appraisal of his virtues difficult to render. Wolsey has gone down in record as a corrupt figure of superhuman dimensions, a personality dear to the hearts of play-wrights for, having been raised on Fortune's wheel to colossal eminence, Wolsey was just as surely thrown down again. *A Mirror For Magistrates* included him as the thirty-third subject of tragedy, prefacing the moral lesson with the title:

HOW THOMAS WOLSEY did arise unto great authority and government, his maner of life, pompe and dignity, and how hee fell downe into great disgrace, and was arested of high treason

which indicated that here was a real-life example of the pride that goes before a fall and, moreover, a very recent instance of Fortune's fickleness. Wolsey tells his own story ponderously, dwelling on his errors remorsefully:

> O let mee curse, the popish Cardnall hat,
> Those myters big, beset with pearle and stones,
> And all the rest, of trash I know not what,
> The saints in shrine, theyr flesh and rotten bones,
> The maske of Monkes, devised for the nones,
> And all the flocke, of Freers, what ere they are,
> That brought mee up, and left mee there so bare.
>
> O cursed priestes, that prate for profits sake,
> And follow floud, and tyde, where ere it floes:
> O marchaunts fine, that do advantage take
> Of every grayne, how ever market goes . . .
>
> Your fault not half, so great as was my pryde,
> For which offence, fell *Lucifer* from skyes:
> Although I would, that wilfull folly hyde,
> The thing lyes playne, before the peoples eyes,
> On which hye heart, a hatefull name doth ryes,
> It hath beene sayde, of olde, and dayly will,
> Pryde goes before, and shame comes after still.
>
> (337–64)

and then goes into an anguished denunciation of pride, which he abuses in the style of a medieval satirist:

> Pryde is a thing, that God and man abores,
> A swelling tode, that poysons every place,
> A stinking wounde, that breedeth many sores,
> A privy plague, found out in stately face,
> A paynted byrd, that keepes a pecocks pace,

A lothsome lowt, that lookes like tinkers dog,
A hellish hownd, a swinish hatefull hog

That grunts and groanes, at every thing it sees,
And holds up snowt, like pig that coms from draffe . . .

(365–73)

In the person of Wolsey, her proliferating critics found a perfect symbol for attacking the more blatant shortcomings of the Church. He seemed to have concentrated in himself the grosser side of Rome's material power and, without intending to bring it about, was by his own intemperate actions preparing the ground for the subordination of Church to State. He was a skilled administrator and perfected the machinery of justice by developing the traditional efficiency of the Court of Star Chamber. This was a medieval court revived by Henry VII to maintain law and order; Wolsey used it to repress the corruption of lower courts. He tried to halt land enclosure and consequently made enemies among large land-owners; as Lord Chancellor he was an active and continuous legislator. As Papal Legate he ruled the Church in England with an iron hand but in ecclesiastical matters a man having Wolsey's weaknesses and lack of scruple was the last person likely to remedy the obvious abuses of clerical jurisdiction and privilege since, after all, he cultivated them both himself. He has been described as 'a one-man powerhouse', who had few friends and who generated hostility in every class of English society.

But his secular power came from the King, who used him and, in the end, discarded him after the Cardinal's Papal authority clashed with Henry's in the matter of divorcing Catherine of Aragon and marrying Anne Boleyn. More succeeded Wolsey as Lord Chancellor and in November, 1529, the latter's chequered career came to an abrupt halt. He died in 1531 while on his way from York to London to answer charges of high treason which would almost certainly have resulted in his condemnation and execution. Reference has already been made to Skelton's *Magnyfycence*, usually thought to be at least in part a satire on Wolsey, but in fact the play was conceived too early to fulfil this role as precisely as some literary historians would like to believe. Skelton composed *Magnyfycence* about 1515 but Wolsey's really ambitious period came in the 1520s, when *Speke, Parrot, Colin Cloute* and *Why Come Ye Not To Courte?* were written. The latter undoubtedly did have Wolsey as a target, but a recent study of the play, William O. Harris's *Magnyfycence and the Cardinal Virtue Tradition* (1965) finds little evidence in favour of the theses that Skelton's plot was a mirror of the first seven years of Henry VIII's Court, corresponded with any historical pattern or even had Wolsey cast as villain. *Magnyfycence* is (on this scholar's argument) to be more accurately interpreted as a play in the 'advice to a prince' category written in the medieval morality tradition and aimed at Henry VIII. By 1515 Henry had revealed himself as intemperate and lacking in the cardinal virtue of fortitude thought essential to kingship. Fortitude, according to Cicero's *De Officiis* (taught by Skelton to Henry as a young boy and recommended by Elyot and others as an important manual for the education of young noblemen), was a virtue which enabled a man to hold both prosperity and adversity in contempt. Contemporary definitions of fortitude brought in 'magnificence' or magnanimity and Alexander Barclay used the terms synonymously in his version of Mancinus' *Four Virtues*, published in about 1517. Older interpretations of magnificence as an Aristotelian quality, of Wolsey as the villain and Henry as the symbol of over-lavishness are now made suspect or at least only partially tenable. (See in this connection R. L. Ramsay's Early English Text Society ed. of *Magnyfycence* [1908], preface; and this writer's *Medieval Drama* [1968], 131–4.)

.   .   .   .   .   .

The second half of Henry's reign saw him break with Rome, dissolve the monasteries, and declare himself Head of the Church— a process first set in motion in 1524 under Wolsey which became an accomplished fact in 1539. These acts were accomplished with the aid of another unpopular man of power, the industrious Thomas Cromwell, a violent hater of clergy helped to promotion by Wolsey in the 1520s who shared some of the Cardinal's qualities. Unlike Wolsey, however, Cromwell sought power alone, never its outward shows. Machiavelli would have approved of his methods;

he was a prodigious drafter of legal statutes, for the Reformation Parliament required an exhaustive network of legislative measures to ensure that Crown and State spoke with one voice.

Wolsey had done much to strengthen the hatred of the ordinary Englishman for the Church's material influence. Henry had sought the aid of Parliament, which he had long regarded as a thorn in his flesh and a spoiler of his projects, in order to combat Papal authority. Now he wanted it developed as an institution that would support the Crown's supremacy and in this Reformation Parliament the King discovered an authority representative of the national will to change and in particular to expel foreign influence. In a succession of Acts, of which the 1534 Acts of Succession and Supremacy were the culminating ones, he gave statutory sanction to the dissolution of his marriage to Catherine and to his intention to marry Anne Boleyn, whose children would enjoy rights of succession; he asserted that he himself was and should be Head of the Church of England, an office which to all intents and purposes he already filled.

Refusal to take the oaths of Succession and Supremacy resulted in the execution of a number of priests for high treason under yet another newly constituted Act. One of these men was Sir Thomas More, beheaded in 1535, whose dogmas supported him to the bitter end on Tower Hill. Henry's avowed motives were to maintain Christian unity, to crush rebellions and rebels, to chase away the spirit of anarchy from a land wherein allegiance might easily be divided and to establish his new-style monarchy as the undisputed symbol of England's government. In effect he was saying, like Louis XIV, '*l'état, c'est moi!*' and proclaiming the doctrine of absolutism.

The dissolution of the monasteries and the ratification of their seizure was completed under the supervision of Cromwell, appointed deputy to the Supreme Head of the Church under the title of 'Vicar-General'. Excommunicated by a Papal Bull of August, 1535, Henry immediately launched two investigations, one into the conduct of monks, the second into Church revenues. Henry's real object was to get his hands on the monastic estates. The monasteries themselves had ceased to be centres of culture or even luxurious palaces for idle clerics and by this time had de-generated into places wherein the country's unemployables, the untalented, the shiftless and even the criminal could establish themselves out of harm's way. Their connection with religious observance had in many respects become purely nominal. The end of monasticism brought great wealth to the Crown and made up for the denuding of Henry's treasury during the first half of his reign. It resulted in a distribution of property, in exchange for money, among a number of individuals, initially about a thousand persons, of whom about half were nobles, royal officials and court-iers, the remainder mostly professional men and civil servants of the new era. About five thousand monks, sixteen hundred friars and two thousand nuns were pensioned off. Few of them suffered personally and the majority emerged from the upheaval to their material advantage. Buildings and movable property, including furniture, gold plate, leading from roofs and stonework were sold by the government, pillaged or simply ruined or defaced. The extensive monastic libraries were destroyed or broken up in acts of vandalism committed by ignorant louts whose efforts resulted in the disappearance of untold MS treasures which, had they sur-vived, would greatly have enriched medieval literature.

Fortunately, not all of these were permanently lost, and anti-quaries like Leland, Cotton and Camden performed a magnificent task of rescue and reconstruction. One may wonder, nevertheless, if a work like *Sir Gawain and the Green Knight*, existing in a single MS unheard-of until the late seventeenth century, might not have been rivalled by others lost forever in this first furious wave of 'icon-breaking'. The MSS of miracle-play cycles that have sur-vived represent only a proportion of what was originally available for performance in English and Scottish towns, and it is surely not coincidence that the cycles which remain complete are all of northern English origin. The fate of copies made in the south, nearer to the centre of Tudor government, and in Scotland, where the teeth of the Reformation were particularly sharp, is obscure. None are now extant.

However, the desire to suppress the old monastic communities did not mean that miracle cycles were fundamentally attacked as being wrong, even when the campaign of Cromwell was at its height. The Reformation of Henry was an attempt to change Church government, not doctrine, and had not yet become a theological struggle. Provided that the content of a play did not appear to constitute a political threat or to imply criticism of the new movement performances were not censured. Occasionally, plays staged in the presence of a popular audience, as interludes often were, turned out to provide a focus for local uprisings, though this was truer of Edward IV's reign than of Henry's, as Holinshed's *Chronicle* makes clear. The 'Pilgrimage of Grace', in which the Earl of Surrey took part, was an early manifestation of northern English resentments against Henrician policy designed to break down the old order. Miracle cycles, which were not political in content except for certain interpolations of a topical character which could easily have been excised without interfering with the main action of the drama, were left alone until after Elizabeth's accession.

Performances of cycles were first stopped in the eastern counties and the last pageant-spectacles at Chelmsford and Romney were held in the 1560s. In this part of the country official religious policy was closely followed and supervision was strict. Later, the running-down of the cycles reached the north, which had enjoyed a long tradition of municipal independence dating back to the fourteenth century. The beleaguered civic authorities which kept the plays going, in, for example, Newcastle, Doncaster, York, Wakefield, Chester and Lincoln, tried to maintain the still popular pageants for as long as they could but, in the end, the arm of suppression reached out to break the ancient links between theatre and old Church. This was done by a series of local pressures, first by censorship of the texts on doctrinal grounds, then by specific authority of austere prelates of the new school like Archbishop Grindal of York, a strict Puritan. The ecclesiastical conflicts of the 1570s and 1580s brought Puritanism to the forefront and pheno-mena like the miracle cycles and the colourful Corpus Christi procession which normally accompanied them were obvious targets. Grindal was as typical of his time as Cromwell had been forty years earlier. The same destructive forces operated in every country in Europe, even in those that remained faithful to Rome, where a cleansing process was felt necessary. Only in Spain did the religious drama manage to survive in anything like its old splendour; everywhere else, it was made to disappear while still beloved of the popular audiences who sustained it both by taking part and as detached spectators.

. . . . . .

In Scotland, the miracle cycles were harder to suppress and isolated performances went on until the end of the century in defiance of official prohibitions. In 1574 the General Assembly of the new Kirk stated weightily that

> Forasmuch as it is considered that the playing of clerk-plays, comedies or tragedies, upon the canonical parts of the Scriptures, induceth and bringeth with it a contempt and profanation of the same, it is thought meet and concluded that no clerk-plays, comedies or tragedies be made upon canonical Scriptures, either New or Old, in time coming, other (*either*) upon the Lord's Day or upon a work day, that the contravenors, if they be ministers, be secluded from their functions, and that others be corrected by the discipline of the Kirk. (Quoted in Harold C. Gardiner, *Mysteries' End* [1946, reprinted 1967], p. 89)

In Perth, where the conservative element seems to have been particularly stubborn, the Kirk Session records informed posterity that it had convened a meeting

> because certain inhabitants of this town as well against the express commandment of the civil magistrates in counsel as against the Minister's prohibition in pulpit has played Corpus Christi play upon Thursday the vi of June last (1577) which day was wont to be called Corpus Christi Day to the great slander of the Church of God and dishonour to the whole town. And because the said play is idolatrous, superstitious and also slanderous as well by reason of the idle day. (*Ibid.*, 90)

and in 1588 the same body refused baptism to children in order to enforce the obedience of their fathers in the matter of prohibition. Hatred of Popery was more radical than it was in England, yet the old religious drama died hard in the north and there are suggestions of 'underground' performances as late as 1617; the passing of the Corpus Christi play left an unfilled emotional vacuum in the hearts of popular audiences in both countries.

Turning back to Henry VIII's reign, it is important to note that Henry was a professed believer in Roman dogmas until the end of his life and that the feelings of the ordinary man in England remained essentially unchanged until the latter half of Elizabeth's reign. Cromwell, whose popularity eventually sank almost as low as Wolsey's had done, clashed with Henry over concessions to the Protestants. He had started to effect changes in Catholic doctrine, to have religious images removed, to make the sermon an essential part of the church service ritual and to have texts taught in English, not Latin. Above all, he lent strong support to Bible translations, first Coverdale's, then the 'Great Bible', and sought an alliance with the German Lutherans—far more extreme doctrinal innovators than the English Protestants of the time ever dreamed of becoming—and so laid himself open to a charge of treason. Henry's marriage to Anne of Cleves, whose brother occupied an important Protestant territory on the lower Rhine, was arranged by Cromwell but was a failure. The King withdrew his favour, Cromwell's parliamentary enemies 'attainted' him for treason on the grounds that he had encroached on royal authority and in 1540 he was executed, ironically enough under the provisions of an Act which six years earlier he himself had been responsible for drafting.

At no time did Henry allow disaffected elements to combine, produce an influential leader and rise up against him. Of unsuccessful uprisings there were many, generated by members of the hereditary aristocracy whose sympathies lay with Rome, like the Howards and the Wriothesleys. Henry married a Howard, Catherine, niece of the Duke of Norfolk, in 1540, after his marriage with Anne of Cleves had been dissolved. Early in 1542 she was executed for adultery, expressed formally and legally as 'high treason', as had been the case with Anne Boleyn six years before. In 1543 the King took his last bride, Catherine Parr, who survived him. The roll-call of his six wives, expressed in terms of a medieval pageant, might have provided an attractive subject for later dramatists, for the fact of his successive marriages is usually the first thing that one remembers about Henry—only his third wife, Jane Seymour (by dying after giving birth to the future Edward VI), escaped marital disgrace or execution while Henry lived. His divorces and annulments were political acts, declarations of independence from Rome; Shakespeare's *Henry VIII*, a mediocre play only partly of his authorship, deals cryptically with the divorce from Catherine of Aragon, the fall of Wolsey and the marriage to Anne Boleyn, culminating in the birth of the child Elizabeth—no further motive than this is sought.

The last years of Henry's reign witnessed a continuous struggle between the Reformers and their opponents, with each side gaining occasional advantages. The King himself maintained a balance of power between the two factions, taking action only when he felt threatened. In 1545 he told his Parliament that Papist, Lutheran and Anabaptist were but names devised by the Devil to separate one man's heart from another's and urged the practice of charity, which he said was the foundation of all religion. Yet he was in these final years inclined towards Protestantism and, when he died in January, 1547, aged fifty-five, England had already taken decisive steps towards becoming a Protestant country.

.   .   .   .   .   .

After 1533 both Cromwell and Archbishop Cranmer encouraged politically suitable plays. An ultra-Protestant German drama called *Pammuchius*, written by Thomas Kirchmeyer ('Naogeorgos') in 1536, was dedicated to Cromwell in its translated form two years later and from this time forth anti-Catholic plays appeared in England with increasing frequency. The translator of *Pammuchius* was John Bale (1495–1563) an ardent Reformer, who wrote a number of morality plays having a clear historical background. The best known of these is *King John*, written in the late 1530s, often referred to as the first English play to combine real characters with moral abstractions. The *dramatis personae* include King John, England, described as 'a widow', and Clergy, all four played by one actor; Sedition, Civil Order, Stephen Langton and Com-

monalty (one actor); Nobility, Cardinal Pandulphus and Private
Wealth (one actor); Dissimulation, Raymundus and Simon of
Swinsett or Swinstead (one actor); Usurped Power and the Pope
(one actor) and an Interpreter, Treason, Verity and Imperial
Majesty. Of these John, Langton, Pandulphus, Raymundus and
Simon were presented as historical characters. Imperial Majesty
was a thinly disguised Henry VIII.

This play shows obvious signs of the influence of *Panmuchius*
and of Cromwell's encouragement. The language used in reference
to the Pope is intemperate and contains many farmyard analogies,
usually to 'pigs' or 'swine'. A conversation near the beginning of
the action between John, England and Sedition will illustrate this
abusive quality in the speeches:

ENG.   . . . the wild boar of Rome—God let him never
to thee! Like pigs they follow in fantasies, dreams
and lies; and ever are fed with his vile ceremonies.

SED.   Nay, sometimes they eat both flauns[1] and pigeon pies.

K. JOHN By the boar of Rome, I trow, thou meanest the
Pope?

ENG.   I mean none other but him; God give him a rope!

K. JOHN And why dost thou thus compare him to a swine?

ENG.   For that he and his to such beastliness incline.
They forsake God's word, which is most pure and
    clean,
And unto the laws of sinful men they lean;
Like as the vile swine the most vile meats desire
And hath great pleasure to wallow themselves in mire,
So hath this wild boar with his church universal;
His sow, with her pigs and monsters bestial,
Delight in men's draff and covetous lucre all;
Yea, *aper de silva*[2] the prophet did him call.

SED.   Hold your peace, ye whore! or else, by Mass, I trow
I shall cause the Pope to curse ye as black as a crow.
(ed. J. S. Farmer; modernised reprint by Charles W.
Traylen)

[1] pancakes   [2] the boar out of the wood

and a short time afterwards England tells John how 'these vile Popish swine hath clean exiled my husband' (*i.e.* God) and how 'the Pope's pigs' suppress God's word.

Sedition, the clown of the play, tells the audience how many different parts he performs:

SED.   In every estate of the clergy I play a part
            Sometime I can be a monk in a long side cowl;
            Sometime I can be a nun, and look like an owl;
            Sometime a canon in a surplice fair and white;
            A chapterhouse monk sometime I appear in sight.
            I am our Sir John, sometime, with a new shaven
                crown;
            Sometime the parson, and sweep the streets with a
                wide gown;
            A grey friar sometime with cut shoes and a rope;
            Sometime I can play the white monk, sometime the
                friar,
            The purgatory priest and every man's wife desire . . .
            Yea, to go farther, sometime I am a cardinal;
            Yea, sometime a pope; and then am I lord over all,
            Both in heaven and earth and also in purgatory.

—an utterance that reveals the political character of the play, for its concerns were not with doctrine but with secular power. On behalf of the Pope, Sedition, as his ambassador, appears in every country in Europe:

SED.   . . . For his holy cause I maintain traitors and rebels,
            That no prince can have his people's obedience
            Except it stand with the Pope's pre-eminence.

King John tells him to get out, exclaiming that he has no place in England but Sedition explains that he (John) will be deposed and that the power of Rome is everywhere, in the Church, the State and even in the Law. John, represented as a Protestant whose relations with Rome were not unlike those of Henry VIII before his excommunication, emerges in Bale's hands almost as a tragic hero.

The uniting of several parts under one player not only keeps the cast small in number but has the dramatic function of making clear the untrustworthiness of individuals. As it is the plot eventually becomes hard to follow, and at the close of the first act, the Interpreter utters a *résumé* of what has happened and forecasts what is to happen in the second:

INTERP.   In this present act we have to you declared
            As in a mirror, the beginning of King John:
            How he was, of God, a magistrate appointed
            To the governance of this same noble region,
            To see maintained the true faith and religion;
            But Satan the Devil, which that time was at
                large,
            Had so great a sway that he could not it
                discharge.
            Upon a good zeal he attempted very far,
            For wealth of this realm, to provide
                reformation
            In the Church thereof; but they did him debar
            Of that good purpose; for, by
                excommunication,
            The space of seven years, they interdict this
                nation.
            These blood suppers thus, of cruelty and spite
            Subdued this good king for executing right.
            In the second act this will appear more plain:
            Wherein Pandulphus shall him excommunicate
            Within this his land, and depose him from his
                reign.
            All other princes they shall move him to hate,
            And to persecute after most cruel rate.
            They will him poison in their malignity,
            And cause ill report of him always to be.

He concludes by likening John to Moses bringing his people out of the desert to the land of milk and honey, and to David striking down Goliath (*i.e.* the Pope) with his sling, thereby

> . . . restoring again to a Christian liberty
> His land and people, like a most victorious
> king;
> To her first beauty intending the Church to
> bring,
> From ceremonies dead to the living word of
> the Lord.

The second act is dominated by Imperial Majesty, who is made to declaim strong Reformers' propaganda, composed in the terms of the 1534 Act of Supremacy:

> IMP. MAJ.   No man is exempt from this, God's ordinance—
> Bishop, monk, canon, priest, cardinal nor Pope:
> All they, by God's law, to kings owe their
> allegiance
> . . . a king is of God immediately;
> Then shall never Pope rule more in thus
> monarchy.

and then to extract the oath of allegiance from Clergy and Nobility:

> CLERGY.   We detest the Pope, and abhor him to the
> fiend.
> IMP. MAJ. And ye are well content to disobey his pride?
> NOBILITY. Yea, and his lousy laws and decrees to set
> aside.
> IMP. MAJ. Then must ye be sworn to take me for your
> head

to which Civil Order replies:

> We will obey you, as our governor, in God's stead.

As a 'mirror' of current doctrine *King John* could hardly be less opaque though it is cumbrous in its presentation and vastly inferior to Lyndsay's contemporary *Ane Satyre of the Three Estates* both in design and execution. It is full of topical allusions, to the Anabaptists, the Catholic fanatics of Munster, who in 1533 tried to establish an independent religious monarchy under John of Leyden, and to the ignorance of bishops regarding the Old Testament. Many phrases are taken from the Vulgate (*aper de silva*, for example) and the line 'Of the Christian faith, play now the true defender' refers to the title *Fidei Defensor*, bestowed by Pope Leo X on Henry VIII in 1521, when he was an active supporter of doctrinal orthodoxy against Luther. *King John* provides the literary historian with an interesting example of how historical facts were early adapted to fashion political propaganda for an active cause. Bale's portrait of John bears little resemblance to that of Shakespeare, who followed Holinshed and made of this early thirteenth-century king a villain and usurper—nor to the real historical John, whose name Bale appropriated for his strictly contemporary purposes.

The playwright, called by his adversaries 'bilious Bale', apparently spoke naturally in the gross and acid terms of his stage characters. He was befriended by Cromwell and protected from the worst persecution, but after the latter's disgrace Bale fled the country to escape Catholic vengeance in England. He returned in 1547, on the accession of Edward VI, who in 1552 made him Bishop of Ossory in Ireland. Again persecuted by the Catholics, Bale left after only six months and led a precarious existence until 1558 when Mary Tudor's death made it possible for him to return and settle in Canterbury for the remaining five years of his life. He wrote over a score of plays, of which only about six remain, in both Latin and English, and left extensive polemical material. *King John* is the first of the 'chronicle' plays and any study of Shakespeare's 'histories' must start with Bale.

Where the stage was concerned Edward VI kept surveillance strict, and during his short reign the first bill of censorship was passed, directed mainly against the Catholics and requiring a license for the printing, selling or playing of interludes. The power of censorship was hardly invoked at all against the Protestants, for it was neither a moral nor a literary criticism which Parliament wished to direct at the increasing spate of printed books. The stage polemic supported by Cromwell and kept alive by public interest and its own momentum went on into Elizabeth's reign. Mary's accession in 1553 saw a savage attempt on her part to reverse the process of emancipation from Rome but her reign was too short to have much effect on prevailing trends in favour of Protestantism. The only drama of any note to be written and performed during her five years on the throne was *Respublica*, acted in 1553, a condemnation of Protestant rapacity in disposing of Church property. The author is unknown, though a slight case was made out by an early twentieth-century editor for Nicholas Udall, Headmaster of Eton from 1534–41, better known as the author of *Ralph Roister Doister*. Although dismissed from Eton for embezzlement, Udall later became Headmaster of Westminster. Once an exponent of Lutheran doctrine, he changed his views, or affected to change them, when Mary acceded, and is one of those personalities of whom we know little but desire to know more, for his career, judging from the scant evidence available, must have been a chequered one.

The stage in Henry VIII's time had proved its uses as a vehicle for spreading fashionable opinions, and the subject-matter of the drama, which in the fifteenth century had been predominantly religious, was rarely free of political or topical matter. The old morality plays, at first speaking tableaux presenting some easily grasped moral lesson in which virtue triumphed over vice or death over the human condition, developed into dramatisations of some contemporary problem or interest. Although the moral arguments and justifications for action remained nominally Christian in character, the real values emphasised were wordly and material, so that conventional morality-play injunctions to reject riches and power since all paths lead but to the grave lent a presumably unintentional irony to the conclusion. This is apparent even as early as *Magnyfycence* and becomes more obvious as the century proceeds. *A New Interlude of Impatient Poverty*, printed in 1560, is an excellent example of the style of the late moral interlude, which claims to present the same moral as *Everyman*, but in fact equates virtue with riches.

Elizabethan drama laid more emphasis on human relations and domestic incident—this was in large measure due to the influence on classical drama of Plautus, Terence and Seneca, revived in Italy in the last quarter of the fifteenth century, which spread to

T

England and was responsible for the introduction of classical stage conventions, such as the division into five acts, the use of Chorus and Messenger to comment on or report action not taking place on the stage itself and the dependence on blank verse, as employed by Seneca. *Gorboduc* (1557) was the first English play to display this pattern. *Ralph Roister Doister* (1533), a Plautean play by Udall, is a comedy free of any political undertones, classical in conception, but owes far more to English precedents. The anonymous *Gammer Gurton's Needle* (c. 1550) is more formally classical, reminiscent less of Plautus than of Terence, of whom Erasmus said: 'No-one has ever become a good Latinist without Terence'. Terence's *Phormio* was the model for the first comedy in English prose, *Supposes* by George Gascoigne, printed in 1566. The comedies of Plautus and Terence, especially the latter, were played in schools throughout Europe, and both *Ralph Roister Doister* and *Gammer Gurton's Needle* were intended to be performed by adolescents.

However, English classical drama before *Gorboduc* had nothing to do with either politics or religion and, apart from noting it as one more way in which the Italian Renaissance affected literature, we should not dwell upon it here. Vernacular influences, a greater lavishness of scene, the Italian backgrounds, the sunny southern European climate of romance as depicted by Chaucer in *Troilus and Criseyde* and a greater Continental sophistication were united with native English traditions of playwriting after 1500 to form a new and sturdy growth from which the poetic drama of the Elizabethans was later to evolve.

12 : Conclusion

A volume like this, made up as it is of so many different elements and treating by its nature of so many diverse subjects and authors, ought surely to have a conclusion even as it has been accorded a preface. Has the chorus of history been a cacophony? Has the connection between history and literature been more contrived than real? Is the truth of the one that of the other, or is the difference between the facts of history and those of fiction irreconcilable? May not some generalities be deduced out of all this material which explain and justify their association in the same book?

Firstly, there are the obvious points of contact. Personal history, or biography, concerning the authors of works dealt with as being literature is in this Tudor period scanty. It would be impossible to write a full-dress account of the 'life' of any one of the poets and prose writers of these years without drawing heavily upon contemporary history in the cases where the subjects themselves are prominent public figures. In other instances, a few bare facts make up the sum total of what is known for certain about Tudor authors. There is nowhere near enough in the way of biographical information to enable conclusions to be drawn about the 'psychology' of a given poet or the relations of life to works of a contemporary prose writer. Private correspondence, such as is available, is chiefly written by poet to patron and as such cannot be accepted as a true reflection of the correspondent's thoughts. Wyatt's despatches to the King allow us to see Wyatt only through a veil. Ascham remains always the courtier, exuding a thin asceticism. Solid personalities they are not and it is hard to say when one is getting a true glimpse of their real selves, for everything they write is to a greater or lesser extent open to interpretation. So-called 'personal' lyrics may not be autobiographical at all, and it is no longer considered critically wise to attach too much importance to what a poet says about himself in his own verses. Tudor prose is too literary, too studied and too much indebted to Latin constructions to allow strong individuality to penetrate it. Prose authors are separated from each other according to the models they admired rather than by powerful eccentricities of style.

Secondly, the facts of history are better known to us than they were to the Tudors, who did not have access to much reliable information. A good deal of what passed for historical writing in Henry VIII's time was quite inaccurate as history and in fact partook of many of the characteristics associated with fiction. The historian was under patronage and revived *a* past rather than *the* past as a service to the Tudor dynasty, though he did not fully realise at the time that what he was producing would one day be considered false or at best propaganda. The most useful historical account was Polydore Vergil's, written in Latin and as such a curiosity out of its own time, for to write in Latin was to cleave to the past, to deny one's talents to the mob. Latin histories were on the whole more meticulous than English ones—propaganda was not so obtrusive, for popular audiences were not being considered. Vergil's history is the only source which has any claim to reliability, but it is not literature. Nor are the chronicles literature, though the later ones by Hall and Holinshed were sources for Shakespeare. Hary's *Wallace*, on the other hand, is not history, in respect of the factual information it offers, but instead an epic poem, composed according to a classical prescription and dealing with events almost two centuries old, beyond the natural range of human memory. Some of these events did take place and the named personages in the work had their counterparts in real life, but actions and characters were not historically true. However, as Elyot pointed out, there is much wisdom in fables. In false history resides a kind of truth, a psychological likeness to life, which gives credibility to characters and reports of deeds which have no basis in fact. *Wallace* was about heroics in times past and was written to fill a vacuum in times present; it may mislead where the facts of the real Wallace's campaign are concerned, but it occupies a place in the history of James III's reign because it is a guide to what popular audiences were thinking in the 1470s. When the poet asks, addressing Scotland:

> Quha sall the defend? quha sall the now mak fre!
> Allace, in wer[1] quha sall thi helpar be!
> Quha sall the kepe? quha sall the now radem![2]
> Allace, quha sall the Saxons fra the flem![3]
>
> (Book XI, xii, 1121–4)

he is thinking far more of his country's present plight, when no champion is likely to offer himself, than of the response of Wallace to English invasion in the late thirteenth century.

Certain works, like *Wallace*, which are heavily dependent upon such formulas, are keys to the psychology of the time in which they were written, even if they exaggerate and distort facts. The poet of James III's reign wished for a Wallace, and Shakespeare celebrated a Henry V, each a convincing symbol of what in retrospect seemed to be a more attractive past, when the issues and problems were apparently clear cut, soluble in naive heroic terms. It has been remarked in the first chapter that historical events are unique, that history does not repeat itself and that the heroes of the past are forever past. Only in imaginative literature may they be awarded a second, or third lease of life, very often in order to satisfy a popular craving for something which in reality is no longer there. The popularity of biography in an age of 'faceless' men, of 'hot war' accounts in times of complacent peace and military decline, of nature poetry in a developing industrial society, of the pastoral as a comment on political and social intrigue, of the romance of high ideals, conceived tongue-in-cheek, and offered as a criticism of contemporary society—all these enthusiasms are themselves the stuff of history. One of the main themes of eighteenth-century criticism was that literary works reflect the age which gave them birth—what is known as the historical approach to criticism, of which the first English exponent was Dryden. The notion that art was a mirror of its age and no more was a limited one, and Coleridge, Arnold and Pater, to name but three major critics who found the standard inadequate, all attacked it. More

[1] war   [2] redeem   [3] cast out

recently, however, studies of authors in relation to their audiences have given the historical approach a revival, though in a modified and much more sophisticated form. Questions of economics, social stratification, political and religious affiliation, industrial background and even geographical influences (as in the case of Conrad) are now taken into consideration by critics, who, thanks to the immense amount of research undertaken by experts in all such matters, are now vastly better equipped to study a given work in its own contemporary setting than they were in the days when the Augustans were at peace.

.   .   .   .   .   .

The period of this volume is the first when such information as this becomes available in sufficient quantity to enable sound judgements to be made regarding trends in popular, that is, not courtly or aristocratic, interests in letters and art. The Tudors were great opportunists. They had an instinct for the useful. Literature and history were there to be used in order that a certain picture, acceptable to themselves, might be compiled and projected for their own and later generations. They were not always sure what they really stood for, and in many ways they disliked change, though open to it. The humanists hated monkishness, which they equated with intellectual unadventurousness or downright ignorance, and sought their standards in the ancient past. In time this backward-looking was to prevail because it came to be coupled with Protestantism, but, for most humanists, especially in a rough society like the English, their loyalty to ancient Greece and Rome meant isolation. Erasmus, a foreigner, brought humanism and Protestantism together. If he had not, the former would have survived only as a purely academic movement, associated with the universities. It was the popular character of Protestantism, sanctioned by Erasmian scholarship, which gave it strength to maintain the struggle against well-entrenched forces, rich and greedy for a century and more previously.

Many of the authors dealt with in this book represent one or the other of these groups—the makers of propaganda, the humanists, the Protestants, the satirical commentators on prominent personalities at Court, the gleaners of useful information who found it in the writings of the ancients and turned it into English for the benefit of influential men, the Bible scholars, who forged a powerful weapon in the cause of Protestant Reform by taking the Scriptures out of the hands of the priesthood, and the dramatists whose plays dealt with practically any topical subject conceivable for the edification of patrons, enlightened members of the universities, the ordinary man of the towns, unaffected by the goings-on at Henry's Court, and the untravelled countryman, illiterate possibly, but not stupid. The drama was a means of spreading opinion and as such it directly reflected contemporary affairs, though most of the allusions are disguised or diluted for the sake of propriety. Even plays which had no topical motives, like the miracles, which had been part of the English scene for two centuries, eventually came to represent an old order, to be compulsorily abandoned because they were making propaganda in reverse.

Of 'non-political' literature there was relatively little. 'Pure lyrical' poetry, expressing personal or quasi-personal emotions, unrelated specifically to contemporary affairs, is not common. Henryson's *Testament*, Dunbar's short moralising poems, Douglas's *Prologues*, Wyatt's love lyrics and a few of the verses of Surrey and of other contributors to Tottel's *Miscellany* fall into traditional literary categories of the 'courtly' type and as such are not historical documents. Even so, the mental anguish and deep melancholy of the Tudors and Stuarts gives to many of these compositions a unique quality not taken from Chaucerian-French sources, or traceable to non-contemporary origins. These are not, on the whole, cheerful poetic personalities—Chaucerian geniality is absent, except in Henryson's *Fables*—and one is made to feel by Dunbar, Wyatt and Surrey, each in his different way, that life is a burden to be endured, not enjoyed. The medieval *memento mori* still haunted the English Renaissance, but the security of vision offered by Catholic Christianity was perceptibly waning. There was an enthusiasm for religious enlightenment but this seemed to promise nothing in the long run—annihilation threatened ecclesiastics who stood up for their beliefs, statesmen fallen from grace, scions of the nobility and even queens, and after 1530.

a deadly fatalism overtook the Court. Both Wyatt and Surrey show it in their poems. One is still in the presence of *wyrd*, in spite of the fact that the prevailing philosophy of the time laid responsibility for political error at one's own door rather than at that of an impersonal *Fortuna*, as later plays like *Respublica* and, more explicitly, *Gorboduc* tried to bring home.

·　　·　　·　　·　　·　　·

The most significant political event of the sixteenth century was the dissolution of the monastic houses and all intellectual activity preceding the 1530s was leading, in most instances unintentionally, to a break with Catholic doctrine and to the encouragement of philosophical and scientific speculation of a kind which the Roman Church would not have sanctioned. Henry's 1534 Act of Supremacy was more than just a bold symbol of English religious independence—in fact, Henry did not seek to meddle with doctrine—for it cut England off from Europe ideologically, politically and intellectually, and prepared a maturing-ground for a strong and arrogant nationalism which had hitherto been inhibited by imported examples of European cultural superiority and achievement in exploration and commerce and a feeling of geographical isolation inclined to breed emotions of inferiority. The economic stability promoted by Henry VII and the enthusiasm for native English institutions generated in his son's reign seeped through all ranks of urban society. The monasteries symbolised a powerful bulwark of medieval Catholicism—the last outpost of Papal power—and with their removal, a new feeling of freedom from foreign influence was released in England. Henceforth the English took their own where they found it. The flow of literature in translation rapidly increased during the second half of the century; French, Italian and eventually Spanish domestic habits were accepted without the accompanying self-consciousness of the earlier years. The Elizabethans held no-one in awe and their superiority complex came to be more and more ascendant. The defeat of the Spanish Armada in August 1588 provided historians with another striking symbol of English triumph over the forces of anti-Christ and added to the legend of invincibility which contemporary chroniclers sought to create. The xenophobia of the earlier part of the century was at last softened or replaced by attitudes of patronising contempt for the foreigner and his un-English customs.

·   ·   ·   ·   ·   ·

The Elizabethan age, too, witnessed the consolidation and stabilisation of the English language. The need to borrow from other tongues, to invent terms, to embellish sentences with extravagant ornament, to overload phrases with double or even triple meaning and all the multiplicity of experiment indulged in by the earlier Tudors continued throughout the remainder of the century. English prose was being perfected as a vehicle for conveying complex ideas, philosophical speculations and elaborate descriptions and gradually moved farther away from Latin. Native poetry before Shakespeare and Spenser was not lively. The example of Wyatt and Surrey was not immediately influential and the anthologies of the next fifty years—volumes like *The Paradyse of Daynty Devyses* (1576)—contained few flowers worth preserving. Spenser's *Shepherd's Calendar* of 1579 was filled with most of the 'devices', dainty and otherwise, employed by Elizabethan courtly versifiers whose immediate model was Tottel's *Miscellany*. The 'conceits' of these poetasters were eventually parodied by Shakespeare and especially by Donne, whose love lyrics celebrated not constancy, according to the old courtly tradition carried over from Wyatt, but inconstancy, in epigrammatic language, with many incongruous comparisons and all the eccentricities of style which later earned Donne's school the title of 'metaphysical'. There is no better example of the increased subtlety of which English was capable than that given by Donne; the vocabulary of Wyatt is in comparison a blunt instrument.

Dictionary-making, begun by Elyot, whose Latin-English dictionary was the first of its kind to be published in England, contributed to the firm founding of a standard vocabulary. Elyot intended it to be used not only by students but also by professional men. Expanded in 1552 by Thomas Cooper it became the basis for later publications of the kind, for it was designed to improve the study of Latin by helping pupils to understand English words more clearly. Furthermore, its secondary effect was to make available materials for writing a history of the English language by recording current forms and meanings. Elyot became what Vives had said a teacher ought to be—'the guardian of the treasure-house of his language' (*praefectus quidam aerarii linguae suae*). In lexicography, history emerges in the form of philology, though it took another century and a half before the latter was developed scientifically by the 'Oxford Saxonists'.

.   .   .   .   .   .

Some of the actual 'history' of events in the fifteenth and early sixteenth centuries becomes the stuff of literature, but with an inevitable delay in time of at least fifty years. The Plantagenets and the early Tudors were well shrouded in the past before they became subjects for imaginative writers to recreate with the poet's own kind of truth. Contemporary history is on the whole left alone for time and legend to mellow and only very occasionally is one afforded a direct glimpse of a current happening—such as Dunbar provides in his marriage-allegory, or Skelton in his criticisms of Wolsey. Henryson's *Fables* are heavily disguised narratives, not to be accounted for by merely topical explanations, and the courtly poets, Wyatt and Surrey, are rather cryptic, reticent when it comes to specifying analyzable facts and conveying impressions of cautiousness—not surprising in the hothouse atmosphere of Henry's Court. The figures who turn up in *A Mirror For Magistrates* are historical characters in name only and reveal no more animation than their counterparts in street-pageants and dumb tableaux. Though the poetry and drama of the time is well supported by topical references and 'wise' political observations, one rarely feels that a poem or play has been composed with no motive other than that of passing comment. Bale's *King John* is first and foremost an actable play, as are Lyndsay's *Ane Satyre*, Skelton's *Magnyfycence* and other plays in the morality tradition. Moral questions treated are very general, being largely concerned with the award of justice in the public weal and the results of neglecting to see that this is done. *Gorboduc* is a good example of such a play and although the authors' purpose, as we have re-

marked, was to encourage Elizabeth to marry and beget an heir—
succession was never far from the minds of the Tudor monarchs—
Gorboduc is a morality with a much wider application and the
pattern of its action is practically archetypal. The tragedy of Gorboduc, a legendary King of Britain, is later elaborated in that of
King Lear, another of Albion's ancient monarchs. Neither can be
called history, though both contained and presumably were intended to convey, one of history's lessons.

．　　．　　．　　．　　．　　．

One all-embracing characteristic of the Tudors, carried over
from the Middle Ages, was an impulse to didacticism. They were
ready, willing and able to instruct and lost no opportunity to pass
on information on any subject that interested them. The earliest
continuous records are narrow streams compared with the flood
of writings of all kinds which poured out from poets, philosophers,
scholars, pedagogues, sermon-makers, civil servants, students of
natural science, lawyers, churchmen and courtiers. The joy of new-
found knowledge and the establishment of new methods brought
out the expert desirous to impart his expertise. The legacy of
Erasmus was weighty—in fact, in the hands of lesser men, his
didactic impulse later resulted in the production of rather tedious
works—but much of the earlier material has about it an attractive
freshness, inspired by delight in new discovery, new ideas and a
learned naïveté which one may associate with the exuberance of
intelligent youth, sensitive to criticism, easily cast down, but
never long daunted. This first flush of excitement at what may be
known took, in the sixteenth century, a literary and historical turn;
in the century following, the Renaissance was to be scientific and
mathematical, culminating in the advanced theories of Newtonian
physics, but under the Tudors the man of letters was licensed to
preach his new, or rather modified ancient, values. Most of them
must have known one another personally, for the sixteenth century
had brought into being the elements of a society centred on
London, the Court and the newly sprung mercantile houses, with
spacious estates situated within a few days journey from the
capital, owned by the older aristocracy and smaller gifts of land

latterly awarded to successful members of the middle class ennobled by Henry after 1535. The capital was still relatively small and the population only three or four times what it had been in Chaucer's day, but the houses and lands of prominent personalities were dotted around the City in places which nowadays would be regarded as being well within central London. In those colourful times, they were well out in the country, on either side of the river Thames, which stream provided the most easily negotiable means of contemporary transport. More's house at Chelsea, where the famous group of early humanists used to gather in the early years of Henry's reign, was then truly rural in setting, and Hampton Court Palace, far out of the City, could be reached by the royal barge in a few hours. The importance of the Thames as a means of swift communication between the King and his chief ministers, and between lesser ranks of society, who were ferried by professional boatmen up and down the few miles on water on either side of Chelsea Reach from Greenwich to Richmond is not remarked upon by poets before Spenser, but the extent to which this waterway facilitated social intercourse in London should be noted. Henry's Court was scattered up and down the river and its members could easily be gathered in whenever he felt like doing so. From Richmond to the Tower was but a little way.

·　　·　　·　　·　　·　　·

In contrast, the Scots Court was itinerant, and moved around from one place to another as the King fancied. In the case of James IV, this was a frequent occurrence, for James was very restless, was moved by an over-abundance of nervous energy, and was genuinely interested in the intimate doings of his subjects. He was a popular and well-liked monarch who was known to the people by sight and did not hide himself away as his father had preferred to do. His Court was much more loosely knit than Henry's and attachments based on name alone, encouraged by the clan system, made it possible for Scottish noblemen and Scottish peasants to mingle in a manner impossible in English society. The importance of pedigree was far greater in Scotland and it would have been impossible to have created an artificial aristocracy in such a short time as Henry VIII found expedient to do. The rush to display armorial bearings generated by his foundation of a new gentry was an English phenomenon, an object of derision for the older families who scorned the *parvenu*. In Scotland the sharp divisions of 'class' separating noble from gentry, bourgeois from artisan, landowner from yeoman farmer and peasant, were not well defined. Demarcation lines existed, undoubtedly, separating clergy from laity, townsmen from 'uponlandis' or country dwellers, owners of castles and stone houses from people who lived in poor cottages, but these were traditional barriers of long standing. The upstarts of a *nouveau riche* mercantilism were not very significant figures in sixteenth-century Scotland, though they existed in and around east coast ports like Leith. The lairds and the peasants formed a closely knit community in each area, did not venture far from their own localities, spoke the same language undivided by class accents or vocabulary and seem in general to have enjoyed a higher level of elementary education than was the case in England before the nineteenth century. What did ail the Scots, however, were factions, splitting the nobles into groups owing allegiance to one or the other cause and producing extra-territorial alliances, which, in James III's reign particularly, caused both laird and peasant to hold the King and his supporters in contempt. Patriotism as Shakespeare understood it was a popular emotion, not an aristocratic one. The noble fought over his own landed possessions, never for any abstract ideal; nor were the feudal levies of English peasants to be described as fired by any warm patriotic duty. They were simply fulfilling their legal and traditional obligation to their lord who, if he wanted to make sure that they did not desert at the earliest opportunity, was forced to pay them. A reliable army, even in the fourteenth century, was a professional army, regularly paid, well equipped and kept fit by some form of training. In the fifteenth century, very few nobles were able to maintain armies—in practice only the king or a contender for the throne, like Henry VII when Duke of Richmond, looked upon as a sound investment by backers whom he was later expected to reward with titles and lands.

Scots armies seem to have been more comradely and more

consciously devoted to the cause of protecting their king or leader, more capable of appreciating the significance of the abstractions 'freedom' or 'Scotland' which Barbour and the poet of *Wallace* employed. Some historians hold that sentimental Scottish nationalism existed as far back as the ninth century, and it is reasonable to assume that if a poet writing in 1375 knew that his audience would understand and respond to such rhetoric the concept itself was no novelty. English invasions of Scotland under Edward I had, however, been harsh in their effects and it was perhaps easier to equate subsequent threats from the same source with loss of liberty and the state of vassal to the King of England with undignified servitude—'foul thraldom', as Barbour called it. Wallace's fate at the hands of the English was part of legend, known to all Scots. He was condemned as a traitor to the English King on an indictment which, on current standards of legality, was not hard to prove satisfactorily since he had given Edward I's emissaries a great deal of trouble. He was executed and mutilated and contemporary accounts inform us that according to the sentence, his head and limbs were cut off and placed on public view in London and four northern towns, Newcastle, Berwick, Perth and Stirling, where he was known to the people. This gruesome retribution (not especially appalling by contemporary standards) helped to make Wallace a Scottish martyr and a convenient symbol with which later generations might be fired to revive old hatreds. Lines from Hary's lament for the dead Wallace, composed about 1474, have already been quoted in this chapter. They are addressed to 'Scotland'. The emotions which the poet was trying to generate were not to be found in English literature until Shakespeare wrote *Henry V*. The history plays and 'epics' like Daniel's *Civil Wars* expressed national feeling proudly and confidently; in *Wallace* the sentiments are tragic, heavy with foreboding, as though the writer were looking back at a past that was gone forever and not, like Shakespeare, celebrating the triumph of England over her adversaries and the impregnable security of her realm.

Select Bibliography

1. *Authors*

Ascham, Roger, *English Works;* ed. William Aldis Wright (Cambridge University Press 1904).

Barbour, John, *Bruce;* ed. for the EETS by W. W. Skeat (Trubner: London 1870–89 3 vols: STS ed. 1894, 3 vols). *Barbour: The Bruce* (Selections from Books I–XIII) ed. A. M. Kinghorn (Oliver & Boyd: London and Edinburgh 1960).

Barclay, Alexander, *Eclogues;* ed. for the EETS by Beatrice White (OUP 1928: reprinted 1960).; *Ship of Fools* (William Paterson: Edinburgh 1874). A reprint of Pynson's ed. of 1509.

Brant, Sebastian, *Ship of Fools* (*Das Narrenschiff*); translated into rhyming couplets by Edwin H. Zeydel (Dover Books: New York 1967). Includes original woodcuts and a commentary. First published 1944.

Douglas, Gavin, *Virgil's Aeneid;* ed. for STS by David F. C. Coldwell (Blackwoods: Edinburgh and London 1957–64, 4 vols). One-volume ed. (Clarendon Medieval and Tudor series: Oxford 1964).

Dunbar, William, *Poems;* ed. W. Mackay Mackenzie (Faber: London 1933, reprinted 1960).

Elyot, Sir Thomas, *The Boke Named the Governour* (Everyman's Library ed. Dent: London n.d.).

Froissart, Jean, *Chronicles;* translated by John Bourchier, Lord Berners (one-volume ed. by G. C. Macaulay: London, Macmillan and Co.; New York, Macmillan Co. 1899).

Hary's Wallace, ed. for the STS by M. P. McDiarmid (Blackwoods: Edinburgh and London 1959–61, 2 vols.).

Henryson, Robert, *Poems and Fables;* ed. H. Harvey Wood (Oliver & Boyd: London and Edinburgh 1933; 2nd ed. 1958). *The Testament of Cresseid;* ed. Denton Fox (Nelson's

Medieval and Renaissance Library, London and Edinburgh 1968).

Lyndsay, Sir David, *Ane Satyre of the Thrie Estaitis;* ed. J. Kinsley (Cassell: London 1954). Modernised ed. M. P. McDiarmid (Hutchinson, London 1967).; *Works,* ed. for STS by Douglas Hamer (Blackwoods: Edinburgh and London 1931–6, 4 vols).

Malory, Sir Thomas, *Works;* ed. Eugene Vinaver (OUP 1933, 3 vols).

Skelton, John, *Magnyfycence;* ed. for the EETS by R. L. Ramsay (OUP 1908).; *Poems;* ed. Philip Henderson (Dent: London 1931, 3rd ed. 1959). Spelling modernised.

Surrey, Earl of, *Poems;* ed. F. M. Padelford (rev. ed. University of Washington Press 1928).; *Poems;* ed. Emrys Jones (Clarendon Mediaeval and Tudor series: Oxford 1964).

Tottel, Richard, *Miscellany;* ed. Hyder H. Rollins (Harvard University Press 1929, 2 vols).

Vergil, Polydore, *Anglica Historia;* ed. and translated by Denys Hay (Camden series: Royal Historical Society: London 1950).

Wyatt, Sir Thomas, *Collected Poems;* ed. Kenneth Muir (Routledge and Kegan Paul 1949); *Sir Thomas Wyatt and His Circle,* unpublished poems); Kenneth Muir from the Blage MS (Liverpool University Press 1961); *The Life and Letters of Sir Thomas Wyatt;* ed. Kenneth Muir (Liverpool University Press 1963). Most of the material in the 1949 and 1961 volumes has been re-edited by Kenneth Muir and Patricia Thomson, *Collected Poems of Sir Thomas Wyatt* (Liverpool University Press 1969).

2. *Collections*

ed. Boas, F. S., *Five Pre-Shakesperean Comedies* (Oxford: World's Classics 1934). Includes *Ralph Roister Doister, Gammer Gurton's Needle.*

ed. Campbell, Lily B., *The Mirror For Magistrates* (Barnes & Noble: New York 1938). Reprinted 1960.

ed. Cunliffe, J. S., *Early English Classical Tragedies* (Oxford: Clarendon Press 1912). Includes *Gorboduc.*

ed. Farmer, J. S., 1905–7, *Reprints of the Early English Drama Society* (Charles W. Traylen, Guildford, 5 vols n.d.). Includes

Four Elements, King John, Respublica, and other well-known plays of the period.

ed. Gairdner, James, *The Paston Letters* 1422–1509 (Chatto & Windus: London; James M. Commin: Exeter 1904, 6 vols). A two-volume ed. without notes is published in Everyman's Library series: Dent: London n.d.).

ed. Hughey, Ruth, *The Arundel Harington Manuscript* (Ohio University Press, 2 vols 1960).

ed. Kinghorn, A. M., *The Middle Scots Poets* (Edward Arnold: London 1970). Includes texts of *Christ's Kirk on the Green, The Testament of Cresseid, The Goldyn Targe, The Twa Mariit Wemen and the Wedo* and other works to which reference is made.

ed. Williams, C. H., *English Historical Documents,* 1485–1558 (Royal Historical Society: London 1967). Vol. V. in the series.

3. *Secondary Sources*

Aurner, Nellie Slayton, *Caxton, Mirrour of Fifteenth-Century Letters: a Study of the Literature of the First English Press* (Russell & Russell, New York 1965). First published 1926.

Blake, N. F., *Caxton and His World* (Deutsch: London 1969).

Burke, P., *The Renaissance Sense of the Past* (Arnold: London 1969).

Charlton, Kenneth, *Education in Renaissance England* (Routledge & Kegan Paul and University of Toronto 1965).

Crane, Ronald S., *The Vogue of Medieval Chivalric Romance During the English Renaissance* (Wisconsin Collegiate Press 1919).

Donaldson, Gordon, *Scottish Kings* (Batsford: London 1967).; *Scotland: James V–VII* (Oliver & Boyd: Edinburgh and London 1965).

Herford, C. H., *Studies in the Literary Relations of England and Germany in the Sixteenth Century* (Cambridge 1886).

Hunt, Percival, *Fifteenth-Century England* (University of Pittsburgh and Oxford University Press 1962).

Kinghorn, A. M., *Mediaeval Drama* (Evans: London 1968).

Kingsford, C. H., *English Historical Literature in the Fifteenth Century* (Oxford: the Clarendon Press 1913).

306 · SELECT BIBLIOGRAPHY

Lass, Roger ed., *Approaches to English Historical Linguistics* (Holt, Rinehart & Winston: New York 1969). Chapter 6.

Lee, Sidney, *The French Renaissance in England: An Account of the Literary Relations of England and France in the Sixteenth Century* (Clarendon Press: Oxford 1910).

Lathrop, Henry Burrowes, *Translations from the Classics Into English From Caxton to Chapman 1477–1620* (Octagon Books: New York 1967). First published 1932.

Lewis, C. S., *English Literature in the Sixteenth Century* (Clarendon Press: Oxford 1954).

Mackie, R. L., *James IV of Scotland* (Oliver and Boyd: Edinburgh and London 1958).

Murison, W., *Sir David Lyndsay: Poet and Satirist of the Old Church of Scotland* (Cambridge University Press 1938).

Plomer, Henry Robert, *Wynkyn de Worde and His Contemporaries from the Death of Caxton to 1535* (Grafton, Coptic House: London 1925).

Stearns, M. W., *Robert Henryson* (Columbia University Press: New York 1949).

Steinberg, S. H., *500 Years of Printing* (Pelican Books 1961. First published Faber: London 1955).

Scott, Mary Augusta, *Elizabethan Translations From the Italian* (Houghton Mifflin: Boston & New York 1916).

Stevens, John, *Poetry and Music in the Early Tudor Court* (Methuen: London 1961).

Underhill, John Garrett, *Spanish Literature in the England of the Tudors* (Macmillan Company: New York 1899).

Weiss, R., *Humanism in England During the Fifteenth Century* (Blackwell: Oxford 1957). First published 1941. With bibliography.

Wilson, F. P., *The English Drama 1485–1585* (Clarendon Press: Oxford 1969).

Woodward, W. H., *Studies in Education during the Age of the Renaissance* (Cambridge 1924). First published 1906.

Wyld, Henry Cecil, *A History of Modern Colloquial English* (Blackwell: Oxford 1956).

Index

Bold figures refer to illustration numbers (between pp. 176 and 177)

fortune, as element in history, 19; Froissart's belief in, 34–5; Shakespeare comments on, 35; role of in romantic history, 36–7; in *A Mirror For Magistrates*, 266–8; Wolsey as example of change in, 274–5; *and see* Wyatt; Surrey; Henryson; *Testament of Cresseid*

Fortunes of Men, The, Old English poem, passage translated from, 15–16

Four Elements, A New Interlude of the (John Rastell's), 12–22, 40, discussed and quoted from, 119–28

Fourteenth-Century Verse and Prose (K. Sisam's), referred to, 192

Four Virtues (Mancinus's), use of terms in Barclay's translation of, 277

Fox, Richard, Bishop of Winchester and Durham (*c.* 1448–1528), referred to by Barclay, 169; commissioned to arrange Margaret Tudor's marriage, 217

Foxe, John, martyrologist (1516–87), 53, 70; anecdote about Barclay told by, 173–4

France, Lyndsay and Wyatt ambassadors in, 241, 251–2; relations with England, 173, 218, 273; with Scotland, 218–20 *and see* 'auld alliance'; cultural influences, English

Francis I, King of France (1515–47), 257, 258; meets Henry VIII, 173

Franciscanus (George Buchanan's), 236

Fraternitye of Vagabonds (Awdelay's), 81

Freiris of Berwik, The, 193

French influence on Middle Scots, *see* Middle Scots

French Revolution, historical uniqueness of, 19

Freudian theories of psychology, *see* psychology

Froissart, Jean, chronicler (*c.* 1337–*c.* 1404), 29, 32–8; poem by, 34; *and see* Berners, Lord

Frontinus, Sextus Julius (*c.* 40–103), printed, 112

Gaelic, 186–7, 222

Galilei, Galileo, astronomer (1564–1642), 128

Gammer Gurton's Needle, 181, 290

'garden metaphor', 95

Gardiner, Stephen, Bishop of Winchester (*c.* 1482–1555), 162; letter by Ascham to, 185

Gascoigne, George, dramatist (1525?–77), 290

Gau, John, translator (*fl.* 1533), 188

Gaunt, John of, 1st Duke of Lancaster (1340–99), 270

Gay, John, poet and dramatist (1685–1732), use of *ottava rima* by, 252

Genealogia Deorum Gentilium (Boccaccio's), 207, 231

genealogy, of Stuarts, 31; of Tudors, 270–1

Genoa, economic power as trading port, 85; loss of, 118; birthplace of Columbus, 118

Geoffrey of Monmouth, chronicler (1100–54), 29

Geoffrey de Vinsauf, grammarian (*c.* 1210), 177

geography, medieval conception of world, 116–17

Gervase of Canterbury, chronicler (d. *c.* 1210), distinguishes between types of history, 23, 56; ideal of history approached by Berners and Froissart, 32

Ghent, 75

Ghiberti, Lorenzo, artist (1378–1455), 68

Ghirlandajo, the family, artists (Domenico, 1449–94; Ridolfo, 1483–1560), 68

Gigli, Silvestro, Bishop of Worcester (d. 1521), in service of Henry VII and VIII, 82

Gilbert, Sir Humphrey, explorer (1539–83), 91

Gilbert, W. S., librettist (1836–1911), quoted, 17–18

Gildas, historian, author of *Gildas . . . de calamitate, excidio et conquestu Britanniae* (*fl. c.* 500), 48

'Giocosa, La Casa', 90 *and see* da Feltre, Vittorino

Giotto, (Giotto di Bondone), painter (1267–1337?), 14, 67

Glamis, Lord of, in opposition to James III, 204

Glasgow, 87

Glencairn, (Alexander Cunningham, 5th Earl of, d. 1574), as author, 236

Glendower, Owen, Welsh leader (*c.* 1359–1415), in opposition to Richard II, 267

glengore, *see* syphilis

Godwin, William, novelist and political writer (1756–1836), cited as admirer of Henryson, 211

Goethe, Johann Wolfgang von, (1749–1832), ideal of translation of, 11, 109, 263

Golden Ass (Apuleius's), referred to, 146

Golden Book of Marcus Aurelius, The, see de Guevara

Golden Legend, The (*Legenda Aurea*), printed by Caxton, 139, 153